THE MINNESOTA VIKINGS ALL-TIME ALL-STARS

THE BEST PLAYERS AT EACH POSITION FOR THE PURPLE AND GOLD

CHRIS TOMASSON

LYONS PRESS

Guilford, Connecticut

An imprint of Globe Pequot, the trade division of
The Rowman & Littlefield Publishing Group, Inc.
4501 Forbes Blvd., Ste. 200
Lanham, MD 20706
LyonsPress.com

Distributed by NATIONAL BOOK NETWORK

British Library Cataloguing in Publication Information available

Library of Congress Cataloging-in-Publication Data available

Names: Tomasson, Chris, author.
Title: The Minnesota Vikings all-time all-stars : the best players at each
    position for the purple and gold / Chris Tomasson.
Description: Guilford, Connecticut : Lyons Press, [2021] | Includes
    bibliographical references.
Identifiers: LCCN 2021017865 (print) | LCCN 2021017866 (ebook) | ISBN
    9781493052257 (Paperback : acid-free paper) | ISBN 9781493052264 (ePub)
Subjects: LCSH: Minnesota Vikings (Football team)—History. | Minnesota
    Vikings (Football team)—Miscellanea. | Football players—United
    States—Statistics. | Football players—United States—Rating of. |
    Football teams—Records.
Classification: LCC GV956.M5 T66 2021 (print) | LCC GV956.M5 (ebook) |
    DDC 796.332/6409776579—dc23
LC record available at https://lccn.loc.gov/2021017865
LC ebook record available at https://lccn.loc.gov/2021017866

CONTENTS

FOREWORD
AHMAD RASHAD

My first introduction to the Minnesota Vikings was after my rookie season of 1972 when I was with the St. Louis Cardinals. We had played the Vikings during the season and I had scored two touchdowns in that game, and then in the offseason I ended up at a tennis tournament in California with Vikings quarterback Fran Tarkenton.

I had never met Fran before, but he came up to me and he singled me out and we just sat and talked. We talked about football. We talked about life. We talked about a bunch of stuff and we just got on famously and had a great time. I remember thinking, "Boy, I wish had a quarterback like that." I had idolized Fran and I was thinking it would be great to be one of his receivers.

I ended up playing in Buffalo in 1974, and then I got hurt and I sat out a season and became a free agent. Seattle got an expansion team in 1976; I grew up in Tacoma, which is 30 miles from Seattle, and so I ended up signing with the Seahawks.

One day during training camp, I get a call from Seahawks coach Jack Patera and he said, "I've got some good news and I've got some bad news, what do you want to hear first?" I said, "How about the good news." He said, "We're trading you to Minnesota." And I said, "Minnesota? Fran Tarkenton's Minnesota?" I don't even know what the bad news was, probably that I was going to have to leave where I had grown up, but hearing I was going to the Vikings made my day.

The first year I was there, we got to the Super Bowl, and lost to Oakland 32–14. The Vikings had gone to four of the first 11 Super Bowls, and the atmosphere of the team was that they expected to go to the Super Bowl.

I had never been on a team that was so prepared the way they were and had such a businesslike attitude. They were all about winning. To have a quarterback like Fran was just a dream. He ran the offense. Jim Marshall was the defensive leader. And we had Carl Eller and Alan Page. All of those guys were household names. And head coach Bud Grant was the best I'd ever seen. He got the best out of me because he challenged me every week to do something better.

After I had been named MVP at the Pro Bowl in Los Angeles following the 1978 season, Bud said I was the best receiver in the league, and that meant a lot to me. He's not one of those guys that's full of baloney and just says things to say things. I cut the article out of the paper that he said it in and I still have it in my house.

The Vikings were such a close-knit organization and you always felt like once you were a Viking, you were always a Viking. I felt like that was the only real team I played for in the NFL. I enjoyed playing in Buffalo, but I was only there one season. At Minnesota, it was a family affair; the whole team was together.

When we lost that Super Bowl to Oakland, my feeling was, "It doesn't matter. We'll be back next year or we'll be back the year after that." It turned out we never did get back. That was frustrating, but I felt like we had legitimate chances during the course of my career in Minnesota to go to the Super Bowl.

When I was in Minnesota is when my broadcasting career started in 1977. I had a show right after the game on Sunday night with local broadcaster Mark Rosen on WCCO. It was called the *Rashad-Rosen NFL Report*. I worked there pretty much year round at the television station. And I had a radio show.

When I decided to retire after the 1982 season, I had opportunities to go to all three networks before I chose NBC. When people saw me on television, they thought it was my first time on TV and I was pretty good, but they didn't realize I had spent five years in Minnesota doing TV.

NBC got the NBA rights starting in 1990 and I began to do that. Some people forgot that I had played for the Vikings. I remember one time my daughter Condola came home from school when she was 12 and said, "Hey dad, there's a guy at school who wants your autograph. He said you played football for the Vikings. Did you?"

I love Minnesota, and I was proud to be a Viking. The fans in Minnesota always made me feel good, and I feel like I'm a Minnesotan. Even after I left, I felt I was still representing Minnesota through my television career, and I did it with enthusiasm.

Being inducted into the Vikings Ring of Honor in 2017 was probably the biggest thing that's ever happened to me. It's the most important thing to ever happen to me and I've won Emmy awards, I've won receiving titles.

I never miss a Vikings game on television at my home in Florida. I'm the biggest Vikings fan ever. That's my favorite team and always will be. I bleed purple. I've got my Vikings hat on every Sunday. If I could go out there and play and help them now, I would.

Chris Tomasson has done a great job in this book of compiling the Minnesota Vikings all-time All-Star team, as well as capturing the rich history of this storied franchise. I am honored to be one of the Vikings all-time All-Stars.

INTRODUCTION

It all started for the Vikings on September 17, 1961, before some curiosity seekers at a half-full Metropolitan Stadium.

The Vikings had entered the NFL as an expansion team, and their first game figured to be an ugly one. They faced the mighty Chicago Bears, coached by the legendary George Halas. Two weeks earlier, the teams had met in a preseason game and the Bears won 30–7.

"They thought they were going to come in and whip us," said Frank Youso, a starting tackle that afternoon. "And a lot of people in our own stadium were hollering, 'They're going to kick your butt.' But we didn't think so."

In one of the most shocking upsets in NFL history, the Vikings won 37–13. Rookie quarterback Fran Tarkenton, who came off the bench late in the first quarter, threw for four touchdowns and ran for another after Mike Mercer had kicked a 12-yard field goal for the first points in team history.

"I kicked the first field goal in the history of the Super Bowl," said Mercer, who had that distinction for Kansas City in Super Bowl I in January 1967. "So I guess I'm the answer to two trivia questions."

Youso said Halas, who would win his fifth NFL championship with the Bears two years later, was "madder than hell" about the loss. The Vikings, of course, were elated.

They would finish that first season 3–11, including being walloped by the Bears 52–35 in the finale. But that first win had gotten the franchise going.

"It was a great first victory for us, but even more importantly for our fans and Minnesota," said defensive end Jim Marshall, who would play a team-record 19 seasons with the Vikings. "We showed them we were ready to compete in the NFL. Minnesota embraced us from that game forward."

Yes, the state did. For six decades, fans have lived and died with the Vikings. They haven't been able to reward them yet with a Super Bowl win, having lost in each of their four appearances, but year after year they keep trying.

The Vikings usually have been competitive. Since second-year coach Bud Grant led them to their first playoff appearance in 1968, they never have gone more than four years in a row without a playoff berth. Since 1987, the longest dry spell has been three years.

Overall, the Vikings have made 30 playoff appearances. Counting the postseason, they have an all-time record of 516–442–11. That's a strong winning percentage of .538.

The Vikings have had 15 Hall of Famers who did most of their best work in Minnesota. They are Grant, general manager Jim Finks, Tarkenton, defensive tackles Alan Page and John Randle, defensive ends Carl Eller and Chris Doleman, safety Paul Krause, wide receivers Randy Moss and Cris Carter, center Mick Tingelhoff, tackles Ron Yary and Gary Zimmerman, and guards Randall McDaniel and Steve Hutchinson.

The Vikings have had their share of exhilarating moments. Joe Kapp tied an NFL record by throwing seven touchdown passes in a 1969 game. Tarkenton set a then NFL career record for TD passes in 1975. Cris Carter caught a then record 122 passes in 1994. Adrian Peterson ran for a single-game record 296 yards in 2007 and then gained 2,097 in 2012, the second-best seasonal showing in league history.

In the playoffs, there have been some thrilling wins. The Vikings in 1987 stunned the mighty San Francisco 49ers, an

11-point favorite, 36–24. Ten years later, they trailed the New York Giants 22–13 before scoring a touchdown with 1:30 left, recovering an onside kick and winning on a last-second field goal.

But that dramatic win was nothing compared to the one that featured the Minneapolis Miracle, without question the greatest play in team history. On the final play of a 2017 divisional playoff against New Orleans at U.S. Bank Stadium, Case Keenum uncorked a desperation pass down the right sideline to Stefon Diggs, who hauled it in against a falling Saints player and stumbled slightly before running the final 34 yards to complete a 61-yard touchdown reception in a 29–24 win.

"It's tough to top the Minneapolis Miracle and what that meant and all that," said Vikings wide receiver Adam Thielen. "I'm sure that will be shown for years and years to come."

Two years later, the Vikings stunned the Saints again in the playoffs on the last play of the game. On the first possession of overtime in a wild-card game at the Superdome, Kirk Cousins hit Thielen on a 43-yard pass to the New Orleans 2. Three plays later, Cousins found Kyle Rudolph in the left corner of the end zone for a four-yard touchdown pass and a 26–20 win.

"I played a lot of basketball in my life," Rudolph said. "And they brought all-out pressure and Kirk gave me a chance and I just go up and get the rebound."

Many of the Vikings' playoff memories, though, have been painful. There was the 17–14 loss to Dallas in 1975 on Roger Staubach's 50-yard Hail Mary pass to Drew Pearson in the waning seconds. There was the 30–27 overtime defeat to Atlanta in the 1998 NFC Championship Game when Gary Anderson, who had previously made all 39 of his field-goal attempts that season, missed a 39-yarder late in regulation that could have wrapped things up.

There was another devastating overtime loss in an NFC Championship Game, this one 31–28 at New Orleans after the 2009 season. There was another kicker who faltered, with Blair Walsh missing a 27-yarder in the waning seconds of Minnesota's 10–9 loss to Seattle in a 2015 wild-card game.

The four Super Bowl losses in the 1970s were mostly just ugly. The Vikings have been outscored 95–34 in the big game, starting with Super Bowl IV in January 1970, when they were a 12-point favorite over Kansas City before being taken apart 23–7. They also fell 24–7 to Miami in January 1974, 16–6 to Pittsburgh in January 1975, and 32–14 to Oakland in January 1977.

"It's unfortunate that we didn't win one," said Eller, one of 10 Minnesota players to have played in all four of the Super Bowls. "We were not happy about the losses, but we were there and we have some great memories."

The Super Bowl memories that elicit chuckles mostly happened off the field. Before the Super Bowl IX loss to the Steelers in New Orleans, several Minnesota players dumped a large trash can of water on legendary ABC broadcaster Howard Cosell.

Cosell was interviewing Tarkenton at the Hilton. It was a two-story hotel and Cosell was sitting with his back facing away from the second floor, where Page, linebacker Wally Hilgenberg and defensive lineman Bob Lurtsema had sprung into action.

"Alan Page, of all people, he says, 'Hey, Lurts, Wally, go to your rooms and fill your waste baskets with water,'" Lurtsema said. "So we said, 'Okay.' We went to our rooms to get our waste baskets with water. Then the three of us tiptoed from our rooms out and we're behind Howard. Then all three buckets of water hit him. It moved his toupee back two inches."

Two years later, after the Vikings fell to the Raiders in yet another Super Bowl defeat, all Tarkenton could do was laugh about it. He went on *Saturday Night Live* three weeks after the game and said in his opening monologue, "I guarantee we'll be in the Super Bowl, and I predict we'll lose again."

Since then, the Vikings haven't even been back with a chance to lose again. But they continue to do everything they can for a shot at winning it all.

The Wilf ownership group has been behind the building of luxurious U.S. Bank Stadium, which welcomed the Vikings in 2016, and the TCO Performance Center, a state-of-the-art training facility that opened in 2018. The Vikings have handed out plenty of lucrative contracts. That included in 2018 signing Cousins to a three-year, $84 million deal, making him for a period the highest-paid player in NFL history. He then signed a two-year, $66 million extension in 2020.

Whether Cousins finally can take Minnesota to the top remains to be seen. But while the Vikings look to the future, they continue to embrace the past, even though it can be bittersweet.

In 2018, they brought back coaches and players for a 20-year reunion of the 1998 team that had gone 15–1 and set an NFL record by scoring 556 points before the stunning loss to the Falcons. And in 2019, they welcomed back 50 years later members of the first Super Bowl team.

The Vikings also took note in 2019 of having won the 500th game in team history, including the playoffs, and they celebrated their 60th season in 2020. But that was the first season that Jerry Reichow, who had been the only person associated with the Vikings for each of their first 59 years, wasn't with the team.

As a wide receiver, Reichow caught three passes for 103 yards and a touchdown in Minnesota's first game. He later served as a scout, player personnel director, and consultant for the team before finally retiring at age 85.

"I remember when we got started, people would just come out to see, what is this pro football?" Reichow said. "The University of Minnesota was very good back then and people said, 'Let's go look at this Viking outfit and see what they've got.'"

People have been looking at them for six decades, and it's been a most interesting ride.

A NOTE ON PLAYERS FROM DIFFERENT ERAS

This All-Star team will consist of 14 players on offense and 12 on defense. The punter will be included with the defense and the kicker and the kick returner with the offense. And there will be a head coach.

We are comparing different eras, which is important to note. Statistics should be looked at differently from the early days of the Vikings compared to today. Dave Osborn rushing for 972 yards in 1967 in a 14-game season in a three-yards-and-a-cloud-of-dust era placed him second in the NFL. In 2020, that figure would have ranked 13th.

Things are even quite different since the NFL's first 16-game season in 1978. Tarkenton led the NFL in passing yards that year with 3,468. In 2020, that figure would have placed him 19th.

So players will be judged in the context of their era. When Mick Tingelhoff entered the NFL in 1962, he was a 237-pound center. Minnesota's current center, Garrett Bradbury, weighs 305 pounds.

Hopefully, you will enjoy this trip down memory lane as the greats in Vikings history are remembered. Let's get started and name a head coach for this bunch. . . .

1

HEAD COACH

In 1961, the expansion Minnesota Vikings were looking for their first head coach, and they reached out to Bud Grant.

Grant had been very successful in the Canadian Football League and had won two Grey Cups for the Winnipeg Blue Bombers. He was popular in the Twin Cities, having starred in football and basketball at the University of Minnesota and played for the NBA's Minneapolis Lakers. He looked to be a great choice.

There was just one problem. Grant told Max Winter, one of the Vikings owners, he didn't want the job.

"He had been one of the owners of the Lakers, so he knew me," Grant said. "He asked me if I would be interested in coaching the Vikings when they got the franchise. And I thought about it, and I don't know if I said this to him or not, but I said, 'First-year coaches of teams don't really last long. They do the groundwork and then they get fired and the next guy comes in and benefits from all that work that had been done.'"

Grant was right. With the most obvious exception of Tom Landry, who led the Dallas Cowboys for their first 29 seasons, expansion coaches usually don't last long.

"I don't know if I said this (to Winter), but I said, 'Call me the next time you need a coach,'" Grant said.

That next time was in 1967. When Grant had turned down the job in 1961, the Vikings hired Norm Van Brocklin, a future Hall of Fame quarterback who had led Philadelphia to the 1960 NFL title before retiring. Brocklin went 29–51–4 in six seasons and failed to make the playoffs before resigning under pressure.

When the Vikings courted Grant the second time, he had won two more Grey Cups. He could see that Minnesota, which went 8–5–1 in 1964 and 7–7 in 1965 before slipping to 4–9–1 in 1966, had some pretty good players.

"I had followed the Vikings, and I knew Van Brocklin vaguely," Grant said. "I used to go down there during the off-season for a couple of years and look at film. Well, one day over Christmas, I went down there, and Van Brocklin was kind of a volatile guy. He said, 'Get your butt out of here. I don't want to see you anymore.' Well, they eventually let Van Brocklin go, and Max called me again and they had some good players and I said, 'Well, yeah, I'd be interested.'"

It turned out to be great fit. In 18 seasons, Grant led Minnesota to a 158–96–5 record and to four Super Bowls. Since Grant stepped down for a second time after the 1985 season, the Vikings have not been back to the big game.

Counting Les Steckel, who served as coach in 1984 when Grant retired for the first time, Minnesota has had seven coaches since Grant's departure. Some have teased fans who have been hungering for a championship for six decades.

Jerry Burns, Dennis Green, Brad Childress, and Mike Zimmer took the Vikings to NFC championship games. But they went 0–5 in such games, with Green having lost twice.

There have been cruel finishes in those games. In 1987, a dropped Darrin Nelson pass in the final minute doomed the Vikings in a 17–10 loss at Washington. In 1998, Gary Anderson, who had made all 39 of his field-goal attempts during the season, missed a 39-yard chip shot late in regulation that could have clinched the game, and the Vikings lost 30–27 in overtime to Atlanta. In 2009, a Brett Favre interception late in regulation proved fatal in a 31–28 overtime loss at New Orleans.

The loss in the 2017 NFC Championship Game, 38–7 at Philadelphia, wasn't close but nevertheless fits well into the lost-opportunity category. A win would have enabled Minnesota to become the first team to play the Super Bowl in its home stadium (Tampa Bay earned that distinction three years later).

Zimmer, the coach of that team, continues to soldier on. The ultimate goal remains a championship, but the first step is to just get to the Super Bowl again more than four decades after Grant was last there.

BUD GRANT

A new generation of fans got a feel on January 10, 2016, for what Bud Grant was all about.

The Vikings were about to face Seattle in a playoff game at TCF Bank Stadium, an outdoor stadium used temporarily for two seasons until U.S. Bank Stadium opened for the 2016 season. The temperature was minus six degrees, tied for the third-coldest game in NFL history.

The legendary former coach, then 88, was brought out for the opening kickoff. He walked to midfield wearing a short-sleeve shirt.

"It was a spur-of-the moment thing," Grant said. "They asked me to go out for the coin toss, and that's a symbolic thing. You walk out and you walk off and what do you do? So I thought, 'What could I do to juice this thing up a little bit?' So I took my coat off and put on a short-sleeve shirt. It wasn't a grandstand play. It was more of an acknowledgment of the weather and this is Minnesota."

During his coaching stint, from 1967–1983 and in 1985, Grant was the face of Minnesota. Grant, known for not allowing heaters on the sideline when the Vikings played outdoors at Metropolitan Stadium through 1981, headed a team known for its toughness.

Grant is the winningest coach in Vikings history and led them to four Super Bowls.
ST. PAUL PIONEER PRESS

Grant coached with a stoic face that looked as if it had been frozen by Minnesota winters. He always seemed to be in control, but to some of his players was considered a distant coach. That's because Grant believed in delegating authority, and usually had his assistants deal more with players.

"Bud was a great coach," said safety Paul Krause, who played for the Vikings from 1968–1979. "He was the best coach I ever played for. He knew football, but he also knew what he didn't know."

Despite the icy facade, Grant was known as a prankster. His longtime offensive coordinator Jerry Burns was afraid of insects, and Grant often didn't hesitate to slip one on him and watch him jump.

There was much less to laugh about when it came to Grant's four Super Bowl appearances, the only ones in team history. They lost all of them, and the combined margin was 95–34. Nevertheless, Grant, the winningest coach in Vikings history, was inducted into the Pro Football Hall of Fame in 1994.

Harry Peter "Bud" Grant Jr. was born May 20, 1927, in Superior, Wisconsin, just across the state line from Duluth, Minnesota. After being a star athlete at the University of Minnesota, he played for the NBA's Minneapolis Lakers before going to the NFL, where he starred for the Philadelphia Eagles as a defensive end in 1951 and wide receiver in 1952. After leading the NFL with 997 receiving yards, he got into a contract dispute and bolted to the CFL, where he was a star receiver for four years with Winnipeg.

Grant then coached the Blue Bombers for 10 years before returning to the NFL on March 10, 1967, when he took over in Minnesota for Norm Van Brocklin. Grant inherited a team that had just lost star quarterback Fran Tarkenton.

Tarkenton had feuded with Van Brocklin, who didn't like the quarterback's propensity to scramble, and demanded to be traded. Even though Van Brocklin resigned February 6, Tarkenton said he didn't want to return and be known for having driven out a coach. So he was shipped to the New York Giants on March 7 for four draft choices.

"I had some trepidations about coming down because they didn't have a quarterback," Grant said. "But [general manager] Jim Finks had originally signed Joe Kapp to go to Calgary and Joe was the kind of guy that was good for two or three years but then he was very volatile and would do stuff that wasn't good for a long-term arrangement. He played in Calgary and they got rid of him and he went to British Columbia and won a Grey Cup there and burned his bridges, and he was available for us."

Well, the Vikings did get three years out of the hard-living, tequila-drinking Kapp before he burned bridges in Minnesota by getting in a contract dispute and was traded to the Boston Patriots. But those were the years that really got the team going.

The Vikings went just 3–8–3 in Grant's first season of 1967 before they made the playoffs for the first time in 1968 at 8–6. In 1969, everything came together. With Kapp leading the way on offense and the defense giving up 9.5 points per game, then a record for a 14-game season, the Vikings went 12–2 and advanced to their first Super Bowl.

That didn't go too well. The Vikings, despite being a 12-point favorite, were stunned 23–7 by the Kansas City Chiefs in Super Bowl IV. Still, Grant had made great advances in his first three seasons.

"I remember when he came from the Canadian Football League, the Vikings offered him a five-year contract, but he said, 'No, I'll take a three-year contract. If I can't turn this team around in three years, I probably can't do it,'" said former Vikings cornerback Bobby Bryant.

Bryant helped in the turnaround. He was part of Minnesota's decorated 1967 draft class, the best the team has had. The

Vikings in the first round selected reliable running back Clint Jones (second pick), future All-Pro wide receiver Gene Washington (eighth), and defensive tackle and future Hall of Famer Alan Page (15th). They later got wide receiver Bob Grim, who made a Pro Bowl, in the second round, and Bryant, chosen to two Pro Bowls, in the seventh round.

Page joined forces with defensive tackle Gary Larsen and defensive ends Carl Eller and Jim Marshall, whom Grant inherited, to form the Purple People Eaters, one of the greatest defensive lines in history.

"We were lucky we got a guy like Page, and could put him with Marshall, Eller, and Larsen," Grant said. "We also had three good linebackers in (Roy) Winston, (Wally) Hilgenberg, and (Lonnie) Warwick. They weren't blitzing linebackers but they were good run stoppers. But we had four good rushers, so we didn't have to rely on a lot of blitzes. And we started using a zone defense when nobody was using much of a zone before. We got Paul Krause [in a trade with Washington] and he roamed back there."

From 1969–1971, the Vikings had the best defense in football, leading the league in fewest points allowed each of those three seasons. But in 1970 and 1971, the Vikings had the same problem Grant had hoped to avoid when he first arrived. They didn't have an upper-echelon quarterback, and they were upset each time at home in their playoff opener.

That was rectified when the Vikings reacquired Tarkenton in 1972 from the Giants for Grim, quarterback Norm Snead, fullback Vince Clements, and first- and second-round draft picks. Tarkenton's first season back was one of adjustment and great frustration. The Vikings lost five games by three or less points and finished 7–7.

But then they took off. Between 1973 and 1976, the Vikings made it to three out of four Super Bowls. Some believe the 1975 team, which was stunned by Dallas 17–14 on a Hail Mary pass to open the playoffs, actually was the best of those four teams. Tarkenton that season threw a league-high 25 touchdown passes and was named NFL MVP, beating out his fullback, Chuck Foreman, who rushed for 1,070 yards, led the NFL with 73 catches, and scored 22 touchdowns.

"We were ahead of the curve a little bit then," Grant said of that four-year stretch for the Vikings. "We went to the short passing game, had a great running back who could catch the ball and a quarterback who was mobile."

It didn't help, though, in Super Bowls. The Vikings lost Super Bowl VIII 24–7 to Miami, Super Bowl IX 16–6 to Pittsburgh, and Super Bowl XI 32–14 to Oakland. That left Grant 0–4 in the big game.

"A lot of coaches go to their grave replaying games, and I don't think I've ever looked at the film of a Super Bowl loss," Grant said. "I would tell the players that if we lose a game, you're frustrated and you're mad but come back Monday and forget about it. The one thing you've got to learn in this business is to learn to lose. I didn't want to embrace losing, but you've got to learn how to get over losing. You've got to move on."

Grant did that, but the Vikings began to age as a team. They made it to the NFC Championship Game in 1977, a 23–6 loss at Dallas when Tarkenton was out in his next-to-last season with a broken leg, but after that Grant never got out of the divisional round. In three of his final four seasons as coach, Minnesota didn't make the playoffs.

Grant stepped down as coach after the 1983 season, one reason being he thought Burns would take over. Surprisingly, wide receivers coach Les Steckel got the job, and it was a disaster. The Vikings went 3–13, and Grant agreed to return as coach in 1985 for a salary of $500,000.

After a 7–9 season, Grant retired for good. He made sure Burns got the job.

"It was an easy transition to give it to Burnsie," said Grant, who departed at age 58. "He had been here the whole time, he was a great coach and a good friend, and it was a good move."

Did Grant miss coaching when he stepped away first for one year and then for good?

"No, because I was in North Dakota hunting ducks," he said.

Grant long has been an avid outdoorsman. He has continued to hunt and fish into his nineties.

Grant missed a reunion in 2015 of players and coaches from all four of the Super Bowl teams because it conflicted with duck hunting season. But otherwise he gets to most big Vikings functions, including in 2019 a 50th reunion of the first Super Bowl team.

At these events, his former players always seem to have Bud Grant stories.

"I was a rookie, and it was snowing and all of sudden he walks up to me and says, 'Has anybody told you about the snow?'" said guard Ed White, a California native who played with the Vikings from 1969–1977. "I said, 'No.' He said, 'Well, don't eat the yellow snow.' That was the first thing he said to me the whole year."

White learned that Grant sometimes was a man of few words, but commanded attention when he did speak.

"Another time, I felt him come up from behind me in practice, and I'm all nervous," White said. "Finally, he just says, 'You're fighting a losing battle.' I asked him what he meant and he goes, 'Your sideburns are too long.'"

Grant was known for being a disciplinarian. He told his players they couldn't smoke, chew tobacco, or spit in public. He had the team each year practice standing at proper attention during the national anthem. He appointed Eller as sergeant at arms to oversee the anthem, and it became known as the Viking Formation.

Still, Grant was known to look the other way at times if it might help the team. Grant didn't want heaters on the sideline at often-frigid Metropolitan Stadium because he believed it led to players not focusing on the game. He also wasn't fond of them bundling up with sweatshirts under their jerseys. After wide receiver Ahmad Rashad came to the Vikings in 1976, it began to get cold late that season at practices.

"It was like 14 degrees," Rashad said. "So I went to the equipment manager, Stubby Eason, and I said, 'Can I get a long sleeve shirt or a sweatshirt or something or a turtleneck?' He said, 'Oh, no, we don't give those out until it gets cold.' So I went to the store and bought some long johns and long sleeves, and I said to myself, 'I'm going to wear these until somebody makes me take them off.'"

Teammates said to Rashad, "Bud doesn't allow that." But Rashad played through 1982, and Grant never said anything.

"About 20 years later, I asked Bud why he didn't tell me to take them off, and he said, 'Because I knew I would get the best of you by letting you wear it,'" Rashad said.

Despite his reputation for being a disciplinarian, Grant didn't have long practices, believing they weren't effective and that it was important for players and coaches to get time at home with their families. He liked players who didn't make mental mistakes, sometimes keeping veterans for an extra year or two as they aged.

"He was a disciplinarian but he was very loyal to his players," Eller said. "Having played for Bud Grant just grows and grows on you and it is something you never leave behind."

It took a while, though, for young players to get comfortable with Grant. But if they stuck around long enough, it usually happened.

Steve Jordan, a Minnesota tight end from 1982–1994, said Grant at first was "almost like this icon who was unapproachable." Eventually, though, players would see some melting of his perceived frigid exterior.

"Bud was a little bit of a prankster," Jordan said. "I was standing next to him in practice once and he reached into his jacket pocket and showed me a caterpillar in his hands and he said, 'This is Fuzzy.' I didn't know how to take that. But then he goes and puts it on Jerry Burns's shoulder, and Burnsie freaks out because he did not like bugs and spiders. Bud was having fun."

After all these years, Grant even is able to have some fun with all the Super Bowl losses.

"We weren't good enough on those particular days and that's why I've got gray hair," he said with a laugh.

JERRY BURNS

When the Vikings made it to three Super Bowls from 1973–1976, they had the Purple Offense. When the San Francisco 49ers advanced to four Super Bowls in the 1980s with a similar style, it was called the West Coast Offense.

So why was West Coast Offense the name that stuck? Well, the Vikings lost all their Super Bowls, whereas the 49ers won each time.

The innovator of the Purple Offense, which relied on a short passing game, was Jerry Burns, who was hired as offensive coordinator in 1968 and was around for all four of Minnesota's Super Bowl losses (including Super Bowl IV after the 1969 season and before the Purple Offense came to fruition). He later served as head coach of the Vikings from 1986–1991, and continued to use the offense with success, making the playoffs three times and going 52–43. He died in 2021.

"Bill Walsh got credit for Jerry Burns's offense," said Chuck Foreman, a star Vikings running back from 1973–1979. "That was our offense. That wasn't their offense. We incorporated that to take advantage of my abilities as a receiver, so we were throwing that way before the West Coast Offense."

Walsh did get tenets of his offense from legendary coach Paul Brown when he was a Cincinnati assistant from 1968–1975 and continued to build it up after becoming 49ers coach in 1979. But he got plenty of credit as an innovator because he won three Super Bowls before his San Francisco successor, George Seifert, added two titles.

Burns's Purple Offense got going after the versatile Foreman arrived in 1973. He began to catch plenty of passes out of the backfield, including an NFL-high 73 in 1975. And the Vikings also began to spread the ball around to a multitude of other receivers with Fran Tarkenton.

"Everybody was a receiver, everybody was involved, and it really worked because Chuck Foreman could do everything," said Ahmad Rashad. "And they don't give Burnsie credit. He'd been running that West Coast Offense for years."

It wasn't the only time in his career Burns was overlooked. After serving as defensive backs coach under Green Bay's legendary Vince Lombardi in 1966 and 1967 and winning two Super Bowl rings, Burns was Bud Grant's loyal assistant for 16 years. After the 1983 season, Grant stepped down as coach, and he thought his replacement would be Burns, then 57. Instead, general manager Mike Lynn hired Les Steckel, 20 years younger.

"I wrongly assumed that Burnsie was going to be the coach," said Grant, who had known Burns since he was Iowa's head coach from 1961–1965. "That's all I really wanted."

Jeff Diamond, who was then in the Vikings front office and later general manager, said Burns was "obviously disappointed" at being passed over. He considered going to Cleveland to serve as offensive coordinator under Marty Schottenheimer, but Grant and Steckel convinced him to stay.

Steckel, who had a military background, had a disastrous 3–13 season in 1984 and alienated players with his boot-camp-like methods. He was fired, and Grant came back in 1985. After the Vikings went 7–9, Grant retired for good, and he made sure of one thing.

"Mike Lynn kind of screwed that up [in 1984]," Grant said. "The second time I said, 'Listen, I'll step down again but Burnsie has got to be the coach.' And he did a great job. They came within a dropped pass of going to the Super Bowl."

That was in 1987, Burns's second season on the job. The Vikings lost the NFC Championship Game at Washington when Darrin Nelson dropped a pass at the goal line in the final minute on fourth down.

That was a big disappointment, but the Vikings had nothing to be ashamed about during their surprise playoff run. They had gone 8–7 during a regular season that was shortened by one game due to a players strike, and were hampered by an awful replacement team that went 0–3.

The Vikings opened the playoffs as a 6½-point underdog at New Orleans, but cruised to a 44–10 win. Then, in the biggest playoff upset in franchise history, Minnesota won 36–24 at San Francisco after being an 11-point underdog. Those were the 49ers with the West Coast Offense, but Burns's passing attack looked a lot better that day. Anthony Carter caught 10 passes for a then playoff record 227 yards.

"I just remember that Burnsie kept saying the entire game, 'Get the ball to A.C., get the ball to A.C.,'" said Hall of Fame Vikings tackle Gary Zimmerman.

At least Burns remembered his star receiver's initials. Zimmerman said Burns often couldn't recall the names of even his best players.

"He didn't know anybody's name," Zimmerman said. "He'd say, 'Hey, Big Boy.' [Tackle] Tim Irwin was Big Boy. Everybody was Big Boy. One funny story was at a Christmas party my wife was talking to Burnsie, and he says, 'Your husband is the best in the business,' and then he goes and on. At the end, he goes, 'What's your husband's name again?'"

Plenty of his former players have stories about the eccentric but likable Burns. Some have to do with how Burns could cuss up a storm. After a 1989 game, when Minnesota didn't score a touchdown but beat the Los Angeles Rams 23–21 on an overtime safety after Rich Karlis had kicked seven field goals, Burns went on a rant defending offensive coordinator Bob Schnelker. Burns threw out a dozen f-bombs in the first two minutes, and it remains a staple on YouTube.

Many of the stories have to do with Burns being afraid of spiders and insects. Players would put moths and once a butterfly inside a film canister to get a big laugh when Burns opened it.

"Once we got a fishing pole and [safety] Karl Kassulke put a spider on the end of it," defensive lineman Bob Lurtsema said of an early 1970s stunt when Burns was offensive coordinator. "Then when the film starts up, Kassulke drops the spider down from the fishing pole right over the screen. Burnsie just about jumped out of his pants, and all of us of course were roaring."

Burns, though, also could dish it out. In 1986, he concocted an elaborate scheme in which defensive tackle Keith Millard pretended to get in a heated argument with linebackers coach Monte Kiffin at training camp in Mankato, Minnesota.

Later, according to plan, Millard and Kiffin got on a roof where players below had a partial view of the two continuing to argue. Suddenly, Millard threw off the roof what players thought was Kiffin. Instead, it was a mannequin dressed just like him.

"It looked just like a person," Millard said. "Dennis Ryan, our equipment manager, did a good job picking a really lifelike one. When the guys saw me throw it off, they freaked out. They literally thought I had thrown him off the roof. And then the trainers are running out to check on him to see if he's dead or not. But then me and Monte were laughing our butts off as we walked out the door onto the field, and everybody started to crack up."

While there were plenty of laughs when Burns was the coach, there weren't as many wins as had been hoped. Burns never got his team back to the NFC Championship Game after 1987. At midseason in 1989, Lynn thought running back Herschel Walker would be the final piece to winning a Super Bowl. So the Vikings traded a boatload of draft picks to Dallas for Walker in what turned out to be a deal involving 18 players and picks.

"Our general manager made the worst trade in the history of professional sports," said Steve Jordan.

The draft choices helped the Cowboys win three Super Bowls in the 1990s. With the Vikings, Walker didn't fit the offense and lasted just two and a half uninspiring seasons. In 1989, the Vikings finished 10–6 but were walloped 41–13 at San Francisco to open the playoffs.

That would be Burns's last playoff game. After seasons of 6–10 in 1990 and 8–8 in 1991, he retired just shy of his 65th birthday.

DENNIS GREEN

On January 10, 1992, Dennis Green, in his first day as head coach of the Vikings, stepped to the microphone and declared,

"There is a new sheriff in town." Soon, commercials aired in the Twin Cities with Green repeating his message.

Boy, did he ever mean it. Green immediately took charge and began a purge of many veteran Vikings players.

Did it work? Mostly. In 10 Vikings seasons, Green, who died in 2016, went 97–62 and led the Vikings to the playoffs eight times. He couldn't get them to the Super Bowl, but still followed Bud Grant as the second coach inducted into the Vikings Ring of Honor. Green died in 2016.

"Denny's thing, saying he was the new sheriff in town, was to come in and shake things up," said Steve Jordan. "He came in and got rid of some solid people right off the bat. He got rid of Wade Wilson, Keith Millard, Joey Browner, Leo Lewis sight unseen. He didn't even bring them into the facility. He just said, 'Hey, I'm the new guy. I'm going in a new direction, and unfortunately you're not a part of it.'"

In his decade on the job, Green wasn't shy about making unpopular moves. He cut future Hall of Fame guard Randall McDaniel after the 1999 season and he finished his career with Tampa Bay. He low-balled future Hall of Fame defensive tackle John Randle on a contract offer in 2000 and he headed to Seattle.

Randle wasn't happy with what happened and gained great satisfaction when he made the Pro Bowl in his first season with the Seahawks. Looking back years later, though, Randle had nothing but appreciation for Green.

"He was a coach who cared a lot about his players, not just on the field but off the field," Randle said. "He was concerned about your personal life. He was a coach that players could talk to. And he really opened up a lot of doors as a Black coach."

Following Art Shell, who coached the Los Angeles Raiders from 1989–1994, Green was the second Black coach in modern NFL history. He also had been a trailblazer before he got to Minnesota.

At Northwestern from 1981–1985, Green served as the first Black football coach in the Big Ten. He later was the first Black football coach in the Pac-12 at Stanford, where he was from 1989–1991.

"Dennis crushed barriers," said Marie Green, his wife. "Dennis's opinion was that it was hard to believe someone hadn't done it before, but if he had to be the first, he was going to be the first to pave the way."

Green at times coached with an iron fist, and sometimes he used that fist for other things. Former punter Mitch Berger recalled the fiery pregame speeches Green gave in the locker room and the night before at the team hotel.

"He was telling a story one Saturday night and there was one of those four-legged wooden tables that they put the video machine or whatever on," Berger said. "He smashed it with his hand and the whole table just shattered. He hit it so hard it broke in half. He would get us so fired up for a game, and it was still 18 hours before we played."

Green made an immediate impact with the Vikings, leading them to an 11–5 mark in 1992 and a playoff berth after they had stayed home for two straight years under Jerry Burns.

Playoff trips followed in 1993, 1994, and 1996, but Green by then still hadn't won a postseason game. The Vikings were 0–4, and there was plenty of grumbling in the postseason.

Green didn't help the situation when in October 1997 he released his autobiography, *No Room for Crybabies*. He devoted 10 pages in the first chapter to saying he would sue Minnesota's 10-person ownership group if he wasn't sold 30 percent of the team. Green was upset that reports had surfaced before the season of two owners trying to hire former Notre Dame coach Lou Holtz, who once coached at the University of Minnesota, as his replacement.

Some thought Green might be fired, but he survived after the Vikings went 9–7 in 1997 and he won his first playoff game, 23–22 at the New York Giants. The Vikings stormed back from a 22–13 deficit by scoring a touchdown with 1:30 left, recovering an onside kick, and winning on Eddie Murray's last-second 24-yard field goal.

In 1998, Red McCombs bought the team and gave Green a three-year contract extension. Green wasted no time making the move look good.

In 1998, the Vikings had the greatest regular season in their history. They went 15–1 and scored an NFL-record 556 points. Helping lead the way was rookie receiver Randy Moss, a future Hall of Famer who had slipped in the draft due to off-the-field issues before Green took him with the No. 21 pick.

But the Vikings were stunned in overtime by Atlanta in the NFC Championship Game, denying Green a chance to become the first Black man to coach in a Super Bowl. Eight years later, two Black coaches faced off in the Super Bowl. Tony Dungy, a former Vikings defensive coordinator under Green, led Indianapolis to a win over Chicago, coached by Lovie Smith.

The loss to the Falcons was the most devastating of Green's career. At least there was some consolation after the game when he got a call from President Bill Clinton. Green had served on a panel Clinton put together on equality in sports, and the two had become friends.

"That evening, Dennis didn't speak at all, and that's when you worry is when Denny gets quiet," said Marie Green. "Then we got a call from the White House that night and President Clinton was calling to talk to Dennis, and that was first time I saw him smile all evening. And he had a nice talk with the president, and that was kind of a nice way to end such a challenging day."

Green never could get the Vikings back to their 1998 level. They went 10–6 in 1999, and lost in the divisional round of the playoffs. They went 11–5 in 2000 and returned to the NFC Championship Game but were destroyed 41–0 at the New York Giants.

In 2001, it all came undone. Star tackle Korey Stringer died after a training camp practice due to complications from heatstroke. The Vikings were 5–10 when Green's contract was bought out with one game left in the season.

"Denny was very close to Big K, and that was very tough on him," said Mitch Berger, who called Green a "father-figure type." "It was just an awful year. But I think it was absolute garbage that Denny wasn't there any more after that season. I think he should have been the coach for a lot longer."

Green was replaced by Mike Tice, who had been the offensive line coach. Green returned to coaching with the Arizona Cardinals from 2004–2006, but went just 16–32 in his final NFL stint.

When Green died on July 21, 2016, at the age 67 due to complications from cardiac arrest, there was an outpouring of support. In 2017, when Moss was informed he would be inducted into the Vikings Ring of Honor, he became emotional when talking about Green having died the year before.

"The man passed away without me really, really giving him my love and thanks for what he was able to do for me and my family, man," Moss said. "There were a lot of teams out there that passed on me for wrong reasons. Coach Green gave me that opportunity."

The following year, Green was inducted into the Ring of Honor in an emotional ceremony at halftime of a game against Buffalo.

"Dennis Green will live forever in our hearts. . . . He will live forever in this magnificent U.S. Bank Stadium," Kevin Warren, then a Vikings executive and now Big Ten commissioner, told the roaring crowd.

MIKE ZIMMER

Mike Zimmer knows quite well how starved fans are for the Vikings to finally win a Super Bowl.

Zimmer is reminded of it plenty. That included when he once went to a horse race in Minnesota.

"A guy says, 'If you win the Super Bowl, we're going to elect you governor,'" Zimmer said. "I said, 'I don't want to be governor. That's the last thing I want to do.'"

Zimmer simply wants to get the feeling as a head coach he once had as an assistant. When Zimmer was in his second NFL season and served as Dallas's defensive backs coach, the Cowboys defeated Pittsburgh 27–17 in Super Bowl XXX after the 1995 season.

Barry Switzer was then the Cowboys' head coach, and had given Zimmer his first NFL job the year before as assistant defensive backs coach. He has been rooting for Zimmer to get to the Super Bowl to help pay him back for giving him 10 of his tickets to Super Bowl XXX to sell at a price much higher than the face value of $350.

"If he gets to the Super Bowl with the Vikings, he owes me some Super Bowl tickets because he wasn't making any money [as an assistant] and I'm sure he made a few thousand bucks off those," Switzer said with a laugh. "So he owes me some tickets so he can pay me back some day."

Zimmer came close to making it after the 2017 season. But the Vikings lost 38–7 at Philadelphia in the NFC Championship Game, denying them the chance to become the first team to play in a Super Bowl in its home stadium. Instead, the Eagles defeated New England 41–33 in Super Bowl LII at U.S. Bank Stadium.

Zimmer, though, keeps pressing on. He was set to enter his eighth season with the Vikings in 2021, making him the

Zimmer has has had some top defenses as Vikings coach and led them to the 2017 NFC Championship Game.

ST. PAUL PIONEER PRESS

third-longest tenured coach in team history behind Bud Grant (18 seasons) and Dennis Green (10).

"I've been very fortunate," Zimmer said. "I've got a lot of good people around me. The fans have been great, so we've been fortunate that we've played decent. But we have a lot of things we haven't accomplished yet that we need to accomplish."

In his first seven seasons, Zimmer went 64–47–1 for a winning percentage of .576. Only Grant (.620) and Green (.610) have been better for the Vikings.

"He's done an outstanding job," said New Orleans coach Sean Payton. "I think you always know you're getting a well-coached team."

Zimmer has taken the Vikings to the playoffs three times and gone 2–3. The wins were both over the Saints on the last play of the game. In a 2017 divisional playoff, the Vikings won

29–24 at U.S. Bank Stadium on the Minneapolis Miracle, Case Keenum's 61-yard touchdown pass to Stefon Diggs. In a 2019 wild-card playoff, the Vikings won 26–20 in overtime at the Superdome on a four-yard touchdown pass from Kirk Cousins to Kyle Rudolph.

But the Vikings flopped after both of those dramatic wins. They were walloped at Philadelphia after the first one and lost 27–10 in a divisional playoff at San Francisco after the second one.

Then came the 2020 season, when the Vikings stumbled to a 7–9 record, their first losing mark since Zimmer's first season in 2014. But after the season, Zimmer vowed he was "going to work like crazy on getting a couple of areas fixed and coming back with a vengeance."

When Zimmer needs advice, he often turns to his mentor, Hall of Fame coach Bill Parcells, a defensive wizard who won two Super Bowls with the New York Giants. Zimmer, also a defensive specialist, has patterned plenty of what he does as a coach from what he learned from Parcells. After being a college assistant for 15 seasons and entering the NFL with the Cowboys in 1994, Zimmer got to know Parcells when he served under him with Dallas from 2003–2006. Zimmer was the defensive coordinator.

"He's very workmanlike, he's very dedicated," Parcells said of Zimmer. "He likes football very much. Football is very important to him. He takes pride in his players performing well. He's a beaver. He really is, and I like beavers."

Parcells worked to help Zimmer get a head position after he retired as a coach following the 2006 season. But it took awhile to happen. Zimmer, who was Atlanta's defensive coordinator in 2007 and Cincinnati's from 2008–2013, was passed over for jobs five times before the Vikings finally hired him in January 2014 when he was five months shy of his 58th birthday.

Zimmer perhaps had trouble getting jobs because he was brutally honest in interviews and would tell team officials everything that was wrong with a franchise. He didn't shy away from using the same approach with the Vikings, but they had plenty of problems and were all ears. Zimmer looked to be the perfect fix for a team that had ranked 32nd and last in the NFL in scoring defense and 31st in total defense during a 5–10–1 season in 2013 that cost Leslie Frazier his job.

When he was hired, Zimmer called himself, "The Fixer." And that's what he soon was able to do with the Vikings. They finished in the top four in the NFL in total defense three straight seasons from 2016–2018. In 2017, they were No. 1 in both total and scoring defense.

"You think of Bud Grant and the Purple People Eaters when it all began in the earlier days of the Vikings, and that's the kind of toughness that he's brought back," said Vikings safety Harrison Smith. "So I think it fits the franchise, the area, the weather. It's old school."

Zimmer has taken an old-school approach with the Vikings, opting to have a run-first offense. In 2019, Dalvin Cook rushed for 1,135 yards, and in 2020 he was even better, rolling up 1,557. When Cook is running well, that has opened things up for quarterback Kirk Cousins, who threw a career-high 35 touchdown passes in 2020. Put it together, and the Vikings, with since-retired offensive coordinator Gary Kubiak calling the plays, finished fourth in the NFL in total offense in 2020, their best finish since they were No. 4 in 2004.

"For the first time in my seven years, I thought we had a very, very explosive offense," Zimmer said.

But the Vikings missed the playoffs with their 7–9 record because the defense fell apart. They were 29th in the NFL in scoring defense and 27th in total defense.

It didn't help that three Vikings defensive stars had battled injuries. Defensive end Danielle Hunter was out all season with a neck injury, linebacker Anthony Barr missed the final 14 games with a torn pectoral muscle, and linebacker Eric Kendricks missed the final five games with a calf issue. After the season, Vikings defensive players vowed to get the unit back to where it usually has been under Zimmer.

"Zim, being his defensive background and his defensive prowess, we've had a lot of success, and we're not used to not being toward the top in defense," Smith said. "I think there's a lot of people here that are eager to get back to that spot."

And you better believe Zimmer, who signed a three-year extension before the 2020 season to put him under contract through 2023, was planning to tell players he expects to get back to that level. He has remained his usual no-nonsense self.

"There's no gray with Mike Zimmer," said Vikings co-defensive coordinator Andre Patterson. "You know where you fit. He's going to tell you, whether you want to hear it or not, he's going to tell you the truth of what you're doing good, what you're doing bad, and what you need to improve on."

Zimmer's players mostly have liked that approach. Barr was criticized by Zimmer in 2016 when the coach said "sometimes he has a tendency to coast a little bit." Barr said he used that as motivation to get better. When he became a free agent in March 2019, Barr initially agreed to sign with the New York Jets before deciding to come back to Minnesota on a five-year, $67.5 million deal. That was less than the Jets' offer.

"It's something I appreciated greatly about Zim," Kyle Rudolph, a Vikings tight end from 2011–2020, said of his tell-it-like-it-is approach. "If you're out of line, even if it's the slightest bit, he calls your attention to it."

Rudolph said that "everybody in the organization has one goal and that's to win the first championship in franchise history." If it happens under Zimmer, don't even bother asking if he wants to run for governor.

AND THE WINNER IS . . .

Obviously, it's Bud Grant. He has been the most legendary figure in the history of Minnesota sports. He has gone down as one of the greatest coaches in both NFL and CFL history.

Grant's legend has continued to live on three and half decades after he coached his last game. At his home in Bloomington, Minnesota, he has a popular garage sale each spring. People come from many miles away to buy items related to Grant's Vikings years and from his life spent hunting and fishing.

COACHES WHO DID NOT MAKE THE CUT

Even though he went just 29–51–4, fiery Norm Van Brocklin deserves note for steering the Vikings through six seasons after they entered the NFL in 1961 as an expansion team. They never made the playoffs during that period, but did go 8–5–1 in 1964. During Van Brocklin's watch, the Vikings acquired many players that helped successor Bud Grant. They included Mick Tingelhoff, Jim Marshall, Carl Eller, Grady Alderman, Bill Brown, Dave Osborn, and Fred Cox. After resigning in February 1967, Van Brocklin later was Atlanta's coach from 1968–1974. He died in 1983.

Mike Tice took over as interim coach from Dennis Green for the final game in 2001 and then got the regular gig. He went 32–33 before being fired after the 2005 season, when Minnesota failed to make the playoffs at 9–7. The cruelest season was in 2003, when the Vikings started 6–0 before finishing 9–7 and missing the playoffs. They were knocked out with an 18–17 loss at Arizona in the finale, when Josh McCown on fourth-and-25 threw a 28-yard TD pass to Nate Poole, who made a diving catch while going out of the end zone on the final play. The

Vikings went 8–8 in 2004, but did record a 31–17 playoff upset at Green Bay before falling 27–14 at Philadelphia.

Brad Childress replaced Tice in 2006 and led the Vikings to the brink of the Super Bowl in 2009. With the NFC North champions tied 28–28 with 19 seconds left in regulation in the NFC Championship Game at New Orleans, they had third-and-10 at the Saints 33 but were penalized five yards for 12 men on the field. Brett Favre threw an interception on the next play, and Minnesota would lose 31–28 in overtime, never getting the ball in the extra session. Things fell apart after that, and Childress was fired when the Vikings started 3–7 in 2010. Childress finished 39–35, also having led Minnesota to an NFC North crown in 2008.

Leslie Frazier replaced Childress on an interim basis midway through 2010 and had the tag removed after the season. He lasted through 2013, going 21–32–1. Frazier had one season of note. With Adrian Peterson rushing for 2,097 yards, the second most in NFL history, the Vikings won their final four games in 2012 to earn a wild-card berth at 10–6. But starting quarterback Christian Ponder was out with an arm injury, and the Vikings fell 24–10 at Green Bay in the playoffs.

2

QUARTERBACK

THE CANDIDATES

Fran Tarkenton
Kirk Cousins
Tommy Kramer
Daunte Culpepper

At least Fran Tarkenton was a homegrown quarterback for the Vikings. Well, mostly he was.

Tarkenton began his career with the Vikings, playing with them from 1961–1966 before being traded to the New York Giants. But he returned to Minnesota for a 1972–1978 stint and had his best seasons.

For much of their history, though, the Vikings have picked up quarterbacks who already had their greatest days elsewhere.

In 1993, they signed Jim McMahon eight years after he had won a Super Bowl with Chicago. But McMahon lasted just one season.

In 1994, Minnesota signed Warren Moon after he had great success with the Houston Oilers. Moon made Pro Bowls at ages 38 and 39 but was unable to lead the Vikings to a playoff win in his three seasons.

In 1997, former Philadelphia star Randall Cunningham arrived for a three-year stint. He had a magical season at age 35 in 1998, when the Vikings went 15–1 and made the NFC Championship Game, but fizzled after that.

Sound familiar? In 2009, the Vikings brought in former Green Bay star Brett Favre, and he had an amazing run that season at age 40, with the Vikings again making it to the NFC Championship Game. But he flopped the next year and then retired.

In 2011, the Vikings brought in another former Eagles star in Donovan McNabb, but that was a disaster.

In 2018, they turned to Kirk Cousins, who had played six years with Washington. Cousins hadn't had the previous success of some other Minnesota quarterback signees, although he had made a Pro Bowl in 2016. But at 30 when he played his first Vikings game, he was a lot younger than the other guys.

Cousins, who signed a three-year, $84 million contract and then a two-year, $66 million extension in 2020, might end up working out as a rare long-term Minnesota quarterback. In his second season of 2019, he was fourth in the NFL in passer rating at 107.4, made the Pro Bowl, and steered the Vikings to a dramatic 26–20 overtime win at New Orleans in the playoff opener. The Vikings finished 7–9 and didn't make the playoffs in 2020, but Cousins threw 35 touchdown passes, the second most in team history.

FRAN TARKENTON
Late in the first quarter of a September 17, 1961, game at Metropolitan Stadium, Francis Asbury Tarkenton was introduced to the NFL.

The quarterback had been selected in the third round of the 1961 draft out of Georgia by the expansion Vikings. He thought he would start their initial game against Chicago, but

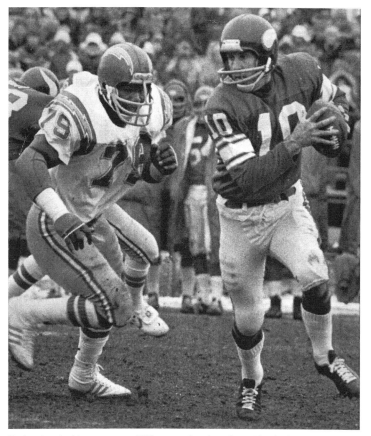

Tarkenton held numerous NFL records when he retired after the 1978 season, including for touchdown passes and yards passing.
ST. PAUL PIONEER PRESS

head coach Norm Van Brocklin made a late switch and decided to go with journeyman Bob Shaw.

Shaw didn't do much early in the game, so Van Brocklin sent in Tarkenton. The Bears didn't know what hit them. The scrambling Tarkenton completed 17 of 23 passes for 250 yards and four touchdowns and also ran for a TD. The Vikings won 37–13 in one of the most stunning upsets in NFL history.

"Tarkenton was running around and he drove (the Bears) crazy," said Jerry Reichow, then a Vikings wide receiver. "They had never seen a quarterback like him."

Nobody had. Tarkenton scrambled like no quarterback had before. He tired out defensive linemen whose attempts to catch him often were in vain.

"Tarkenton was the best scrambler I'd ever seen," said former Vikings halfback Dave Osborn. "He had eyes in the back of his head, so he could see people coming at him."

Tarkenton's act played out for nearly two decades in the NFL and landed him in the Hall of Fame. He was with the Vikings from 1961–1966 and from 1972–1978 with a stop in between with the New York Giants. His second Vikings stint was his most productive as Tarkenton led them to three Super Bowls.

When Tarkenton retired in 1978, he held every significant NFL career passing record, including having thrown for 47,003 yards (33,098 with Minnesota) and 342 touchdowns (239 with the Vikings).

"He was one of the best that ever played," said Hall of Fame tackle Ron Yary, who played for the Vikings from 1968–1981. "He knew what plays to call in what situations. He knew when to audible. He was as good as any quarterback you could ask for. He was the perfect quarterback for our team."

Van Brocklin didn't necessarily think that was the case when he was the coach from 1961–1966. Even though Tarkenton was putting up good passing numbers and made Pro Bowls in 1964 and 1965, the two clashed.

Van Brocklin, who had been a Hall of Fame quarterback with the Los Angeles Rams and the Philadelphia Eagles, was an old-school guy who wanted Tarkenton to stay in the pocket. He didn't like his scrambling nature.

The Vikings weren't very good under the fiery Van Brocklin, having only one winning season. So that fueled the tension between the coach and quarterback.

"There was a lot of friction there," said Hall of Fame defensive end Carl Eller, who played for the Vikings from 1964–1978. "They didn't agree with each other and they had difficulty coming to terms on how to play the game."

It came to a head after the 1966 season when Tarkenton said he no longer would play for the Vikings. In *Every Day is Game Day*, his 2009 autobiography written with Jim Bruton, Tarkenton wrote that Van Brocklin "taught me the game of professional football" and was a "brilliant strategist" but that it became "time to go" from Minnesota.

"Our relationship, pure and simple, did not work," Tarkenton wrote. "I was miserable. And so I came to the decision that my days with the Minnesota Vikings were over."

Van Brocklin ended up resigning, but that didn't change Tarkenton's mind. He didn't want to stay in Minnesota and potentially be dubbed as the guy who drove out a coach.

So Tarkenton was traded to the Giants for two first- and two second-round picks, and Bud Grant replaced Van Brocklin. Tarkenton ended up playing against the Vikings three times with the Giants, going 1–2.

The one win was memorable. In the 1969 opener at Yankee Stadium, Tarkenton in the final minute threw a desperation long pass and then the winning touchdown in a 24–23 victory.

"I actually got the game ball from that game," said Bob Lurtsema, then a Giants defensive lineman and later Tarkenton's teammate on the Vikings. "Fran said, 'I know you got the game ball, but you'll never know how good I feel. You'll never know how much this game meant to me.'"

After that game, the Vikings reeled off 12 straight wins. They finished the season 12–2 and eventually lost 23–7 to

Kansas City in Super Bowl IV, their first appearance in the big game.

The Vikings looked set at quarterback at the time with Joe Kapp, who was named to the Pro Bowl in 1969. However, Kapp ended up being traded to the Boston Patriots due to a contract dispute after that season, and the Vikings had struggles at quarterback over the next two years. They had the top defense in football but didn't win a playoff game in 1970 or 1971 because of inadequate play at the position.

"We had the nucleus of a great team, but we needed a quarterback," Grant said. "I said to [general manager] Jim Finks that if Tarkenton was available, that's the kind of guy we wanted. That of course was a great move on our part."

The Vikings acquired Tarkenton for quarterback Norm Snead, wide receiver Bob Grim, fullback Vince Clements, and first- and second-round draft picks. After missing the playoffs in all five of his seasons with the Giants, he was glad to go to a Super Bowl contender.

Grant, influenced by coaching in the more wide-open Canadian Football League, embraced Tarkenton's scrambling. And by that time, Tarkenton had become a more mature quarterback, primarily scrambling in order to better set up to pass.

"The reason Tarkenton moved around a lot is because he was only 5-foot-10 and three quarters," Grant said. "So you move right or left or back so you can see to throw the ball."

Tarkenton's first season back didn't go too well as the Vikings went just 7–7. But they ended up going to the Super Bowl in three of the next four seasons, although they lost each time.

The one season during that stretch when Minnesota didn't make the Super Bowl was the best individual one of Tarkenton's career. In 1975, he was named NFL MVP, first-team All-Pro for the only time in his career, and to his eighth of nine career

Pro Bowls. He led the NFL with 25 touchdown passes as the Vikings went 12–2.

The season, though, ended in bitter disappointment. The Vikings were stunned 17–14 by Dallas at home in the play-off opener when Roger Staubach threw a 50-yard, last-second Hail Mary pass to Drew Pearson for the winning touchdown. Tarkenton then learned that his father, Dallas Tarkenton, had died during the game in the family's native Georgia from a heart attack.

After losing their fourth straight Super Bowl 32–14 to Oakland after the 1976 season, the Vikings began to age as a team. Tarkenton missed the final five games in 1977 after suffering a broken leg. He returned in 1978, but the Vikings went just 8–7–1. Tarkenton elected to retire after an ugly 34–10 play-off loss to the Los Angeles Rams.

Tarkenton had tried to put on a brave face about not having won a Super Bowl, even appearing on *Saturday Night Live* in 1977 to joke about it. In reality, though, the losses hurt.

"I am very disappointed we didn't win the Super Bowl," Tarkenton said in his Hall of Fame induction speech in 1986. "There has been a void in my life ever since. But once you get to the top of the mountain, you look for another mountain to climb."

Tarkenton did just that. He became a television personality, which included being an analyst on *Monday Night Football* and cohost of the popular show *That's Incredible!* He became a very successful businessman, including founding the annuity marketing firm Tarkenton Financial in Atlanta.

Tarkenton follows the Vikings regularly on television and gets to their games when he can. He has spoken to players about the upset of the Bears in 1961.

The night before Minnesota's 14–9 win at Atlanta in 2017, Tarkenton gave a pep talk at the team hotel. He showed off his game ball from 56 years earlier.

"He talked about the importance of team," said sideline analyst and former punter Greg Coleman, who was on hand. "He didn't start that game, but as part of the team, you never know when your number is going to be called. And when his number was called, he came in and threw four touchdown passes."

KIRK COUSINS

Kirk Cousins was leaving a stadium after a game on the Vikings team bus when he gazed out the window and saw a fan wearing a T-shirt.

The T-shirt didn't mention the Vikings or anything about football. But the quarterback knew exactly what the message implied.

"The T-shirt was purple with yellow letters and it said, 'Just Once in My Lifetime,' and that was all the shirt said," Cousins said. "But I knew exactly what it meant. And I thought that summed up what it would mean to the fan base to win a world championship."

Minnesota fans are starved to one day win it all. The Vikings have been around for 60 years, and have lost in all four of their Super Bowl appearances. And they haven't been to the big game since January 1977.

Cousins is reminded of the team's drought seemingly every day. When he goes to a coffee shop, a shopping center, or even to church, he invariably hears the same thing from fans.

"They say, 'Bring us a Super Bowl, bring us that ring,'" he said.

When the Vikings signed Cousins as a free agent to a three-year, $84 million contract, which for a short period made him the highest-paid player in NFL history, it was believed he would be the final piece to put them over the top. After all, the Vikings were coming off having gone to the NFC Championship Game in 2017.

"They brought him in to try to win the Super Bowl," said Joe Theismann, who won Super Bowl XVII as Washington's quarterback in January 1983 and got to know Cousins well when he played for Washington from 2012–2017.

The Vikings stumbled in Cousins's first year, going 8–7–1 and not even making the playoffs. In 2019, they at least won a playoff game, a first in Cousins's career, and he made the Pro Bowl. That was enough for Minnesota to sign him to a two-year, $66 million contract extension in March 2020, taking him through the 2022 season.

In 2020, the hope was the Vikings would make the playoffs in consecutive years for the first time since 2009. So much for that. They went 7–9 for their first losing season since Mike Zimmer's first year of 2014.

It was hard, though, to pin much blame in 2020 on Cousins. The Vikings had elected to get younger and clear up some of their salary-cap issues, so they didn't bring back a lot of veterans on defense. The defense ended up being what Zimmer called the "worst one" he's ever had. But the Vikings did rank No. 4 in the NFL in total offense, their best finish since they were No. 4 in 2004.

Cousins threw for 4,265 yards and 35 touchdown passes, the most in his nine-year career and the second most in team history following Daunte Culpepper's 39 in 2004. He had a passer rating of 105.0, the second best of his career, and it raised his rating after three Minnesota seasons to 103.6, the best in team history.

True, Cousins threw 10 interceptions as the Vikings got off to a 1–5 start. But he tossed just three in the last 10 games, although he did end up equaling his career high with 13 picks.

"He probably started out a little slow at the beginning of the season," Zimmer said. "I think at the end of the year, he's had some big-time games, made some big-time throws, he's taken much better care of the football. I think he's had a good year. It's unfortunate that we couldn't do a little bit better and win a few more games, so he could showcase himself even more."

For his part, Cousins mostly shrugged off his gaudy 2020 statistics.

"It's nice to have positive statistics, but ultimately that's not what it's really about," Cousins said after the season. "Ultimately, you want to win games and that's where my focus is and will be going forward."

It hardly was the first time in his Vikings tenure that Cousins downplayed statistics. But there was one statistic he brought up before the 2019 season that he said he wanted to rectify.

At the time, after having gone 26–30–1 as a starter for Washington and 8–7–1 in his first Vikings season, Cousins had a 34–37–2 mark. He lamented, "I'm pretty much a .500 quarterback in my career so far, and I don't think that's where you want to be."

Cousins helped shake off that stigma in 2019. He went 10–5 as a starter, sitting out the final game of a 10–6 season when starters rested, and won his first playoff game in dramatic fashion.

The Vikings were 7½ point underdogs at New Orleans in a wild-card game at the Superdome. With the score tied 20–20, Cousins led the Vikings on a 75-yard drive on the first possession of overtime, and threw a four-yard touchdown pass to Kyle Rudolph for a 26–20 win. The winning points were set up by a 43-yard pass from Cousins to Adam Thielen to the Saints 2.

"It was a thrill for our team, something we had worked hard to do," Cousins, who completed 19 of 31 passes for 242 yards and a touchdown, said of the win. "It was a difficult, hard-fought game, and it was gratifying to win in a tough environment against a good football team."

Cousins, though, wasn't able to build upon the victory. The following week, the Vikings were walloped 27–10 at San Francisco in the divisional round as Cousins completed 21 of 29 passes for 172 yards with an interception and a touchdown and was sacked six times. And once again there was plenty of talk by critics about his big contract.

Cousins also has faced scrutiny in his career for not being able to win prime-time games. At least he got one monkey off his back in November 2020, when he steered Minnesota to a 19–13 win at Chicago. It marked his first win as starting quarterback on *Monday Night Football* after a 0–9 start.

Cousins's legacy as a Vikings quarterback will come down to how much he will be able to win. After just three seasons, he already was fourth in team history with 12,166 yards passing and 91 touchdown passes. But his record as a starting quarterback was an unimpressive 25–21–1.

"Once somebody stamps you one way, you're just that way forever," said former NFL quarterback Brock Huard, who has served as a Fox analyst for Vikings games. "And I think for him, people just say, 'Yeah, he's good but he'll never be great.' I just hate that stamp, but the only way you change that is ultimately to get to and win a Super Bowl."

Tommy Kramer

They called him "Two-Minute Tommy."

Tommy Kramer's nickname actually was born when he was a junior in high school in San Antonio and led several comeback victories. But it really gained popularity early in his Vikings career.

In the fourth game he played as a rookie in 1977, Kramer led the Vikings to a dramatic 28–27 win over San Francisco. They had trailed 24–0 and Kramer entered when it was 24–7 early in the fourth quarter.

In the next-to-last game of the 1980 season, Kramer threw a 46-yard desperation pass to Ahmad Rashad on the final play for a 28–23 win at Metropolitan Stadium. The Vikings had gotten the ball back with 14 seconds left, and Kramer drove them 80 yards on two plays with no timeouts left for the win that clinched the NFC Central.

"He had a great disposition as a quarterback," Rashad said. "He wasn't afraid of anything. He was fearless. He was a swashbuckler."

Cornerback Carl Lee called Kramer an earlier version of Jim McMahon. From 1977–1989, Kramer took Vikings fans on a wild ride. Sometimes he was very good, other times he was woefully inconsistent. But it was always entertaining.

Often, when Kramer started to get rolling, he would get hurt. After taking over as the starter from the retired Fran Tarkenton in 1979, Kramer played in just 118 of a possible 165 games over the next 11 seasons.

Kramer also had off-the-field issues. He was charged with drunken driving twice while with the Vikings, and had two stays in rehabilitation clinics.

Through it all, Kramer emerged as second in Minnesota history behind Tarkenton in yards passing (24,775) and touchdown passes (159). He played in the Pro Bowl after the 1986 season, when he led the NFL with a passer rating of 92.6. He was the first quarterback in NFL history to have two 450-yard passing games.

"The way I look at it, I accomplished a dream of what I wanted to do," said Kramer, who finished his career by playing

Kramer was the first NFL quarterback to pass for 450 or more yards in
a game twice.
ST. PAUL PIONEER PRESS

one game with New Orleans in 1990. "I gave it all I got every
game. I didn't have any more to give."

Kramer was selected with the No. 27 pick in the 1977 draft
out of Rice and earmarked to be the heir apparent to Tarkenton. Tarkenton was lost for the season in the ninth game in
1977 with a broken leg, and veteran Bob Lee initially took over
as the starter because Kramer said Bud Grant "didn't like rookies very much, especially quarterbacks." But in Week 12, Grant
yanked Lee against the 49ers with 12 minutes left when Minnesota trailed 24–7.

Kramer led the amazing comeback. He threw three touchdown passes in the fourth quarter, the last a 69-yard strike deep
down the middle to Sammy White with 1:47 remaining.

"That's probably my greatest memory because I was a rookie," Kramer said. "So for me to be a rookie and come off the bench and do that, that's pretty darn good."

When Kramer eventually replaced Tarkenton for good, he downplayed there being a lot of pressure. He said Tarkenton had been preparing him.

"The media said things like he isn't helping Kramer and all that, but that wasn't the case," Kramer said of his first two seasons. "When I had a question, he would give me an answer."

Kramer inherited a team in transition. Many top players from the teams that made four Super Bowls from 1969–1976 had retired. Still, Kramer had some solid seasons. In a three-year span, from 1979–1981, he threw for 10,891 yards and 68 touchdowns.

Kramer led the Vikings to the NFC Central title in 1980 in most dramatic fashion. In the legendary win over the Browns in the Miracle at the Met, he offered bold words in the huddle to start the final drive when the Vikings were facing what seemed to be impossible odds.

"I looked in eyes of my offensive linemen and I said, 'They're scared of us, you understand that,'" Kramer said. "That got their attention."

Kramer first rifled the ball to tight end Joe Senser at the Minnesota 30, who latereled to fullback Ted Brown at the 27. Brown ran the ball down the left sideline and out of bounds at the Cleveland 46 with five seconds left.

Kramer then called Squadron Right, and heaved the ball down the right sideline. It was tipped and landed in the hands of Rashad on the goal line.

"That was one of the most miraculous comebacks ever," Kramer said. "That one was really good because it put us in the playoffs. We had practiced it. It was pure luck, but we were prepared."

Brown said Kramer always seemed prepared when the game was on the line.

"He had a calm about him," Brown said. "He never got flustered. He never got rattled. It was like he almost always knew that something good was going to happen."

As the 1980s went along, not a lot good happened when it came to Kramer's health. He was limited to just three games in 1983 after suffering a torn medial collateral ligament in his knee and to just nine games in 1984 when he separated his shoulder.

Kramer bounced back to play a full season in 1985. Then he had his impressive 1986 season, when he threw 24 touchdown passes.

After that, injuries returned. That played a role in Kramer starting just 15 times in his final three Minnesota seasons.

Kramer was the starter when the Vikings played at New Orleans to open the 1987 playoffs even though he had started only five games in the regular season. He didn't make his debut that season until November after suffering perhaps the most troublesome injury of his career on a hard hit in the exhibition opener.

"Well, my spine was bent," Kramer said.

Because of the injury, Kramer's arm at times would go numb, and that's what happened in the playoffs against the Saints. Kramer was done after throwing just nine passes. Backup Wade Wilson came in and completed a 44–10 win. Wilson then led the Vikings to a 36–24 upset at San Francisco and in the NFC Championship Game, a 17–10 loss at Washington.

After that, Kramer's body was simply too beat up, and Wilson became the primary starter. Kramer also was continuing to deal with off-the-field issues, although he denies his drinking affected his play.

"People can say whatever they want to say, but I'm the one that lives it," Kramer said. "The only time that I played bad was when I was hurt."

Kramer was a tremendous talent, and it's always been a source of debate how good he could have been.

"The off-the-field problems kind of contributed to the inconsistency, but when he was on fire, there weren't many better," said former tight end Steve Jordan. "But he would get out of the zone and there were some issues, and it just didn't work as well."

Former linebacker Scott Studwell prefers to look back at what the quarterback was rather than what he could have been.

"Tommy had a really good career," Studwell said. "I think people kind of pick up and run with some of the off-the-field stuff and disregard how good of a player he was. Tommy was one of the most competitive people I've ever been around. He was extremely intelligent, had a good arm and a great feel for the game, and was very productive."

DAUNTE CULPEPPER

No quarterback in Vikings history ever has had a better season statistically than Daunte Culpepper. Not Fran Tarkenton. Not Brett Favre. Not Kirk Cousins.

In 2004, Culpepper set every significant single-season passing record in Minnesota history, and they still stand. He threw for 4,717 yards, 39 touchdowns, and had a passer rating of 110.9.

"He was the best in the game at that time," said former Vikings center Matt Birk.

That might be stretching it since Peyton Manning of Indianapolis led the league that season with then NFL records of 49 TD passes and a 121.1 passer rating. But Culpepper did have more yards passing than Manning's 4,557.

"Daunte was unreal that year," said former Vikings cornerback Antoine Winfield. "That was the best I've ever seen a quarterback play, and that includes the year Brett Favre had."

Favre in 2009 threw for 33 touchdowns and had a passer rating of 107.2, third in Vikings history. Second is the 107.4 rating Cousins had in 2019. As for Tarkenton, who played for the Vikings from 1961–1966 and 1972–1978, he had several impressive seasons in an era before quarterbacks were throwing the ball all over the place.

Culpepper, taken with the No. 11 pick in the 1999 draft, looked as if he might be the next Tarkenton in Minnesota. Not only could he pass, he was a running threat. Culpepper made three Pro Bowls in his first five years as a starter, which actually was one more than Tarkenton did in his first five behind center.

But then it all came crumbling down for Culpepper. In the seventh game of the 2005 season at Carolina, he suffered a devastating knee injury.

The 6-foot-4, 260-pound Culpepper never was the same after that. He got into a squabble with Vikings officials, who wanted him to rehab his knee in Minnesota while Culpepper insisted on doing it in Florida. Culpepper asked to be traded, and he got his wish, being shipped before the 2006 season to Miami for a second-round pick.

Culpepper continued to have injury problems and played in just four games with the Dolphins. Then he became a journeyman, being a part-time starter in Oakland in 2007 and for Detroit in 2008 and 2009.

Talk about an ugly way to end an NFL career. Culpepper lost his last 10 starts, going 0–5 in each of his final two seasons. He wasn't helped by the Lions going 0–16 in 2008.

Making his football end even more unceremonious, Culpepper spent the 2010 season with the Sacramento Mountain Lions of the fly-by-night United Football League, who were coached by his former Vikings mentor Dennis Green. Culpepper flopped, throwing 12 interceptions to 10 touchdown passes.

Culpepper never was able to overcome his injuries. He had shoulder issues in both Miami and Detroit. But the worse one remained his 2005 knee injury, when he was hit low by Panthers cornerback Chris Gamble after an 18-yard run. He sustained damage to three of the four major ligaments, the anterior cruciate, medial collateral, and posterior cruciate.

"I was there when he got hurt," said Birk, then on injured reserve with a hip injury. "It was tough. You kind of thought he was kind of indestructible, he was just so big and strong. He was such a competitor, maybe sometimes to a fault. Maybe that's why I think he came back too early from his injury."

Birk, who played for Minnesota from 1998–2008, took over as the starting center in 2000, the same year Culpepper became the starting quarterback. After the Vikings drafted Culpepper out of Central Florida, they elected to bring him along slowly.

Culpepper didn't throw a pass as a rookie in 1999, getting into one game and rushing three times for six yards at the end of a Vikings rout. He spent the year learning under veteran quarterbacks Randall Cunningham and Jeff George.

"I think that helped him," said former Vikings receiver Jake Reed. "Too many quarterbacks, they come in and play right away and the speed of the game is so different. But for him to sit out that first year, get the offense down, and understand the players he had around him, I think that was good for him."

In his first NFL start in the 2000 opener, Culpepper ran for three touchdowns in a 30–27 win over Chicago. He led the Vikings that season to the NFC Championship Game, although they were drubbed 41–0 at the New York Giants. Culpepper threw for 3,937 yards and a league-best 33 touchdowns and made his first Pro Bowl.

Culpepper had his share of struggles in 2001 and 2002 although he was able to bounce back in 2003. He made his second Pro Bowl, and threw for 3,479 yards and 25 touchdowns.

Then came Culpepper's 2004 season, when he also rushed for 406 yards to give him what was then an NFL record of 5,123 combined passing and rushing yards. It was Culpepper's fifth straight season with 400 or more yards rushing, with his career high having been 609 in 2002.

The problem that season was that the Vikings, who started 5–1, finished just 8–8. Star receiver Randy Moss missed three games due to injury and slumped to 767 yards after averaging 1,396 in his first six seasons. Moss had issues with the team, and ended up being traded after the season.

But Culpepper did all he could. He led the Vikings to a 31–17 upset at Green Bay to open the playoffs, throwing for 284 yards and four touchdowns with no interceptions.

"He was one of the best quarterbacks in the game then," said Kevin Williams, then an All-Pro Vikings defensive tackle. "He had a cannon for an arm. He wasn't afraid to make any throws. He could make all the throws and he could run."

But after his knee injury, many former teammates were left to ponder what might have been with Culpepper.

"He could have been a Hall of Famer with the numbers that he was putting up," Winfield said. "I remember watching him drop back and throwing the ball 60 yards downfield. It was just unfortunate he couldn't stay healthy."

AND THE WINNER IS . . .

Fran Tarkenton, of course. He not only goes down as the best quarterback in Vikings history, he also ranks among the greatest in the NFL's first 100 years. While he was known as a scrambler, Tarkenton ran around to help his passing game, and it worked.

Yes, Tarkenton was 0–3 in Super Bowls, but he was 6–2 in other playoff games, including 5–1 at home. When the weather got cold in Minnesota, Tarkenton still could find a way.

Tarkenton, who led the NFL with 3,468 yards passing in his final season of 1978, probably could have played longer. But he went on to a successful career in broadcasting and in business.

QUARTERBACKS WHO DID NOT MAKE THE CUT

Joe Kapp played just three years for the Vikings (1967–1969) but led them to their first Super Bowl, a 23–7 loss to Kansas City in January 1970 that turned out to be his last game for them. An ugly contract dispute resulted in Kapp being traded to the Boston Patriots, and he played just one more season. In 1969, Kapp made the Pro Bowl and tied an NFL record with seven touchdown passes against Baltimore. He was a fiery and much respected leader. He declined his 1969 award for team Most Valuable Player, saying the Vikings had no single MVP.

Few quarterbacks have defied age the way Warren Moon did. He turned 38 in his first Minnesota season of 1994, but threw for 4,264 yards and 18 touchdowns and made the Pro Bowl. Moon made it again in 1995, when he threw for 4,228 yards and finished second in the NFL with 33 TD passes. Injuries limited Moon to just eight games in 1996, and the Vikings figured he finally was too old to keep around. But all Moon did in 1997 was make the Pro Bowl with Seattle at age 41. He was inducted into the Hall of Fame in 2006.

Randall Cunningham came out of retirement to join the Vikings in 1997 as a backup. By 1998, he was leading the most explosive offensive in NFL history. After Brad Johnson was injured in the second game, Cunningham took over and the Vikings went on to a 15–1 mark while setting an NFL record with 556 points scored. Cunningham threw 34 touchdown passes and was named first-team All-Pro and to the Pro Bowl. The magic ran out the next season, though, and Cunningham was benched after six games in favor of Jeff George. His three-year run in Minnesota then ended.

Brett Favre had taken Green Bay to two Super Bowls in the 1990s, winning one. He almost made another Super Bowl with the Vikings. Favre had been traded by the Packers to the New York Jets in 2008, and then was signed by the Vikings in 2009. He beat his old Green Bay team twice that season, and finished with 4,202 yards, 33 touchdowns, and a career-high 107.2 passer rating. He took the Vikings to the NFC Championship Game, but they lost a heartbreaker 31–28 at New Orleans in overtime. Coming back at age 41 in 2010, Favre finally ran out of gas. He had a rough season and retired after Minnesota went 6–10. He was inducted into the Hall of Fame in 2016.

3

FULLBACK

THE CANDIDATES

Bill Brown
Chuck Foreman
Ted Brown

The fullback has become an endangered species. Many NFL teams no longer even have one on the roster.

For those teams that have a fullback, he rarely carries the ball. When Jerome Felton made the Pro Bowl with the Vikings in 2012, he didn't have a single carry that season. His job was to block for halfback Adrian Peterson, who rushed for 2,097 yards, the second-highest total in NFL history.

The Vikings did use fullback C. J. Ham to run some during his Pro Bowl season in 2019. He had a grand total of seven attempts.

It didn't used to be like that. Under the first two Vikings coaches, Norm Van Brocklin and Bud Grant, the fullback often was a focal point of the offense.

BILL BROWN

Minnesota's first great fullback arrived in an unceremonious manner. After he had rushed for just 81 yards as a rookie in

1961, the Chicago Bears traded Bill Brown to the Vikings for a mere fourth-round pick.

In Brown's first Vikings season, it didn't look like much of a deal. He ran for just 103 under coach Norm Van Brocklin.

Eventually, though, Van Brocklin became enamored with the toughness of the 5-foot-11 Brown, who was stumpy and bowlegged and always seemed to lead with his head. In 1964, he rushed for a career-high 866 yards and began a stretch of making four Pro Bowls in five seasons.

Bud Grant took over as coach in 1967 and continued to use Brown plenty. In 1968, he rushed for 805 yards and scored 11 touchdowns.

Brown, who died in 2018, played with the Vikings through 1974, and rushed for 5,757 yards. He also was an adept receiver, catching 284 balls, and a top-notch blocker.

"He was as good of a football player as the Vikings have ever had," Grant said. "He could do everything. When I got here, I didn't realize he was a great pass receiver, and then we went to the short passing game and we started passing to him more. And he was our best blocker."

The NFC Central once was known as the Black and Blue Division thanks to the many rugged, low-scoring battles. The Vikings played Detroit twice a season, and Grant said eventual Hall of Fame linebacker Joe Schmitt dreaded going against Brown. Schmitt played for the Lions from 1953–1965 before becoming their coach from 1967–1972.

"I was talking to Joe Schmitt and he said, 'I hated to blitz against you guys because that darn Bill Brown was always there. He would get lower than I did and I took a beating,'" Grant said.

Because of the physical nature of his play, Van Brocklin gave Brown the nickname "Hammer Head." A sportswriter dubbed him "Boom-Boom," which is the one that stuck.

"He wouldn't run around a player," said former Vikings defensive lineman Bob Lurtsema. "He would rather run through a player."

The 228-pound Brown was a bowling ball on the field. He figured it was just a waste of time to try to fake anybody out.

"I'm not fancy like a halfback, so I'd rather go right at it and get where I can," Brown once told NFL Films.

Brown was a throwback to the days of leather helmets. He wore a crew cut from when he arrived in Minnesota until he left in the mid-1970s, when many players wore their hair long.

In his later years, when the Vikings brought in younger runners, he took over as special teams captain. Brown had just 646 yards rushing in his last four seasons but was invaluable rumbling down on kickoffs and trying to break up the wedge.

"Bill was one of those guys who Bud used to say would have played for nothing," said former Vikings cornerback Bobby Bryant. "He just loved the game. He was just so physical and he used his head as a battering ram. At the end of his career, he suffered a lot of head injuries, but you didn't talk about concussions back then. You just went to the sideline, and as soon as he was cleared, they would send you back in."

Brown spent the final five years of his life in a memory center before his death at age 80 in November 2018. His wife, Darlene Brown, told the *St. Paul Pioneer Press* after his death that "with all the concussions, his body took a lot of beating." His brain was donated to Boston University's Chronic Traumatic Encephalopathy (CTE) Center to see if he had the disease. However, the family elected later not to go public with the results.

"Bill was my roommate in training camp and on the road," said former Vikings safety Paul Krause. "He was a just wonderful person. But on the field he would knock your socks off. He would run as hard as anybody. He was one of the best fullbacks in the game."

Even when the temperatures in Minnesota would drop well below freezing, Krause said that never bothered the rugged Brown.

"He didn't worry about those things," Krause said. "I'd have all the clothes I could get on, and Brownie would be out there in short sleeves."

Brown played in three of Minnesota's four Super Bowls. His last game was against Pittsburgh in Super Bowl IX, when he played on special teams but lost a fumble on the kickoff return to open the second half.

Brown in 2004 was the first running back inducted into the Vikings Ring of Honor.

"He really loved the game," said former Vikings defensive end Carl Eller. "He loved playing. He would do whatever you asked him to on the field. He didn't care what it was. He was a dedicated guy."

Despite his rugged play on the field, Brown was known for his compassion off it. After Vikings safety Karl Kassulke was paralyzed in a motorcycle accident in 1973, Brown spent a great deal of time with Kassulke and organized a fund-raiser on his behalf.

CHUCK FOREMAN

Known for his twisting and turning, Chuck Foreman got the nickname "The Spin Doctor." But he didn't learn those moves from football.

When Foreman was growing up in Frederick, Maryland, his favorite basketball player was Earl "The Pearl" Monroe of the Baltimore Bullets. Foreman began to put what Monroe did into his game.

"He'd always come down the court and he had this spin move, and I tried to emulate that move when I played basketball," Foreman said. "Then I took that move later and I tried it out in football."

It worked. Playing for the Vikings from 1973–1979, Foreman made five Pro Bowls and three times rushed for 1,000 or more yards. He is third in team history with 5,887 yards rushing.

Foreman also was adept as a receiver, with the Vikings going to a short passing game that was ahead of its time. He had 336 receptions for Minnesota, including an NFL-high 73 in 1975.

"For five years, Foreman was as good as any back in the league," said Bud Grant.

However, when Foreman arrived in Minnesota as the No. 12 pick in the 1973 draft, there was no certainty what position

Foreman had three 1,000-yard rushing seasons and led the NFL with 73 receptions in 1975.
ST. PAUL PIONEER PRESS

he would play. He had been a wide receiver as a college senior at Miami, and there was talk he might play there.

What Foreman didn't think was that he would end up at fullback.

"The coaches came to me and said, 'We're going to move you to fullback,' and I said, 'Heck no, I'm not playing fullback,'" Foreman said about his rookie year. "So I went back to the dormitory [at training camp] and I was all upset. But then [running backs] Oscar Reed and Bill Brown came into my room and said, 'Hey, you don't understand. The fullback position in our offense is the guy that is going to get all the best plays.'"

The Vikings wasted no time calling Foreman's No. 44. He rushed for 801 yards in 1973 and was named NFC Offensive Rookie of the Year.

By 1975, Foreman was one of the top players in the NFL. In addition to leading the league in receptions, he rushed for 1,070 yards and scored 22 overall touchdowns.

When the Vikings headed into snowy Buffalo for the nationally televised regular-season finale, it was billed as a battle between Foreman and Bills star running back O.J. Simpson. Both were trying to break the NFL mark then held by Gale Sayers of 22 touchdowns in a season.

Foreman scored four touchdowns to finish with 22, and Simpson got two to finish with 23 and break the record. But Foreman believes he could have gotten at least one more score had he not been knocked out of the game late in the third quarter when a fan threw a snowball from the end-zone stands that hit him in the eye and hampered his vision.

The incident also cost Foreman, who had 85 yards rushing in Minnesota's 35–13 win, from winning the NFC triple crown. He ended up leading the conference in receiving and scoring but was beaten out in rushing by Jim Otis of St. Louis, who had 1,076 yards.

"I don't like to talk about it, but I lost by six measly yards," Foreman said. "Somebody in the stands hit me in the eye with that snowball. I think I could have played more, but they didn't want to put me back in."

Foreman had no idea who had thrown the snowball until he received a call in August 2013 from Joe DeLamielleure, a Hall of Fame guard who played that day for Buffalo and long has been friendly with Foreman. DeLamielleure had been at a Bills preseason game, and struck up a conversation with a security guard.

The security guard admitted that when he was 10 he threw the snowball and had long felt guilty about it. So the security guard was put on the phone and he apologized to Foreman.

Foreman and DeLamielleure can't remember the name of the guy. By the following season, he no longer was doing Bills games.

"At least I got to talk to the guy and I was able to put it to bed for him because he had carried it around for awhile," Foreman said of accepting the apology.

Foreman felt a lot worse after a loss that ended the next season. Foreman shed tears on the field as the clock wound down in Minnesota's 32–14 loss to Oakland in Super Bowl XI.

"I lost a lot of sleep losing one, losing two, and losing the third one was totally devastating for me," Foreman said of playing in three of Minnesota's four Super Bowl defeats.

Foreman's all-around dominance continued through 1977. He had 1,115 yards rushing and 55 catches in 1976 and 1,112 yards rushing and 38 receptions in 1977. He also was a solid blocker.

"I wouldn't have traded Chuck Foreman then for anybody in football," said tight end and longtime teammate Stu Voigt.

Also quite impressed with Foreman then was wide receiver Ahmad Rashad. He had been Simpson's teammate in Buffalo before coming to Minnesota in 1976.

"Chuck Foreman was probably the greatest all-around back that I have ever seen," Rashad said. "He could block, he could catch, and he could run. He was great. He could do it all."

A knee injury, though, would take its toll on Foreman. He also was disappointed that the Vikings after the 1977 season traded star guard Ed White, one of Foreman's favorite blockers, to San Diego. It didn't help him that Minnesota got in return running back Rickey Young, who got some of the touches Foreman once had. Young led the NFL in receiving with 88 catches in 1978.

After seasons of rushing for 749 yards in 1978 and just 223 in 1979, when rookie Ted Brown took over as the primary fullback, Foreman was called into the office of general manager Mike Lynn.

"I left his office and I got to my apartment and my phone rang and he said, 'We just traded you to New England,' and that was that," Foreman said. "It was, 'See you later,' and that was it."

Foreman retired after a 1980 season in which he ran for just 63 yards with the Patriots. He first became eligible for the Pro Football Hall of Fame in 1986, and he's been waiting for a call ever since.

Foreman is only eligible now to be selected as a senior candidate. He believes he's worthy of enshrinement and that selectors have failed to properly take into account his 3,156 career receiving yards. Coupled with 5,950 rushing yards, that's 9,106 from scrimmage in his eight seasons. He also scored 76 touchdowns.

"It bothers me a little but there's nothing I can do about it," Foreman said of not being enshrined. "For the first five or six years of their career, nobody dominated like me [as an all-around running back]."

In his first six seasons, Foreman rushed for 5,664 yards, caught 317 passes for 2,910 yards, and scored 73 of his 75 Vikings touchdowns.

"Chuck had moves we hadn't seen before," said Carl Eller. "He would run to the sidelines and he wouldn't go out of bounds. He would have that whirl and that twirl."

Foreman can thank Earl "The Pearl" Monroe for that.

TED BROWN

When Chuck Foreman began to slow down, the Vikings needed a replacement at fullback. Enter Ted Brown.

Brown was taken with the No. 16 pick in the 1979 draft. He had run for 4,602 yards in four seasons at North Carolina State and seemed ready to start as a rookie.

He soon did. The Vikings benched Foreman early in the season and inserted Brown. Foreman ended up running for a meager 223 yards that year, while Brown gained 551.

Brown would get even better. After Foreman was traded to New England in 1980, Brown rushed for 912 yards. He piled up 1,063 in 1981 to become the second Vikings player after Foreman to have a 1,000-yard season.

"They were going in a new direction. Chuck was a little bit older, and I don't know if Chuck's contract played a part in it but they were literally getting me for peanuts," said Brown, who made about $25,000 as a rookie. "They thought they could get the same results out of me that they got out of Chuck, and I didn't come there to sit on the bench."

Playing for the Vikings through 1986, the 5-foot-10, 206-pound Brown had 4,546 yards rushing in his eight seasons. Like Foreman, he was a top-notch receiver. He caught 339 career passes, including a career-high 83 in 1981 for 694 yards.

"I knew Ted was going to be a really good running back, no question," Foreman said. "He could run and he could catch.

He was a three-down back. He was a good selection because he came in and took my place."

Brown, though, eventually had his place taken as Minnesota's feature back. After the strike-shortened 1982 season, when he played in eight of the nine games and had 515 yards rushing, the Vikings began to change their offense.

Minnesota had taken halfback Darrin Nelson with the seventh pick in the 1982 draft, and he became the primary ball carrier by 1983. Brown remained at fullback but became more of a blocker.

Brown, who didn't have even a 500-yard campaign in his last four seasons, sought to make the best of it. He remembers one game in 1986, when the Vikings defeated defending Super Bowl champion Chicago 23–7 and Brown ran for 33 yards.

"I was picking up blitz after blitz and so they gave me the game ball for blocking," Brown said. "Darrin Nelson had become more of the feature back and so I guess I was on my way out. But I became a very good blocker. My goal was to do whatever I could to help the team win."

Brown did a lot more blocking than running in the second half of his career, but he still often got the ball on the goal line. In 1983, he had 10 rushing touchdowns. In 1985, he had seven rushing touchdowns and three through the air for a team-high 10 overall.

"He had this big butt and he could get in the end zone or get a first down when we were in a short-yardage situation," said former Vikings tight end Steve Jordan. "He was a great athlete and he was going to figure out a way to get into that end zone."

Brown's most notable moment, though, came the play before a touchdown. In the next-to-last game of the 1980 season, the Vikings were trailing Cleveland 23–22 at Metropolitan Stadium and had the ball on their own 20 with 14 seconds left.

Tommy Kramer threw a pass over the middle to Joe Senser, who latereled to Brown at the Vikings 27, and he ran down the left sideline and out of bounds at the Cleveland 46 with five seconds left. On the next play, Kramer threw a Hail Mary touchdown pass to Ahmad Rashad, and the 28–23 victory in the Miracle at the Met clinched the NFC Central Division.

"I thought to myself, 'Maybe I should try to run and score and be a hero,' but then I said, 'Oh, the Cleveland Browns are heading me off at the pass,'" Brown said. "I said, 'I better step out of bounds.' And then, you know, the rest is history."

Brown eventually became history with the Vikings when he was released before the 1987 season. He remained in the Twin Cities and became a hockey dad.

Brown's son, J. T. Brown, has been a pro hockey player since 2011, including spending seven seasons in the NHL. He returned home to play for the Minnesota Wild in 2018–2019.

"I don't like hockey," his father said with a laugh. "I go to one or two games a year now. I did all that stuff when he was growing up. I was taking him all over the place to these tournaments in Canada. I've put in my time and done my papa duties. But, really, I'm very proud of him. He's done pretty well in the NHL. He's a good kid."

AND THE WINNER IS . . .

Chuck Foreman gets the nod for the way he helped revolutionize the game. In addition to piling up plenty of rushing yards, he was a top-notch receiver as the Vikings started throwing the ball to running backs more than any team had before.

The only drawback for Foreman was that his period of being at the top of his game did not last long. Foreman had a lot of touches in his first five seasons, and it began to catch up with him.

After Foreman was done, the Vikings got a 1,000-yard season out of Ted Brown at fullback before he eventually became more of a blocker. Considering how the fullback is now used in the NFL, it could be a long time before Minnesota has another one who puts up the type of numbers Foreman, Bill Brown, and Ted Brown did.

FULLBACKS WHO DID NOT MAKE THE CUT

Jerome Felton played for the Vikings from 2012–2014 and gained a reputation for being Adrian Peterson's bodyguard. An impressive blocker, Felton helped pave the way when Peterson ran for 2,097 yards in 2012 and was named NFL MVP. Felton that season made the Pro Bowl. Felton rarely got any touches. In his three Vikings seasons, he had just four rushing attempts for 27 yards, but he did rumble for 21 yards on one. And he had just nine catches. Felton played nine overall NFL seasons, and retired after playing for Buffalo from 2015–2016.

C. J. Ham was a halfback when he signed in 2016 as an undrafted free agent out of Division II Augustana (S.D.). He was turned into a fullback in 2017. By 2019, Ham became more of a focal point when head coach Mike Zimmer went to a more run-oriented attack. Ham, who blocked well and had 17 catches for 149 yards, made the Pro Bowl that season. He didn't get as many touches in 2020, but did average slightly more snaps per game.

4

HALFBACK

THE CANDIDATES

Adrian Peterson
Robert Smith
Dalvin Cook
Dave Osborn

The Vikings were a mere expansion team in 1961, but at least they had a "King."

The Vikings were looking for some veteran leadership when they entered the NFL, so they picked up future Hall of Fame halfback Hugh McElhenny in the expansion draft. He had gotten the nickname "The King" while making five Pro Bowls in the 1950s with San Francisco.

It wasn't certain how much was left in McElhenny, who had run for just 347 yards while averaging 3.7 per carry in 1960 with the 49ers. But McElhenny gained 570 yards and averaged 4.8 per attempt in 1961 for Minnesota while making his sixth and final Pro Bowl at age 33.

McElhenny lasted only two seasons with the Vikings and had stops with the New York Giants and Detroit before retiring after the 1964 season. But he went down as the first star halfback in team history.

Plenty more have followed. McElhenny helped groom Tommy Mason, the No. 1 pick in the 1961 draft who began in 1962 a streak of three straight Pro Bowl berths. Then Dave Osborn took over the spot, and he landed in the Pro Bowl in 1970.

In 1975, Chuck Foreman became Minnesota's first 1,000-yard rusher, although he was a fullback. So was Ted Brown, who in 1981 became the second to gain 1,000 yards.

Since then, all of Minnesota's 1,000-yard rushers have been halfbacks. The list has included Terry Allen, Robert Smith, Michael Bennett, Chester Taylor, Adrian Peterson, and Dalvin Cook.

Oh, by the way, there's also been a 2,000-yard rusher in Peterson. He reached that milestone in 2012.

Cook took over in 2017 for Peterson. He rushed for 1,135 yards in 2019 and 1,557 in 2020, and showed that the Vikings should be in good hands at halfback for years to come.

ADRIAN PETERSON

On October 24, 2019, Adrian Peterson came to U.S. Bank Stadium for what many have regarded as his farewell to Minnesota. It was emotional, to say the least.

Peterson carried 14 times for 76 yards for Washington in a 19–9 loss to the Vikings. But statistics didn't matter much in that game. For Peterson, it was a chance to thank the fans in Minnesota.

After the game, Peterson embraced Dalvin Cook, the running back the Vikings had drafted in 2017 as his replacement. He blew a kiss to the crowd.

"It was special," Peterson said. "It was kind of, obviously, bittersweet because you come here to win a game. But just coming back and seeing the love that they still have for me and they showed it, man, it felt good. It was definitely a great home welcome. They welcomed me with open arms."

Peterson did return to Minnesota with Detroit on November 8, 2020, but there were no fans on hand due to the coronavirus pandemic, and he was merely an afterthought in that game. He carried just eight times for 29 yards, and said the emotion was nothing compared to the previous year.

Peterson played with the Vikings from 2007–2016, leaving as their all-time leading rusher with 11,747 yards. He set an NFL record for yards rushing in a game with 296 as a rookie. In 2012, he was named NFL MVP when he came back from a torn ACL suffered the previous December and amazingly rushed for 2,097 yards, a league most and the second-highest total in NFL history. He was four times named first-team All-Pro and to seven Pro Bowls.

Peterson holds the NFL record of 296 yards rushing in a game, set as a rookie in 2007.
ST. PAUL PIONEER PRESS

Peterson's Minnesota tenure ended up having an unceremonious ending. He played in just one game in 2014, when he served an NFL suspension after being charged with child abuse for an incident involving his then four-year-old son.

Peterson returned in 2015 to lead the NFL in rushing for the third time, gaining 1,485 yards. But 2016 was a disaster. Peterson, bothered by a knee injury and later a groin strain, played in just three games, and ran for a meager 72 yards. He wanted to return to the team in 2017, but the Vikings elected not to re-sign him.

Peterson showed after his Minnesota departure he still had life left while playing for New Orleans, Arizona, Washington, and Detroit. He rushed for 1,042 yards with Washington in 2018 to become at 33 the oldest running back in 34 years to reach 1,000. Peterson showed signs of slowing down with Detroit in 2020 when at age 35 he rushed for 604 yards. But in the last game of the season, he had seven carries for 63 yards, including a 38-yard jaunt, and scored a touchdown at Ford Field against Minnesota.

Nearly all of Peterson's greatest memories, though, happened with the Vikings. Whenever he retires, he wants it to be with a one-day contract from them.

"Without a doubt, I'm retiring as a Viking, for sure," Peterson said. "I was blessed to play with one team for 10 years. It was a great experience just being around a great organization with some different head coaches and just meeting all the players who went through the organization. And the fan base was so incredibly supportive."

Peterson arrived in Minnesota as the No. 7 pick in the 2007 draft. He had rushed for 4,041 yards in three seasons at Oklahoma, including 1,925 as a freshman.

The Vikings had a solid halfback then in Chester Taylor, who had run for 1,216 yards in 2006. But with a chance to draft Peterson, it hardly mattered who already was on the roster.

"I was real good friends with Chester Taylor," said Antoine Winfield, then a Vikings cornerback. "But when we drafted Adrian, I told Chester, 'You're in trouble because this guy can play.' And then just seeing him come in his rookie year, he was the best back I've seen in person."

In his first game, Peterson ran for 103 yards and caught a 60-yard pass against Atlanta. In his fourth game, he rushed for 224 yards at Chicago. In his eighth game, he made history.

On November 4, 2007, Peterson rushed for his record 296 yards against the San Diego Chargers at the Metrodome. The crazy thing was he had just 43 yards at halftime before erupting for 253 after intermission.

"That was probably like the best game collectively I've been a part of," Peterson said.

Peterson remembers being "pretty wired up" because he was facing his idol, fellow Texas native LaDainian Tomlinson, who was then in his seventh season with the Chargers. Tomlinson, who rushed that day for just 40 yards, was in awe of Peterson during the 35–17 Minnesota victory.

"It was just a special day, and clearly at that time I was already passing the torch to the next great running back in our league," said Tomlinson, who retired after the 2011 season and was inducted into the Hall of Fame in 2017.

Peterson broke Jamal Lewis's 2003 record of 295 yards on a four-yard run up the middle with 1:04 left in the game. Quarterback Brooks Bollinger took a knee on the next play to end the game, although Peterson later wished he had gotten another carry.

"I do look back and I think I could have been the first person to go for 300 yards," he said.

Peterson at least got an unexpected thrill after the final gun.

"What I remember is meeting Prince after that game," Peterson said. "That was one of my great memories. He was a Vikings fan."

Perhaps nobody in the Twin Cities ever will top native son Prince when it comes to adulation, but Peterson at one point made a good run at it. He finished his rookie season with 1,341 yards and then led the NFL in rushing for the first time with 1,760 yards in 2008.

Peterson opened his career with four straight 1,000-yard seasons and was bound for a fifth in 2011. But in the next-to-last game he suffered a season-ending knee injury at Washington and finished with 970 yards.

The way Peterson returned from that torn ACL is the stuff of legends. He came close the next season to breaking Eric Dickerson's 1984 record of 2,105 yards rushing.

"He was a different animal," said Jared Allen, then a Vikings defensive end. "He was just so fully focused on coming back."

Peterson said "a lot of people speculated when I tore my ACL" that he never would be the same again, but he didn't listen to any of that.

"One thing I learned in my time around Adrian is never to bet against him and never to count him out," said tight end Kyle Rudolph, who was a Vikings rookie when Peterson was injured. "Adrian is one of those freak of nature, special athletes, but also works harder than anyone I know."

Peterson's training sessions during the offseason have become legendary. He has his own gym in Houston and rarely takes any time off.

By 2014, Peterson was playing for his third Vikings coach in Mike Zimmer, who had taken over from Leslie Frazier, who had replaced Brad Childress. But one game into Zimmer's tenure, Peterson was indicted on a child-abuse charge after beating his son with a switch while disciplining him. Peterson admitted to hitting the child but said he never meant to injure him.

Peterson sat out the rest of the season, first being placed on the commissioner's exempt list and then being suspended by the NFL for six games. Peterson plea-bargained in court to a misdemeanor charge of reckless assault and received a $4,000 fine and 80 hours of community service.

Overall, he was disappointed with the way the situation was handled. The Vikings had initially reinstated him after he missed one game but reversed course after several businesses dropped sponsorships with the team.

"Of course, I understand [the Vikings] did what they did from a business standpoint, but I had been there [since 2007]," Peterson said. "Those guys knew my passion and what type of person I was. I wasn't perfect but I wasn't a trouble guy."

Peterson had his strong comeback season of 2015. But 2016 didn't go well, and the Vikings elected not to bring him back. Peterson said they didn't even offer him a contract.

"I'd be lying if I said I wasn't disappointed," Peterson said. "After spending 10 years with a team, you would think you would get some type of offer."

At least Peterson's legacy is secure as the greatest runner in team history. Peterson, who entered 2021 fifth in NFL history with 14,820 yards, is a lock for the Hall of Fame, and he's hoping the Vikings one day will retire his No. 28.

"He was a great teammate," said wide receiver Adam Thielen, who joined the Vikings in 2013. "He wasn't a guy that was too big for anybody, which I think is really cool, because he's one of the best players ever to play the game."

ROBERT SMITH

In February 2001, Robert Smith stunned the football world.

Smith, just shy of his 29th birthday, had rushed for 1,521 yards in 2000, second in the NFL. He seemed to have several more seasons left at the top of his game.

But Smith didn't care. He abruptly retired after eight seasons with the Vikings.

"I got most of my major injuries out of the way my first four years," Smith said. "My last four years were my healthiest. The last season was my only season I didn't miss any games, and I still needed knee surgery after the year. So it was definitely time for me."

Smith departed as the leading rusher in Vikings history with 6,818 yards. That record was broken by Adrian Peterson in 2012.

Smith never has had any regrets about not sticking around longer. He has gone on to a successful broadcasting career as a college and NFL analyst.

Smith closed his career with four 1,000-yard rushing seasons and unexpectedly retired after having 1,521 in 2000.
ST. PAUL PIONEER PRESS

It was in college at Ohio State that Smith first began to get national attention, and it wasn't all for what he did on the field. Smith showed then he was a man of principle.

After rushing for 1,126 yards as a freshman in 1990, Smith quit the team during the 1991 season because of a disagreement with an assistant coach, who wanted him to skip two classes to attend practice. Smith returned to the Buckeyes in 1992, and was taken by Minnesota with the No. 21 pick in the 1993 draft.

The speedy halfback had injury issues in each of his first four seasons. He missed 23 of 64 games, and his best season in that stretch was gaining 692 yards in just eight games in 1996.

That led many to wonder how effective Smith could be if he played a full season. He answered that in 1997, when he rushed for 1,266 yards. That was followed by three more 1,000-yard seasons and Pro Bowl berths in 1998 and 2000.

"He was great," said Hall of Fame guard Randall McDaniel. "He didn't look like he was running that fast but once he got in the open field no one could catch him. He was a joy to block for."

Smith, a former track star, had been timed at the NFL scouting combine in the 40-yard dash at 4.39 seconds.

"We would always joke and say who you would be if you could be another person for a day," said former Vikings center Jeff Christy. "I always said, 'I want to run as fast as Robert Smith for one day and see what it feels like.'"

Although the 6-foot-2, 212-pound Smith was known for being able to turn on the afterburners, he could mix it up if needed. Christy said he should have gotten more short-yardage carries.

Because of injuries suffered early in his career, Smith became well aware of the need to take care of his body. Jeff Diamond, Minnesota's general manager for most of his career, said that contributed to how Smith viewed his contract situation.

"Because he had gotten hurt a couple of times, major injuries, he didn't want to go to training camp, and so he always wanted to sign one-year deals," Diamond said. "I knew that he wanted to sign a one-year deal but wanted to hold out until 10 days before the regular season started, and then he would sign. But I was okay with that because I knew he would come into camp in shape, and I knew he was smart as heck and knew the system."

Smith had some memorable games for the Vikings. He had 100 or more yards 29 times, including four games of 160 or more.

Unfortunately for Smith, he got knocked out with an injury in perhaps the biggest game he played because of what he deemed a dirty play. In the 1998 NFC Championship Game, the Vikings, who had gone 15–1 during the regular season, suffered a stunning 30–27 overtime loss to Atlanta. Smith, who had rushed for 71 yards, was unable to play late in the game and in overtime because of an injury suffered when Minnesota was up 27–20.

"It was a cheap shot by [Falcons linebacker] Jessie Tuggle," Smith said. "I checked down underneath and was out of the play, and he goes at my knee, and I got this really deep thigh bruise just above my knee and could barely bend my leg."

Smith's final NFL appearance also was in an NFC Championship Game. But the Vikings never had a chance, being crushed 41–0 at the New York Giants in January 2001. Smith only got seven carries (for 44 yards) because Minnesota fell behind 34–0 at halftime and had to throw on nearly every play the rest of the way.

A month later, Smith unexpectedly retired.

"Robert has always been a guy that the National Football League has been able to count on as a shining example of quality character off the field and 100 percent effort on the field," then Vikings coach Dennis Green said after Smith's announcement. "Robert's decision to retire, as everyone knows, comes off his best season ever as a running back for the Minnesota Vikings. He leaves the game on top and is looking forward to his next challenge."

One of Smith's next challenges would be getting sober. In 2013, Smith revealed he had a problem with alcohol abuse that had stemmed from his playing days. However, he insisted it never affected his performance on the field.

Smith said he had his last drink in 2012. He decided to go public with his story after seeing wide receiver Cris Carter, his longtime Vikings teammate, give an emotional speech at his Hall of Fame induction in 2013 about having overcome substance abuse.

"I thought about how powerful that was," Smith said. "When you're part of the group of alcoholics and addicts, you feel a kinship and a desire to help other people when they're going through similar situations. And so that potential to help other people really kind of outweighed any feelings of protecting my ego. It was very inspiring for me."

Smith, who lives in the Houston area, gets back to see Vikings games when he can. He returned to Minnesota in 2018 for a 20-year reunion of the 1998 team even though he admitted it was "bittersweet." And in 2020 he served as a Fox analyst for two Vikings games.

DALVIN COOK

Before the 2020 season, Dalvin Cook didn't mince words when talking about his abilities.

"I consider myself the best back in the game," he told the *St. Paul Pioneer Press.*

Cook then went out and did a pretty good job backing up what he said. He rushed for 1,557 yards, the third most in a season in Vikings history and second in the NFL behind Tennessee's Derrick Henry, who had 2,027. And he tied for second with 16 rushing touchdowns.

Cook was second in the NFL in yards from scrimmage, with 1,918 to Henry's 2,141, but he played two less games than the Titans star and led the league in average yards per game from scrimmage at 137.0. Cook suffered a groin injury in Week 5 at Seattle, and missed nearly the entire second half before also sitting out a Week 6 game against Atlanta. He also sat out the season finale at Detroit following the death of his father.

When Cook was sidelined with the groin strain, there was talk of "here we go again." Cook had missed 19 out of a possible 48 games in his first three seasons due to injuries.

But Cook, helped by a bye week, quickly shook off the injury and started November off with 163 yards rushing, 227 yards from scrimmage, and four touchdowns in a 28–22 upset at Green Bay. The next week, he had career highs of 206 yards rushing and 252 yards from scrimmage and scored a touchdown in a 34–20 win over Detroit. Not surprisingly, Cook was named NFC Offensive Player of the Month for November.

"I'm not the biggest, I'm not the strongest, but I put myself in position to be the biggest and the strongest in a lot of scenarios," Cook said. "My thing is keep working, keep pounding away, always be ready, so when my team calls upon me to take 30 touches, 40 touches, whatever it is, be ready, and I don't have any limitations on my body. I'm willing to give it my all each and every Sunday.

Cook, a two-time Pro Bowl selection, isn't going to make anybody forget about Adrian Peterson, the legendary halfback he replaced, but he's doing a pretty good job of at least making Peterson's 2007–2016 Minnesota tenure seem somewhat of a distant memory. After the Vikings elected not to re-sign

Peterson as a free agent in March 2017, they took Cook out of Florida State the next month in the second round of the draft.

Cook was considered a first-round talent but fell in the draft due to some off-the-field issues, although he had no convictions. Cook was charged with striking a woman in 2015 while at Florida State and suspended from the team, but he was acquitted by a jury after 25 minutes of deliberation. In 2014, Cook was charged with criminal mischief for a BB-gun incident, but that was dropped. Also dropped were charges for an alleged robbery and allegedly firing a gun when he was a juvenile.

Since he was drafted, Cook has been a model citizen. Plenty of teams no doubt regret not drafting him, including perhaps the Tampa Bay Buccaneers, whom many believed would take him No. 19 in the first round. Instead, his home-state team selected tight end O. J. Howard, who was nothing special in his first four seasons.

"He's showing them what they missed," said Cook's mother, Varondria White.

Cook broke out of the gates as a rookie with 127 yards in his first NFL game against New Orleans, and had 354 yards early in the third quarter in Week 4 against Detroit. But Cook then went down with a torn ACL, ending his season.

In 2018, Cook missed five games and parts of several others with hamstring issues, and finished with 615 yards. But it all started to really come together in 2019.

Cook rushed for 1,135 yards and made his first Pro Bowl. That was despite missing two full games and nearly two full halves of two others with chest and shoulder injuries.

Cook, though, had shown enough for the Vikings to sign him to a five-year, $63 million extension before the 2020 season. And then he looked even better in 2020, making his second straight Pro Bowl with Gary Kubiak calling the plays in his only year as Minnesota's offensive coordinator.

Kubiak retired after the season and was replaced by his son, Klint Kubiak. But the Vikings were expected to run the same attack as they did under the elder Kubiak, who tutored in his career many notable running backs as an offensive coordinator and head coach, including Denver Hall of Famer Terrell Davis.

"It's hard to argue that [Cook's] not the best back in the game now," Davis said. " I just see [the Vikings] using Cook in so many different ways. I see them running multiple screens, and he's perfect for the screen game."

Cook is the consummate three-down back, which has made some point out that even Peterson wasn't a top-notch receiver. Cook caught 53 passes for 519 yards in 2019 and 44 for 361 yards in 2020.

"The things I do coming out of the backfield, the things I do in between the tackles, I block, I pretty much do it all," Cook said. "I don't have to come off the field. I think some guys just don't do as much as I do, and I think that's why I'm today's [top running] back."

Cook hasn't heard a lot of disagreements about that. Former San Francisco star Roger Craig, one of just three running backs to have 1,000 yards rushing and 1,000 receiving in the same season, called Cook "right at the top of the list" among current NFL backs. And Peterson during the 2020 season paid Cook the ultimate compliment.

"He's a lethal weapon," said Peterson, who is bound for the Hall of Fame.

Cook has heard plenty of comparisons to Hall of Fame running backs. Former Vikings star wide receiver Ahmad Rashad compared him to the second-leading rusher in NFL history.

"I see a little bit of Walter Payton in him," Rashad said. "When he gets somebody coming at him, he delivers the blow."

And Vikings coach Mike Zimmer likened Cook to the leading rusher in league history. Zimmer was a Dallas assistant during the final nine seasons of Emmitt Smith's 1990–2002 Cowboys tenure.

"[Cook has] got such quick feet and acceleration," Zimmer said. "He runs hard, and runs physical. He's a good leader. I guess Emmitt was a lot like that. Really good feet, quick accelerator. Powerful runner. Good vision."

DAVE OSBORN

Dave Osborn had plenty to be thankful for during Thanksgiving weekend in 1964. The Vikings drafted him in the 13th round on November 28, 1964, and he went on to play with them for 11 seasons.

Then again, the entire weekend wasn't exactly smooth sailing. Osborn remembers being essentially held hostage in his hotel room until he signed a contract.

Osborn grew up on a farm in Cando, North Dakota (population 1,800), and rode a horse to a one-room school house before going on to star at small-college North Dakota. When he was drafted by the Vikings, that was a big deal.

After he was selected, Osborn went to Minnesota to attend a November 29 game between the Vikings and the Los Angeles Rams at Metropolitan Stadium, and said he and his wife Beverly "nearly froze to death" in the stands. After the game, Vikings officials, wary of the rival American Football League, said they wanted to sign all their draft picks immediately. But Osborn had one big problem.

"I also ran track at North Dakota," Osborn said. "I knew that if I signed then, I couldn't run track in the spring because you're ineligible if you sign a professional contract, so I said I couldn't sign."

That didn't sit well with the Vikings.

"I got back to the hotel and my plane was supposed to leave at 5 o'clock, and they called my room just before 4 and said,

'We just called the airport and your flight has been cancelled,'" Osborn said. "They were doing everything they could to not let me leave until I signed my contract. It seemed like the only way I was going to get home was if I signed. They finally said, 'Well, we'll pay your scholarship.'"

Osborn agreed to sign under the condition the Vikings paid for the rest of the school year since he would be ruled ineligible. His track coach wasn't happy, but at least Osborn got a signed deal worth $9,000 for 1965.

"And 12 years later, I was still carrying the ball," said Osborn, counting the final season he played for Green Bay in 1976.

Osborn carried it quite well. When he left the Vikings, he was the second-leading rusher in team history with 4,320 yards and was sixth entering 2021.

Osborn came up just 28 yards shy in 1967 of being the first Minnesota player to rush for 1,000 yards in a season, a feat not accomplished until Chuck Foreman did it eight years later. He scored five touchdowns in three playoff games in 1969, when the Vikings made it to their first Super Bowl, and was named to the Pro Bowl in 1970.

"He was very, very difficult to tackle," said former Vikings safety Paul Krause. "I always heard [legendary Chicago line-backer] Dick Butkus say that Dave Osborn was probably the hardest running back to tackle. He was all knees and elbows. When we were in practice, nobody even wanted to touch him because he would run right over you."

Osborn also could catch passes, but that took some work. Under coach Norm Van Brocklin, Osborn had just one reception as a rookie in 1965 and 15 in 1966.

"When I came in, I knew he could run the ball but he was not a very good pass receiver," said Bud Grant, who took over as coach in 1967. "So in one of my great coaching lines, I said, 'Dave, we've got to work on your receiving.' I said, 'You've got to concentrate.' Well, Dave did concentrate and he became a very good receiver. That was one of the greatest coaching jobs I ever did was to get Dave Osborn to catch the ball better, and he did lead our team one year in receiving."

That was in 1967, when Osborn had 34 receptions. After barely playing in 1968 because of an injury, Osborn had a stretch from 1969–1972 when he had 20 more catches in four straight seasons, which was good then for a running back.

That helped Osborn last a long time with the Vikings. The only running back to have logged more Minnesota seasons was fullback Bill Brown, who played from 1962–1974 and lined up alongside Osborn in the backfield for much of that time.

"They brought in a lot of top draft choices, but I think it was because of my durability and toughness and that I didn't make mistakes," Osborn said about how he staved off competition for so long. "Bud said everybody makes physical mistakes but he didn't want people making mental mistakes, and I didn't."

The end of the line for Osborn in Minnesota finally came when he was cut before the start of the 1976 season. He finished his career by playing six games for the Packers, and carried just six times for 16 yards.

Osborn's next-to-last career game was at Minnesota. Osborn, known for his pranks with the Vikings, sought to get in a final one.

"I knew that Bud didn't want his players to get to the locker room until an hour before the game, so I got there early," Osborn said. "I kind of wandered around their locker room and tied all their socks and jock straps in knots and stuff like that."

Osborn figured Vikings players would know who did it, and he was right. After Minnesota won 20–9, he was cornered by several, including center Mick Tingelhoff and defensive end Carl Eller.

"They threw me in a snow drift and covered me with snow," Osborn said.

AND THE WINNER IS . . .

No doubt here. Adrian Peterson is clearly the best halfback in Vikings history, and one of the best players overall. And he wants to keep going. Peterson turned 36 after the 2020 season, but was hoping to play multiple additional seasons.

If he does remain in uniform, Peterson could continue to climb the rushing charts. And if he sticks around long enough, perhaps he'll be back for yet another appearance in Minnesota.

HALFBACKS WHO DID NOT MAKE THE CUT

Tommy Mason ran with power and speed. He was the top overall selection in the 1961 NFL draft, making him the first pick ever by the expansion Vikings. After learning the ropes for a year under future Hall of Famer Hugh McElhenny, Mason took over as a starter in 1962 and made his first of three straight Pro Bowls. He played for Minnesota through 1966, and entered 2020 eighth in team history in rushing with 3,252 yards. His top rushing seasons were 763 yards in 1963 and 740 in 1962. He finished his career as a reserve with the Los Angeles Rams from 1967–1971. He died in 2015.

Versatile Darrin Nelson was adept at rushing, receiving, and returning kickoffs while playing for the Vikings from 1982–1989 and 1991–1992. He entered 2020 seventh in team history in rushing with 4,231 yards. His best rushing season was 893 yards in 1985. He also had two 50-catch seasons. Nelson was included in the massive Herschel Walker trade midway through the 1989 season, but refused to report to Dallas. He then was sent to San Diego, where he played for one and a half seasons before returning to Minnesota.

Entering 2021, Terry Allen was one of just five players in Minnesota history with multiple 1,000-yard seasons. The other four were Adrian Peterson (seven), Robert Smith (four), Chuck Foreman (three), and Dalvin Cook (two). Allen bounced back twice from torn ACLs. He hurt his left knee as a rookie in 1990 and missed the entire season before eventually getting 1,201 yards in 1992. He hurt his right knee and missed all of 1993 before gaining 1,031 yards in 1994. Allen only got into Minnesota games in three seasons. He later played for Washington, and had seasons of 1,309 yards in 1995 and 1,353 in 1996.

5

TACKLES

THE CANDIDATES

Grady Alderman
Ron Yary
Gary Zimmerman

During the 2020 season, the lightest offensive tackle on the Vikings was Brian O'Neill at 297 pounds, and he talked about still needing to gain weight. The other tackles on the team weighed between 305 and 325 pounds.

Go back to the early days of the Vikings, and their best tackle in the 1960s, Grady Alderman, weighed 245 pounds. When Ron Yary was taken with the No. 1 pick in the 1968 draft, he weighed 255 pounds.

By 1986, NFL tackles were starting to weigh 300 or more pounds. With that in mind, Gary Zimmerman remembers showing up for his first day on the job at 275, and running into head coach Jerry Burns.

"I said, 'Hi, Coach, my name is Gary Zimmerman. I'm your left tackle,'" Zimmerman said. "He looked at me and said, 'You're too small,' and he walked right on by."

So Minnesota hasn't always had behemoths at tackle, but that often hasn't mattered. The Vikings still have had a rich tradition at the position.

GRADY ALDERMAN

When Grady Alderman played for the Vikings from 1961–1974, some said he looked like an accountant. Actually, he was an accountant.

During a career that saw him make six Pro Bowls at left tackle, Alderman worked as a CPA on the side. He brought the same business-like approach to football.

"I used to call him the 'Intellectual Assassin,'" said former Vikings guard Ed White. "He would come in wearing a suit and tie, and then he would put on his football uniform and practice and then would put his suit and tie back on and go work as a CPA."

While Alderman fit the stereotype of a mild-mannered accountant off the field, he was anything but that when the game started. He was a rugged lineman who protected legendary quarterback Fran Tarkenton during nine of his 13 Minnesota seasons.

Alderman and Tarkenton were longtime friends. When Alderman died in 2018 at the age of 79, he offered a tribute on the Vikings website.

"He was smart, had great talent and was a team-first guy," Tarkenton said then. "Grady was a man of integrity, smart, kind, and generous. He was the best guy you could ever be around."

Tarkenton said Alderman was the first player he met when the quarterback showed up for Vikings training camp in their inaugural season of 1961. Tarkenton had been a third-round pick and Alderman had been selected in the expansion draft after playing for Detroit as a rookie in 1960.

"He was the very first Viking ever. . . . He was the first player picked," Tarkenton said in a taped eulogy that was played at Alderman's funeral in Colorado. "He was the first captain. He was the starting left tackle. . . . He was an incredible football player."

Each team, with the exception of the Dallas Cowboys, who had entered the NFL in 1960, was allowed to protect all but eight players in the expansion draft, and each team would lose three. So Alderman was one of 36 players the Vikings got.

"They gave me 36 stiffs for a football team," then-head coach Norm Van Brocklin grumbled after seeing the list after the expansion draft.

Alderman, the only one of those 36 to last past the 1963 season, hardly would go down as a stiff. But his early years with the Vikings weren't easy.

"They ran so many players through camp that first year, it was hard to know who was coming and going. . . . As for me, I wasn't smart enough at the time to know if I was doing well or if I was on the way out," Alderman said in Jim Bruton's 2012 book *Vikings 50: All-Time Greatest Players in Franchise History.*

Alderman was named one of the "50 Greatest Vikings" for the first 50 years of the team. The left tackle was a fixture in the starting lineup until he lost his job in 1974 and ended up being released after that season at the age of 36.

"When I got here, he was an undersized tackle," said Bud Grant, who took over for Van Brocklin in 1967. "He wasn't very big, but if you had a right-handed quarterback the blind side was always to your left and the left tackle was very important. Grady Alderman was a tenacious blocker. He didn't knock you on your back but he protected the quarterback."

Alderman emerged early as a leader on an expansion team that had plenty of growing pains. He was a longtime captain who commanded respect.

"He was a real student of the game," said former Vikings defensive end Carl Eller. "He had a business-like attitude and that's how he approached both life and football. He really knew the ins and outs of the game and he was really dedicated."

Alderman's best season was in 1969, when he made first-team All-Pro for the only time in his career, and the Vikings advanced to their first Super Bowl before losing 23–7 to Kansas City. He played in two more Super Bowls for Minnesota.

"Grady never made a mistake," said former Vikings halfback Dave Osborn.

Alderman was known for being a technician. Former defensive lineman Bob Lurtsema saw it while playing for the New York Giants from 1967–1971. Then he was Alderman's teammate on the Vikings from 1971–1974.

"He wasn't that big but he just had this technique and he could change his technique up," Lurtsema said. "He would change it each and every week depending on if he needed to be a little more aggressive."

Alderman was very athletic for being an offensive lineman. In the taped eulogy, Tarkenton, who played for the Vikings from 1961–1966 and 1972–1978, recalled the many times Alderman bailed him out.

"I was a scrambler," Tarkenton said. "I ran the ball a lot and when I was running and I would gain some yards and someone would tackle me, I would lateral often the ball to one of my offensive linemen who were trying to keep up with me. Grady Alderman was my most valuable lineman pass catcher. He caught more of my laterals than anybody."

After he was released by the Vikings in 1975, Alderman signed with Chicago. However, he was cut before the season, and his playing career was over.

Alderman continued then to work as a CPA and was the Vikings' radio analyst for four seasons. He served in Minnesota's front office and then was general manager of the Denver Broncos in the 1981 and 1982 seasons.

RON YARY

Ron Yary was the No. 1 pick in the 1968 NFL draft, and he assumed he would start immediately as a rookie.

But that didn't happen. Bud Grant, who never was enamored with rookies, informed Yary before the season that Doug Davis would be the starter at right tackle. That didn't go over well with Yary.

"I came very close to walking," Yary said. "I liked Bud, I liked the coaches, but I should have started right away, period. I almost packed my bags one night and Bob Lee talked me out of it."

Lee was a backup quarterback who also was a rookie in 1968. He convinced Yary to not leave the team and have some patience.

That was difficult for Yary. He did end up starting seven games in 1968 and six in 1969, but didn't become a regular starter until 1970.

By 1971, his career took off. Yary began a streak of making seven straight Pro Bowls, and in six of those seasons was named first-team All-Pro.

"If they would have put me in my first year, that would have started then," Yary said of his Pro Bowl streak.

Yary, though, is glad Lee kept him from leaving the team. He played for the Vikings through 1981 before finishing his career with the Los Angeles Rams in 1982. He was inducted into the Pro Football Hall of Fame in 2001.

Yary, who starred at USC, was the first offensive lineman taken with the top pick in the draft. He remains the only player the Vikings have selected No. 1 overall since the NFL and the AFL had the first common draft in 1967. Minnesota took

Tommy Mason No. 1 in the 1961 NFL draft, but Mason that year had gone third in the AFL draft to Boston.

If the Vikings had their way, though, they would have landed another USC star. In 1967, Yary had paved the way for star running back O. J. Simpson. But Simpson was a junior and not eligible for the draft until the next year.

Yary was named to the second team on the 1970s NFL All-Decade Team.
MINNESOTA VIKINGS

"We actually tried to trade the pick to somebody so we could get O. J. the next year," Grant said. "We thought maybe we could go through the league and we could postpone the pick the next year, but there was no avenue for us. It was more of a fantasy."

After the Vikings realized they had no chance to get the rights to Simpson, who would be drafted No. 1 the next year by Buffalo, they set their sights on Yary. Consider, though, that the draft was much simpler than now. Grant had never met Yary before Minnesota picked him.

"I wouldn't have known Ron Yary from a fence post," Grant said. "I only saw I think one film on him, but we had scouts and they filed reports. It was a consensus for us that Yary was a no-lose option as a pick, and he turned out to be great for us."

On the day of the draft, Grant called Yary to "make sure he hadn't fallen down and broken his leg the day before." When Yary said all was well, he was the pick.

"It was a normal day just like any other," Yary said. "I went to class."

The Vikings worked Yary in at right tackle since they were set on the left side with Grady Alderman, who played for them from 1961–1974. While left tackle might now be considered a more glamorous position, that wasn't necessarily the case when Yary played.

The Vikings often ran behind the 6-foot-5, 255-pound Yary. By 1975, Chuck Foreman began a streak of three straight 1,000-yard rushing seasons.

"Ron Yary was the best offensive tackle I knew," Foreman said. "He was big, he was fast, he was dominant. He had a little bit of a mean streak in him. He was a tough dude, a smart guy and never quit on a play."

Yary sure was tough. During his career, he played with a broken left foot, a broken hand, and broken fingers. He once broke his right ankle and returned to the game, although he later was forced to miss three games after the injury was diagnosed.

"The biggest honor in football is when a coach comes up to you and asks you to play when you're hurt or you're injured," Yary said. "They're saying that you're better injured at half speed or two-thirds speed or three-quarters speed than the guy who's playing behind you. Now, that's a compliment."

Yary said he loved the game so much he would "have played for free if they had just given us room and board."

Yary was selected NFC Offensive Lineman of the Year three years in a row (1973–1975) by the NFL Players Association. He was named to the second team on the 1970s All-Decade Team.

"He was 100 percent committed to being the best," said Ed White. "You could count on him. He was always there. He was unbelievably strong and as good as it gets at that position."

Yary was one of the Vikings' emotional leaders. He didn't always a say a lot, but he made it count when he did.

"His locker was right next to mine, and he would get you so fired up for games," said former Vikings wide receiver Ahmad Rashad. "He would say, 'Come on, Ahmad, come on.' That was his big thing. And during the course of the game, if we needed a big play, he might say, 'Come on, Ahmad.' And that might be the only thing that Yary would say the whole game."

The only downer for Yary, other than not starting early in his career, was the Vikings losing all four Super Bowls they played. He said the fourth one, a 32–14 loss to Oakland in Super Bowl XI after the 1976 season, was especially difficult since the Vikings were then an aging team and he sensed they wouldn't be back soon. More than four decades later, they still haven't returned to a Super Bowl.

Yary first became eligible for the Hall of Fame in 1988. But the wait to get in was a long one, which frustrated him.

"My career was as good as any other lineman who ever played the game at that time in terms of being All-Pro and all the other accolades," Yary said. "But of course it was quite an honor [being inducted]."

Carl Eller, who retired from the NFL after the 1979 season and didn't make the Hall of Fame until 2004, knows the feeling about waiting to be enshrined. But who knows if the left defensive end would have made it had he not gone against Yary regularly in practice.

"He was a tough guy to beat but that made me better," Eller said. "Ron was very agile and he was really intelligent and he was dedicated."

GARY ZIMMERMAN

Playing for the Vikings from 1986–1992, left tackle Gary Zimmerman twice was named first-team All-Pro and made four Pro Bowls. But he didn't talk much about it.

After Zimmerman had emerged as one of the NFL's top offensive linemen, the Vikings had a bad showing in a defeat. He then met with the media.

"They asked me what happened," Zimmerman said. "I said, 'The offense didn't play well enough to win, the special teams didn't play well enough to win, and the defense didn't play well enough to win.' So then they write, 'Zimmerman says defense didn't play well enough to win.' I said, 'That's out of context.' But at that point, I just said, 'You know what, I don't need to be in the papers, so I'll just keep my mouth shut.'"

So Zimmerman stopped talking to the media the remainder of his career. That included when he finished up with Denver from 1993–1997. With the Broncos, he tacked on another All-Pro selection and three more Pro Bowl nods and was on the winning side in Super Bowl XXXIII, his final NFL game.

Zimmerman (No. 65), who played in the decade with the Vikings and Broncos, was named to the 1990s NFL All-Decade Team.
ST. PAUL PIONEER PRESS

Put it all together and Zimmerman was inducted into the Pro Football Hall of Fame in 2008. Ron Yary, enshrined seven years earlier, was thrilled to have Zimmerman join the club.

"I thought he was as good as any offensive tackle who ever played the game," Yary said.

Zimmerman's entrance into the NFL, though, was modest. After playing center and guard at Oregon, the Southern California native elected to play for the Los Angeles Express of the USFL in 1984 and 1985. He had never played tackle until the team's regular left tackle, Mark Adickes, suffered a knee injury, and Zimmerman was moved over.

After his two USFL seasons, Zimmerman was selected by the New York Giants in a 1986 supplemental draft. He wasn't thrilled by that.

"I'm not an East Coast guy," he said. "You drive every two miles and you've got to throw quarters in the machine (at toll booths). That's ridiculous."

After some behind-the-scenes dealings, the Vikings traded for his rights. There were no toll roads in Minnesota then and he was at least closer to the West Coast, so Zimmerman was okay with the deal.

It took some time, though, for the 6-foot-6, 275-pound Zimmerman to impress Jerry Burns, who had thought he was too light.

"It took a whole training camp to win him over and then he kind of put me in there, and he said, 'You're doing okay,'" Zimmerman said. "Then I did a little bit better than okay, and by the first game he had trust in me. I had to prove it with my play."

Zimmerman sure did. After starting all 16 games as a rookie in 1986, he was All-Pro and made the Pro Bowl in his second season and was on his way.

"Going against Gary in practice, he was an impeccable technician," said former Vikings linebacker Scott Studwell. "He had great feet, great eyes, great balance and body control. He was real patient. He was one of those guys that would just kill you softly. He rarely got beat."

Zimmerman was named to the 1990s NFL All-Decade Team. He was joined by Vikings Hall of Fame left guard Randall McDaniel, which made for quite a left side of the line.

"In my opinion, Gary's easily one of the top two or three tackles that ever played," said former Vikings defensive tackle Keith Millard. "What separated him from other guys was his athleticism, his intelligence, his toughness, and his quiet confidence. He didn't say much but you couldn't beat this guy."

Zimmerman wasn't the most vocal guy but was known for being a prankster. He would pilfer the pants of teammates from lockers, wet them, and hang them outside, where they quickly would freeze in the Minnesota cold. Once, Zimmerman got together with some other linemen and they tied kicker Rich Karlis to a goalpost.

The fun, though, eventually came to an end for Zimmerman in Minnesota. He became frustrated playing for a team that had a 10-person ownership group he considered cheap. He said the Vikings put timers on showers, placed locks on lights, and charged players for lost socks.

It reached a head for Zimmerman when he went to talk to then president Roger Headrick about his contract in the summer of 1993. Zimmerman had agreed previously to defer money he had earned to later years for tax reasons. However, after President Bill Clinton took office in 1993 and Zimmerman sensed tax laws might change, he asked for an advance on some of what he had earned. He said others in the organization said that wasn't a big deal.

"I went in there and Roger Headrick is saying, 'We're going to charge you a penalty,'" Zimmerman said. "Then he started belittling me and he said, 'If you weren't playing football, you'd be flipping burgers.' It wasn't a big deal until he called me a 'burger flipper.' I'm not going to work for somebody like that."

Zimmerman refused to play again for Minnesota, and threatened to retire. He started packing up to leave town. Realizing he was serious, the Vikings reached a deal to send Zimmerman to Denver for first-, second-, and sixth-round draft picks.

Zimmerman enjoyed his four seasons with the Broncos, especially getting to "the top of mountain" with the 31–24 win over Green Bay in the Super Bowl in January 1998. As for his relationship with the Vikings these days, there isn't much of one even though he does say the organization now is much improved.

"I look at it like a divorce," he said. "When you get divorced, you're still cordial with the other team but it's not like you go back and have dinner with your ex-wife or stuff like that. So it's kind of like, my loyalty is to the Denver Broncos because they treated me so well. I know the new ownership is doing a great job, but I just don't feel like I'm part of the Vikings anymore."

Zimmerman, though, did visit the Vikings Hall of Fame and Museum in June 2019 for a memorial service for John Michels, once his offensive line coach. The museum had opened in 2018 and features palm prints of the team's hall of famers. The spot for Zimmerman's hand had been conspicuously blank.

"People were thinking that if they didn't have his handprint, he must be dead," McDaniel said with a laugh.

With that in mind, Zimmerman agreed to leave his print, and it's now on display.

AND THE WINNERS ARE . . .

The choices are easy. Yary and Zimmerman are the only two former Vikings tackles in the Hall of Fame.

Need more evidence? Zimmerman, the best left tackle in team history, was named to the NFL's All-Decade first team for the 1990s, and Yary, the top right tackle Minnesota has had, was named to the second team for the 1970s.

TACKLES WHO DID NOT MAKE THE CUT

Grady Alderman and Ron Yary both played 14 Vikings seasons, and Tim Irwin was right behind them with 13. Irwin never made a Pro Bowl playing right tackle from 1981–1993 but was a steady performer and a team leader. He was named one of the "50 Greatest Vikings" when the team celebrated its 50th season in 2010. He is now a juvenile court justice in his native Knoxville, Tennessee.

Todd Steussie played for the Vikings from 1994–2000 and was named to two Pro Bowls. He started 111 times during that period, only missing one game. He was a key lineman on the 1998 team that went 15–1. He helped pave the way for Robert

Smith to have four 1,000-yard rushing seasons, including 1,521 yards in 2000.

Korey Stringer died just as he was beginning to emerge as one of the NFL's best tackles. In his sixth season, Stringer made the Pro Bowl in 2000, and the Vikings advanced to the NFC Championship Game. On July 31, 2001, Stringer was stricken during a heat wave at training camp in Mankato, Minnesota. He died from complications from heatstroke on August 1, 2001, at the age of 27, and the Vikings were devastated. The team retired his No. 77 later that year.

Bryant McKinnie played for the Vikings from 2002–2010, and made one Pro Bowl. He was a key blocker for Adrian Peterson when he opened his career with four straight 1,000-yard seasons from 2007–10, including a 1,760-yard campaign in 2008. Late in McKinnie's tenure with Minnesota, he had weight issues, and he was cut in 2011 shortly after showing up for training camp out of shape.

6

GUARDS

THE CANDIDATES

Randall McDaniel
Ed White
Steve Hutchinson

In their first eight NFL drafts, the Vikings didn't put much stock into guards. They didn't take a single one in the first five rounds of any draft.

Not that they weren't able to find at least one quality guard. They selected Milt Sunde in the 20th round of the 1964 draft (yes, there really once were 20 rounds). He went on to play for Minnesota for 11 seasons, most as a starter.

The Vikings started paying more attention to guards in the draft in 1969. They selected Ed White in the second round, and he went on to make three Pro Bowls with them.

Then they took Wes Hamilton in the third round in 1976 and Dennis Swilley in the second in 1977. Swilley ended up moving to center, and was Mick Tingelhoff's replacement in 1979.

The 1980s began with the Vikings selecting Brent Boyd in the third round. And near the end of the decade they took a guard in the first round of the draft for the only time in their history in Randall McDaniel.

That one turned out quite well. McDaniel, selected with the No. 19 pick, is regarded by one of the greatest guards ever.

RANDALL MCDANIEL

Each year Randall McDaniel played for the Vikings from 1988–1999, there were some unsuspecting rookies to arrive.

They didn't immediately know about McDaniel's tremendous athleticism. They took a look at his 6-foot-3, 276-pound frame and figured no way was he a fast runner.

With that in mind, it became time for McDaniel and other Vikings offensive linemen to make some bucks. They rounded up some young guys who thought they were fast and issued a challenge.

"There were a lot of running backs and receivers who didn't realize that I ran a 4.5 40, and so the other linemen would set up these races," McDaniel said. "They would talk them into giving me a five-yard head start, and they would agree because no running back or receiver figured a lineman could beat them even with a five-yard head start. Well, we would take their money and then laugh about it."

McDaniel estimates he and other linemen won hundreds of dollars in such races.

"Randall was just the best athlete I'd ever seen," Hall of Fame Vikings tackle Gary Zimmerman said of McDaniel, who used to impress teammates with his basketball dunks. "We took some money betting on Randall, but of course it was like a ringer. Nobody could stack up to Randall."

That also was the case on the football field. McDaniel, who concluded his career with Tampa Bay from 2000–2001, was the best offensive lineman ever to suit up for Minnesota.

McDaniel was named to 12 Pro Bowls, tied for the most among guards in NFL history.

McDaniel played in 12 Pro Bowls, which ties Will Shields for the most by a guard in NFL history (Bruce Matthews got into 14 but four were at center). He was named first-team All-Pro seven times. He was inducted into the Hall of Fame in 2009 and in 2019 was named to the NFL 100 All-Time Team in conjunction with the league's 100th anniversary.

"After going against Randall in practice, the games were a lot easier," said legendary Vikings defensive tackle John Randle, also a member of the Hall of Fame and the NFL 100 team. "I'd have Randall to go against on Wednesday, Thursday, and Friday and that made the games a lot simpler."

McDaniel was a star athlete when growing up in Phoenix. In high school, he averaged 28 points per game as a power forward for the basketball team and for the track team ran the 100- and 200-meter dashes, anchored the sprint relay team, and threw the shot put and the discus.

After being a tight end and linebacker in high school, McDaniel went to Arizona State to play tight end. He sat on the bench when he first arrived, and when there was an open tryout at guard, McDaniel raised his hand.

"I just wanted to play and help the team in any way I could," McDaniel said.

McDaniel, who entered college at 235 pounds, was a natural at the position. And while he packed on 40 pounds to play guard, it didn't hamper his speed and athleticism.

The Vikings took McDaniel with the No. 19 pick in the 1988 draft, and immediately inserted him into the lineup at left guard. He made the Pro Bowl in 1989, starting a streak of 12 straight appearances, 11 with Minnesota.

McDaniel's second season also saw him develop his most interesting stance. He stood upright and stuck out his left leg while turning his ankle toward the ground.

"That stance came about from my right knee getting rolled up on in my second year by one of my teammates [Todd Kalis]," McDaniel said. "When I returned [after missing two games], I had to wear a knee brace. The knee brace wouldn't allow me to get down into my stance, so I turned my other foot out so I could get low enough to get my blocking assignments done.

"I remember the D-lineman across from me for the Packers saying he couldn't read my stance. He said he had no clue what I was going to do. I figured if a guy can't figure out what you're going to do in a stance, you need to stay with it. So I didn't change it over the next 13 years."

The stance looked strange, but it was quite effective.

"It was nuts," said former Vikings linebacker Scott Studwell. "It was like, 'What the hell?' But he was a perennial All-Pro guy. He had unbelievable athleticism. He had unbelievable strength, great hands, great eyes, and great balance."

After his knee injury, McDaniel never missed another NFL game, playing in 203 straight. He had a knack of rarely getting hurt.

"For some reason, ever since I was a kid, I could run into a brick wall and walk away without a scratch and be fine," McDaniel said.

McDaniel was like a brick wall on the line. But opponents weren't always fine after they ran into him.

Teammates learned not to mess with McDaniel even when they were joking around. Wide receiver Jake Reed found out the hard way.

"He was the strongest human being I have ever known," Reed said. "We were really good friends, and I tried to wrestle him one time. I tried to grab him from the back and that was one of the biggest mistakes I ever made. He broke my little hold and flipped me around so quick and had me on the floor."

As invincible as McDaniel seemed, Vikings coach Dennis Green eventually soured on him. After the 1999 season, when McDaniel had made the Pro Bowl but was not All-Pro, Green cut him in what was termed a salary-cap move.

"I don't like to talk about it a lot, but I always said, 'I was fired,'" McDaniel said. "They said it was about money, the salary cap, and that they had to let me go. But I got fired. I don't think it was the money. I just think they wanted to make a change and that's how they did it."

McDaniel, a man of tremendous pride, was hurt. But McDaniel soon was signed by the Buccaneers, whose coach, Tony Dungy, had previously been Minnesota's defensive coordinator.

McDaniel in 2000 made the Pro Bowl at age 36. You better believe that felt good.

"It was a great way to finish my career," said McDaniel, who retired after the 2001 season. "I got to play against the Vikings four games my last two years and I graded out well and the guys across from me didn't have good games."

Despite some lingering disappointment, McDaniel chose to remain in Minnesota after he left the Buccaneers. Green no longer was in town, having been fired late in the 2001 season.

While playing for the Vikings, McDaniel had become involved in teaching elementary school kids who had struggles in the classroom. When he returned to Minnesota, he continued in that role, and now has been doing it for two decades. He also has continued to remain quite modest.

"I tell the new students that I used to play a little football but I never say what I accomplished," McDaniel said. "Then they'll Google me later or figure it out and they'll come back and say, 'You didn't tell us you were that good.'"

Ed White

Nobody messed with Ed White on or off the field.

As a rugged guard for the Vikings from 1969–1977, White knocked down his share of defenders while paving the way for running backs and protecting quarterback Fran Tarkenton. Off the field, White took on all comers.

In arm wrestling.

Growing up in Indio, California, White became quite adept at it, and he and his buddies made their share of bets. That carried over when he attended the University of California.

"I won a lot of hamburgers," White said. "Hundreds. What we ended up doing was to see if anybody could last more than a second with me. Not many did. I was a pretty strong guy. My dad was a construction worker, and I grew up doing a lot of physical things."

So when the NFL came up with the idea to have an arm wrestling competition shown at halftime of televised games during the 1975 season, White was in his element. Each team nominated one player for the taped event, and the Vikings chose White.

The 6-foot-1, 269-pound White easily won the competition, defeating New England defensive tackle Julius Adams in the finals. He won $10,000 and used it, among other things, to buy his wife Joan a dining room set for the house.

"That was right down my alley," White said of the competition. "I was so excited. It was perfect."

By that time, those in the NFL knew all about White's strength. He was then in his eighth season, and had been to three of the four Super Bowls he played in for Minnesota. In 1975, he started a streak of making three straight Pro Bowls.

"Ed White was the strongest guy in the league," said former Vikings running back Chuck Foreman.

White also had plenty of technique. Former Vikings defensive lineman Bob Lurtsema said he had the quickest hands he had seen on an offensive lineman, an asset that also had helped him in arm wrestling.

White was selected by the Vikings in the second round of the 1969 NFL draft. He had played the defensive line his last two years in college, so moving to guard was a new experience. He had at least played offensive tackle as a college sophomore.

"I just immersed myself in it," White said of playing guard. "Our defensive line at the time was stacked, and they needed help on offense."

White didn't start any games as a rookie. He broke into the lineup midway through his second season and was a regular starter by 1971.

White was at left guard through 1974 before Vikings coach Bud Grant decided to move him to the right side. That put him next to right tackle Ron Yary, a future Hall of Famer.

"Bud told me he was tired of me beating up [right defensive tackle] Alan Page," White said. "I'm not going to say I beat him up, but we had some pretty good battles in practice and it probably beat both us up, and he wanted Alan to be a little fresher and probably me, too."

Minnesota's running attack really took off with White and Yary playing alongside each other. Foreman in 1975 became the first Vikings back to have a 1,000-yard season, and he duplicated the feat in 1976 and 1977.

But then White was gone. Following a contract dispute, he was traded to San Diego for running back Rickey Young. White played for the Chargers from 1978–1985 and made one more Pro Bowl while becoming more of a pass blocker in Don Coryell's aerial circus.

"When I found out there wasn't payroll integrity, that ticked me off," White said. "Mike Lynn [then the Vikings general manager] was a shady wheeler and dealer and I was lied to."

White had held out in 1977 before returning to training camp when he claimed Lynn, who died in 2012, had promised he would get a new contract. After White said Lynn failed to deliver, he held out again in 1978, and then was traded. His salary eventually was doubled by the Chargers from $50,000 to $100,000 a year.

"I was very sad and disappointed," White said of leaving Minnesota. "It ate me up. I had given everything I had to a team I loved and to a state that I loved, but I had been lied to and there was a lot of hurt and disappointment and anger. But it was then like falling out of a plane and landing on a pile of feathers. I ended up coming home and playing in front of my family in San Diego, and it turned out to be a super thing."

White didn't make another Super Bowl, but did get into two AFC championship games with the Chargers. Meanwhile, it was all downhill for Foreman.

Foreman saw his running totals drop to 749 yards in 1978 and to 223 in 1979 before he was traded to New England.

While Young ended up getting some of his touches and Foreman had some injuries, he pointed to White's departure as the biggest reason for his slippage.

"Then it was all over for me," Foreman said. "I knew it wasn't going to be the same. There was nobody who dominated the offensive line like Ed White. Not only was he intimidating, he didn't take any crap."

Off the field, though, White was known for being a gentle giant.

"He had a great sense of humor," Lurtsema said. "Everybody loved him. We used to kid him that he ran like a duck. We even left a couple of duck decoys in front of his room one time, and he laughed along with us."

While playing in the NFL, White also had time to work as an artist. That became his occupation after he retired.

White has a studio in Julian, California. He does oil and watercolor painting, sculpture and bronze work. He has pieces on display at the San Diego State and University of California–San Diego halls of fame.

Many wonder, though, why Ed White isn't in the Pro Football Hall of Fame. He was known as a top run blocker with the Vikings and then developed into an impressive pass blocker with the Chargers.

"He was as good as any guard in the NFL," Yary said. "He was better than a couple of guys who are in the Hall of Fame in my opinion. Ed was invincible. He was a rock."

So did Yary ever take White on in arm wrestling?

"Yes, I did," he said. "It was hopeless."

STEVE HUTCHINSON

When Steve Hutchinson first opened a Twitter account following his retirement in 2012, his handle was @poisonpill76.

That was catchy for the big guy who once wore No. 76. After all, as great of a guard as Hutchinson was during 12 NFL seasons, he is best known by some for the poison-pill contract he signed with the Vikings in 2006.

Hutchinson had played for the Seattle Seahawks from 2001–2005, his last game with them a 21–10 loss to Pittsburgh in Super Bowl XL in February 2006. The Seahawks then gave the free agent a transition rather than a franchise tag.

That was a big mistake, and the Vikings pounced on it. They signed Hutchinson to a seven-year, $49 million poison-pill deal that had some unique contract language specifically geared for the Seahawks to be unable to match it unless they wanted to guarantee every dollar.

That's how Hutchinson came to Minnesota, where he starred from 2006–2011. He finished his career with Tennessee in 2012, and was inducted into the Hall of Fame in 2020.

Hutchinson was elected to the Pro Football Hall of Fame in 2020 in his third year of eligibility.
ST. PAUL PIONEER PRESS

Hutchinson is now a consultant for the Seahawks, who have cooled down from their initial anger about his departure. And he did drop the @poisonpill76 handle after a few years in favor of another with his former uniform number, @HutchSevenSix.

"People asked me, 'How can you do that? You're just rubbing it in,'" Hutchinson said of his initial handle. "I kind of signed up for Twitter after I retired, so, of course, was trying to get on the Twitter train with everybody and get as many followers as I could. I said, 'How can I create a stir?' But that was probably not very good."

As a player, though, the 6-foot-5, 313-pound Hutchinson was very good. He made four of his seven career Pro Bowls and had three of his five first-team All-Pro selections with Minnesota.

"He was one of the best interior lineman I've ever seen play," said former Vikings defensive end Jared Allen. "He had a different kind of strength."

After starring at Michigan, the native of Fort Lauderdale, Florida, was taken by Seattle with the No. 17 pick in the 2001 draft. He moved into the lineup at left guard as a rookie and by his third year made the Pro Bowl and was first-team All-Pro.

But after his fifth season, contract negotiations broke down and Hutchinson was bound for free agency.

"We could never even get close," Hutchinson said. "They had the option at the tag deadline to transition me, as opposed to franchise tagging me, which left the door open for me to go to another team with Seattle not getting any compensation."

The Seahawks figured they could match an offer and keep Hutchinson. But then agent Tom Condon and Vikings salary-cap expert Rob Brzezinski concocted a plan.

Minnesota offered the seven-year, $49 million deal, the richest ever for a guard. The catch was if Hutchinson wasn't the highest-paid offensive lineman on his team, his entire salary would be guaranteed. If he was the top guy, the guarantee was $18.5 million. The Seahawks had signed star left tackle Walter Jones to a more lucrative deal, so their hands were tied.

"I was apprehensive at first because I just knew what it would do to Seattle, and I didn't want them to mistake me as being purposely malicious because I had no reason to be malicious to that organization," Hutchinson said. "My agent, said, "Hey, listen, if you want to be the highest paid and smash the record for guards, you basically have to sign the clause and the poison pill because Minnesota doesn't want Seattle to match and look silly.'"

Hutchinson signed, and the outraged Seahawks didn't match. They then signed Vikings free-agent receiver Nate Burleson to a poison-pill deal, one that included a stipulation he would get way more money if he played five or more games each season in Minnesota. It was not matched, and the poison-pill maneuver eventually was outlawed by the NFL.

But the Vikings had gotten their man. Hutchinson entered the lineup alongside Pro Bowl center Matt Birk.

"When we got him, I was like, 'Oh, my gosh. We're bringing in the best guard in football,'" Birk said.

Hutchinson said there was plenty of pressure to live up to his big contract at left guard.

"When you sign the biggest contract in the history of the league at that position, you want to show you're worthy," he said.

Hutchinson wasted no time doing that, making the Pro Bowl in 2006 while helping pave the way for Chester Taylor to rush for 1,216 yards. The next year, the Vikings drafted Adrian Peterson. He had four seasons of 1,200 or more yards and four Pro Bowl selections with Hutchinson as a blocker.

Hutchinson developed a reputation as one of the NFL's strongest guards. Just ask Allen, who had scrimmaged against the Vikings in training camp in Mankato, Minnesota, with Kansas City before joining them in 2008.

"Our D-line coach, Tim Krumrie, was like 'Hey, do not run down the middle on this guy,'" Allen said. "[Chiefs defensive tackle] James Reed used to give this stutter step and try to bull rush, and he did that to Hutch, and Hutch grabbed him by his shoulder pads and lifted him up and James' legs were running in the air. He just held him there."

In 2009, the Vikings made it to the NFC Championship Game, and Hutchinson was hopeful of a second trip to the Super Bowl. But they lost 31–28 at New Orleans in overtime.

"I just had a feeling we would have done well against Indianapolis that year in the Super Bowl, so it makes it a little hard to swallow the fact we didn't win," Hutchinson said.

That was the last time Hutchinson appeared in the playoffs and his last season named to the Pro Bowl or All-Pro. He was released in March 2012 with one year and $6.95 million left on his contract.

"I'm still a little bitter about the way that went down to this day," Hutchinson said. "Rick Spielman's the GM, and the person that called me and told me I was getting released was [head coach] Leslie Frazier."

Hutchinson believed it was Spielman's job instead to call. He said Spielman later tried to reach out, but he didn't take his call.

Hutchinson said it ended up being a "blessing in disguise" going to Nashville, Tennessee, since he has continued to live there. After his final season with the Titans, the next stop looked to be the Hall of Fame.

Hutchinson said the wait was difficult. He was passed over in 2018 and 2019 before finally getting the news in 2020 of his selection at Super Bowl LIV in Miami, close to where he grew up.

"I'm floating right now," Hutchinson said on NFL Network after his selection was announced. "It was emotional. You can't help it. It's a whole life's work."

As for fans in Seattle, feelings remain mixed about Hutchinson's career. Some are still ticked off about the poison-pill contract.

"There are still some fans that are pretty bitter about it, which I completely understand," Hutchinson said. "But, I mean, that's why we play this game in front of those passionate fans. But I think as far as the organization is concerned that's all water under the bridge."

AND THE WINNERS ARE . . .

Randall McDaniel and Steve Hutchinson are the picks. Both were dominant on the left side and both were disappointed when their tenures with the Vikings came to sudden ends. But both were later enshrined in the Pro Football Hall of Fame in Canton, Ohio.

McDaniel weighed nearly 40 pounds less than Hutchinson, but he played in a different era. Now, the great majority of NFL guards weigh 300 or more pounds.

Both McDaniel and Hutchinson were known for their strength. However, Ed White might go down as the strongest guard in team history.

GUARDS WHO DID NOT MAKE THE CUT

When Milt Sunde was taken in the 20th round of the 1964 draft, it helped that he was a Minneapolis native who had played at the University of Minnesota. But Sunde soon showed he hardly was a token pick. He played for the Vikings from 1964–1974, including being a regular starter from 1965–1972. In 1966, Sunde became the first Vikings guard named to a Pro Bowl. He died in 2020.

When the Vikings selected Wes Hamilton in the third round of the 1976 draft, they were looking for depth. But little did they know Hamilton eventually would move into the lineup at right guard in place of Ed White, who was traded to San Diego prior to the 1978 season after being involved in a contract dispute. Hamilton did a solid job manning the spot from 1978–1983 before spending one final season as a Vikings reserve.

At 6-foot-5, 343 pounds, David Dixon was one of the biggest guys to ever suit up for the Vikings. Dixon was surprisingly athletic, and it took plenty of work for defensive linemen to get around him. Dixon played for the Vikings from 1994–2004, including 1997–2004 as a regular starter. He played a key role on an impressive offensive line in 1998 that helped Minnesota go 15–1.

7

CENTER

Mick Tingelhoff
Jeff Christy
Matt Birk

No Vikings center ever has approached the longevity of Mick Tingelhoff, but they've had several others who at least stuck around for quite a while.

Tingelhoff took over as the starting center in the team's second season of 1962 and never missed a game until he finally retired after the 1978 season. Then came Dennis Swilley, the starter through 1986. Then it was Kirk Lowdermilk, who manned the spot through 1992.

OK, so Adam Schreiber only held the job in 1993, but then came several more long-term centers. Jeff Christy took over from 1994–1999, Matt Birk from 2000–2008 (minus missing the 2005 season due to injury), and John Sullivan from 2009–2014.

The typical Vikings center is tough and smart and is a mainstay at the position. The Vikings are hoping to have another long-term starter in Garrett Bradbury, who was inserted immediately into the lineup as a rookie in 2019 and continued in that role in 2020. But only time will tell.

MICK TINGELHOFF

Mick Tingelhoff delved out crushing blocks for 17 seasons. Once, he took out a locker.

The Vikings were set to open the 1976 season at New Orleans, and Tingelhoff's streak of having played and started 196 straight games seemed ready to end because of a separated shoulder. Well, he wasn't about to let that happen.

Team medical officials had ruled Tingelhoff out, and Vikings coach Bud Grant was ready to insert backup Doug Dumler into the lineup. In a last-ditch attempt to let him play, Tingelhoff approached Grant at the Superdome.

When Grant wouldn't budge, Tingelhoff sought to show he could use his injured shoulder to block. So he rammed a locker, denting it, and Grant was finally convinced to let Tingelhoff start his 197th straight game.

"By today's NFL standards, he would have been out for three weeks," Fred Zamberletti, the longtime Vikings athletic trainer who died in 2018 said in 2015. "But Mick said, 'I'm playing.' So we rigged up some special pad for him, and he played."

Tingelhoff eventually extended his streak to 240 straight starts, which remains third in NFL history. He started every game he played while with Minnesota from 1962–1978.

During his legendary career, Tingelhoff was five times named first-team All-Pro and six times selected to the Pro Bowl. He was inducted into the Pro Football Hall of Fame as a senior candidate in 2015.

"Mick was about as tough as you could get," said former Vikings safety Paul Krause. "He always had big scars on his forehead where the defensive lineman would knock his helmet right into his head."

Running back Dave Osborn remembers another time the Vikings were convinced Tingelhoff's consecutive games streak was about to end.

"In a Saturday practice, he pulled a tendon and they had to carry him off the field, but he played the whole game the next day," Osborn said. "They taped him up and he couldn't run, but he could snap the ball and block. He never missed a game. It was unreal."

Tingelhoff never missed a game in his 17-year Vikings career, starting 240 straight.
ST. PAUL PIONEER PRESS

Tingelhoff, a native of Lexington, Nebraska, grew up on a farm and walked a mile and a half each way to school. After playing at Nebraska, he went undrafted in 1962 and was thinking about becoming a school teacher. Then he got a call from the Vikings, entering their second NFL season under coach Norm Van Brocklin.

"I was lucky that the Vikings contacted me," Tingelhoff said in 2015. "Van Brocklin needed a center. They just put me in and I played, and things worked out for me pretty good."

It didn't take long for Van Brocklin to become enamored with Tingelhoff. He inserted him into the lineup as a rookie, and by 1964 he was named All-Pro.

The Vikings had other centers on the roster during Tingelhoff's tenure, but they didn't have much to do.

"We had a player, Godfrey Zaunbrecher, who used to say he was the third-string center on the Vikings," tight end Stu Voigt said of the center who played from 1971–1973. "The joke was the Vikings only carried two centers. So Godfrey would say, 'I'm the third-string center behind Tingelhoff and Tingelhoff hurt.'"

Tingelhoff was one of 10 to have played in all four of Minnesota's Super Bowls. He developed a close relationship with Fran Tarkenton, the quarterback from 1961–1966 and 1972–1978. When Tarkenton retired, Tingelhoff followed suit.

Tarkenton was Tingelhoff's presenter at his Hall of Fame induction but ended up doing all the talking. Tingelhoff has suffered from health issues, which have affected his memory, so his family opted that night in Canton, Ohio, to not have him speak.

"It was a last-minute decision," his wife, Phyllis Tingelhoff, told the *St. Paul Pioneer Press.* "We thought it would be fine for Fran just to kind of take the ball. We kind of made the decision just to take the pressure off Mick. It was easier for him to not say anything."

Tarkenton's speech about Tingelhoff was brief but emotional. "Mick's a man of little words but a lot of action," Tarkenton said while holding back tears. "He's so proud to be in this class of 2015. He waited 37 years to get to the hall of fame. He just wanted me to tell all of his teammates who are here and thank them for being here, our great coach and fellow Hall of Famer, Bud Grant, all the Vikings fans who have come from all over the country, and all the rest of you fans, and even you Steelers fans who beat us in that Super Bowl [in January 1975]."

Tingelhoff was undersized at 6-foot-2, 237 pounds, but during his career he took on some of the toughest players in the game. Twice a season, he often faced legendary middle linebackers such as Dick Butkus of Chicago, Ray Nitschke of Green Bay, and Joe Schmitt of Detroit. Tingelhoff used to anger Butkus with his hits, but Tingelhoff never backed down.

Tingelhoff had plenty of agility. Because of Tarkenton's scrambling nature, he often joked that if he missed a block he would just wait until Tarkenton came back around and then he blocked the guy again.

"Mick was as quick as he was tough," said former Vikings linebacker Jeff Siemon. "He was undersized but he made up for it with savvy and experience and with his great quickness."

Off the field, Tingelhoff was generally mild mannered. That is, unless he had a point to make.

Late in his career, when Tingelhoff's contract was up, Vikings general manager Mike Lynn called him into his office. When Lynn low-balled him with an offer, Tingelhoff was furious. He swiped his arm across Lynn's desk, knocking everything onto the floor. Then he stormed out of the office, punching a hole in the wall on the way out.

When Tingelhoff got back to his car, he realized he had left his keys on Lynn's desk, and they had gone flying with everything else. So Tingelhoff quietly went back into the office, got on the floor, found his keys, and walked out.

As for that contract offer, he ended up getting a much better offer than the one Lynn originally had made.

Jeff Christy

Jeff Christy is a former kicker and punter. Oh, by the way, he also was a three-time Pro Bowl selection at center.

Christy had never played center in his life until Vikings coach Dennis Green suggested he take up the position in 1993. Christy had been cut by the Cardinals after they drafted him out of Pittsburgh as a guard in the fourth round in 1992, so he figured he had nothing to lose.

"Denny Green said, 'Just learn how to snap the ball. If it works out, it does. If it doesn't work out, we didn't really invest much money in you,'" Christy said.

It sure did work out. Christy started at center for six Minnesota seasons and made Pro Bowls in 1998 and 1999. He tacked on another Pro Bowl appearance with Tampa Bay in 2000.

Christy had played all over the place in college. He was a guard, tackle, fullback, middle linebacker, and a punter. Yes, a punter. He punted three times in a 1988 game for a less-than-stellar average of 27.3 yards.

Christy had been better as a kicker when he was an all-state selection at Freeport (Pennsylvania) High School. But nobody had ever figured out before Green that Christy was best suited to be a center.

"I was playing out of position," Christy said of why he was cut by the Cardinals. "I wasn't big enough to play guard, and I think it showed in training camp. The way it turned out is that center was my natural position. I just don't think I was good enough to play anywhere in the NFL until they moved me to center, and then I was able to trick them and keep the position."

The 6-foot-3, 275-pound Christy learned how to snap the ball while barely playing in 1993, his first season with the Vikings. He became good enough to become the starter in 1994.

"Christy was more of an overachiever," said Hall of Famer Randall McDaniel, who played left guard alongside Christy. "He was undersized but he was just relentless. He was always getting after you. And he was probably one of the smartest guys out there on the field. Christy was calling defenses and setting the blocking patterns for everybody."

By 1998, Christy was a key cog on one of the best offenses ever. The Vikings went 15–1 and scored an NFL-record 556 points before being stunned in the NFC Championship Game 30–27 by Atlanta in overtime.

"He was just the perfect center on that team in terms of being smart and calling the line assignments," said then general manager Jeff Diamond.

Nevertheless, when Christy became a free agent after the 1999 season, the Vikings did not make much of an effort to re-sign him. So he joined the Buccaneers, then coached by former Minnesota defensive coordinator Tony Dungy.

"It wasn't a stunner," said Matt Birk, who had learned under Christy for two seasons before replacing him as the starting center. "It was just the way things were with ownership at the time, and we weren't paying that many guys to stay."

The Vikings sure weren't. After the 1999 season, they also released McDaniel after a Pro Bowl season, and he also signed with Tampa Bay.

McDaniel and Christy both made the Pro Bowl in 2000. Christy said that was satisfying. Then again, Birk also made the Pro Bowl in 2000, his first of six.

Christy's greatest satisfaction came when the Buccaneers defeated Oakland 48–21 to win Super Bowl XXXVII after the

2002 season, his final game. He said that was a blessing in disguise after the Vikings had essentially shown him the door.

"I obviously had wanted to stay in Minnesota, but they had different plans," Christy said. "But it worked out well. Obviously, that's the ultimate goal is to win a championship. It was an unbelievable feeling."

Christy still keeps in touch with his good friend McDaniel, who retired the year before the Buccaneers won the Super Bowl. They regularly talk about the good days they spent together on Minnesota's offensive line.

While Christy was with the Vikings, he does wish he could have gotten one shot at his old position of kicker. Christy, who used a straight-on style, said he actually got plenty of work at one point early in his career when Fuad Reveiz was nursing an injury but the kicker didn't end up missing any game time.

"I actually kicked all week in practice, extra points and field goals and kickoffs, and got my timing down," Christy said. "If we ever had an emergency in any game I was ready. [Equipment manager] Dennis Ryan always had my shoe in the kicking bag although I don't know if they did that to humor me or I actually could have had a chance to kick."

Had a center also kicked in the modern era of the NFL, Christy said it would have ended up "in some kind of record book." Nevertheless, Christy did go down in the books as being a pretty darn good center.

MATT BIRK

When Matt Birk was growing up in St. Paul, Minnesota, his heroes were Vikings stars Tommy Kramer, Ted Brown, Sammy White, and Joe Senser. Sure, it was a dream to one day play for his hometown team, but how realistic was that?

Birk went on to be an offensive lineman at Harvard. After he had played three seasons with the Crimson, he figured his senior year in 1997 would be his last in football.

"I came home the summer before my senior year and I said, 'I've got one year left and then I'm done forever,'" Birk said. "I was really committed to getting as strong as I could and having a great senior season. And about halfway through my senior year a national scout was watching film on me and I walked into the room and I just asked him point blank, 'Hey, you think I've got a chance to play in the NFL?' He said, 'Yeah, I do.'"

Birk had a strong senior season and was projected to be drafted. He didn't think, though, it would be by the Vikings.

"I had a predraft workout and (offensive line coach) Mike Tice told me they weren't going to draft a lineman," Birk said. "But then to get that call during the draft and have Dennis Green on the other end say, 'You ready to become a Minnesota Viking?' It was like, 'Are you kidding me?' The whole thing was unreal."

Birk came home to play after the Vikings selected him in the sixth round of the 1998 draft. As to what position he would play, that would be figured out later.

The 6-foot-4, 310-pound Birk had been a tackle at Harvard, and he also could play guard. He never had played center before.

"Mike Tice said, 'You're not going to be a starter because we have a dominant offensive line. I think you can play guard and tackle, but why don't you learn to play center so you can play all five positions,'" Birk said.

So Birk set out to learn the ins and outs at center. While playing mostly on special teams in 1998 and 1999, he spent much of his time learning under Jeff Christy, who had been named to the Pro Bowl during each of those seasons.

"Matt was just a very smart kid," Christy said. "Obviously, he graduated from Harvard. He was like a sponge, just able to absorb anything. And he had tremendous size and strength."

The pupil learned well enough that when Christy became a free agent in 2000, the Vikings were content to move on without him. They turned to Birk, who made a much lower salary.

"I had sat with Jeff in every meeting and roomed with him on the road, and I just tried to be like him every day," Birk said. "And so when he left via free agency, they kind of opened it up for competition, but I had spent two years under the tutelage of the best in the game, so I was prepared."

Birk wasted no time in becoming one of the top centers in the game himself. He was named to the Pro Bowl in 2000, his first season as the starter.

The accolades kept coming. Between 2000–2007, Birk made six Pro Bowls. The only time during that stretch he didn't was in 2002 and in 2005, when he sat out the season with a hip injury.

"In my time and my era, maybe I'm a little too prideful, but I don't think there was anybody better (at center)," Birk said.

Birk, though, didn't earn any first-team All-Pro nods. Defensive end Jared Allen believes he should have.

"I think he was an underrated center," Allen said. "I don't think he got his due as far as what he should have. It was probably because he didn't play with a ton of, you know, superstar quarterbacks."

Birk did snap to Daunte Culpepper, who made Pro Bowls in 2000, 2003, and 2004. But after Culpepper sustained a serious knee injury in 2005 and then departed, it was a revolving door of quarterbacks for several seasons.

After the 2008 season, Birk decided to leave as a free agent for Baltimore. That was before the Vikings landed Brett Favre in 2009 and ended up in the NFC Championship Game, a 31–28 overtime loss at New Orleans.

It eventually, though, turned out better for Birk. He played his final four seasons with the Ravens, and his final game was a 34–31 win over San Francisco in Super Bowl XLVII in February 2013.

"When I left (Minnesota), it was sad to leave," Birk said. "I could have stayed but I just felt like Baltimore was better. I didn't have many years left, so I just felt like it was where I needed to finish my career. But it was definitely bittersweet."

Birk was thrilled to have won a Super Bowl. But he doesn't deny he sometimes has thought about what it would have been like to have won it in his native Minnesota.

"I guess in a Hollywood ending, I would have stayed and we would have won the Super Bowl, but it didn't work out," Birk said. "But everything happens for a reason, and leaving and going to Baltimore, that was just part of my journey."

AND THE WINNER IS . . .

Mick Tingelhoff was one of the greatest centers in NFL history, and gets the nod here. It remains mystifying he wasn't inducted into the Hall of Fame until 2015, 31 years after he first became eligible.

Iron men Jim Marshall and Tingelhoff have been called by many the two toughest players in Vikings history. When he retired after the 1979 season, Marshall, a defensive end, held the NFL record for most consecutive starts at 282 and Tingelhoff was second at 240. The two were teammates during each of Tingelhoff's 17 seasons and they banged heads in practice.

CENTERS WHO DID NOT MAKE THE CUT

Dennis Swilley learned under Mick Tingelhoff during his two final seasons of 1977 and 1978. He must have been taught something about durability. Swilley, who played all 28 games in 1977 and 1978 on special teams, took over as the starter and extended his overall game streak to 134 before missing time in his final season of 1987.

Kirk Lowdermilk took over as the starter in 1987 from Swilley. Overall, Lowdermilk played for the Vikings from 1985–1992 before leaving as a free agent and spending his final four seasons with Indianapolis. Lowdermilk got a three-year, $6 million contract from the Colts, the most ever then for a center. Despite being undersized at 6-foot-3, 269 pounds, Lowdermilk was a very physical player.

John Sullivan learned under Matt Birk as a rookie in 2008 before taking over as the starter in 2009. It was quite a first season in that role as the Vikings went to the NFC Championship Game. Another big season came in 2012, when he helped pave the way for Adrian Peterson to rush for 2,097 yards. But Sullivan suffered a season-ending back injury in the 2015 preseason and was cut before the start of 2016. Sullivan did bounce back to start for the Los Angeles Rams when they made the Super Bowl in 2018 before retiring.

8

TIGHT END

THE CANDIDATES

Kyle Rudolph
Steve Jordan
Stu Voigt

Vikings tight ends have run the gamut. Some have been mostly blockers. Some have been pass-catching machines. Some have been both.

That was the case with Steve Jordan and Kyle Rudolph. Jordan once caught as many as 68 passes in a season and Rudolph as many as 83 balls, but both later had years in which they were used more as blockers and their stats were roughly cut in half.

In the beginning, the job for a Minnesota tight end was mostly to block. Gordie Smith was the primary starter from 1961–1965, and never caught more than 22 passes in a season.

Eventually, the tight end became more involved in the offense. John Beasley had 33 catches during Minnesota's first Super Bowl season of 1969. Then Stu Voigt had a pair of 30-catch seasons during the 1970s, including a then team-record 34 in 1975 for a tight end.

Joe Senser eventually blew that record out of the water. After having 42 catches in 1980, Senser had 79 for 1,004 yards in 1981, which stood until Rudolph had his 83 grabs in 2016. But Senser remains the only Vikings tight end to have had a 1,000-yard season.

Knee problems ended Senser's career prematurely, and his last season was 1984. Jordan then took over and had quite a run. Playing for the Vikings from 1982–1994, Jordan made six Pro Bowls. He had 50 or more catches in a season five times and also was a solid blocker.

Jim Kleinsasser, who was mostly a blocker, later also played 13 seasons at tight end for the Vikings, punching the clock from 1999–2011. Kleinsasser's final season was Rudolph's rookie season.

Rudolph looked as if he might challenge the longevity record for a Vikings tight end shared by Jordan and Kleinsasser. But after playing for Minnesota from 2011–2020, he was released in a salary-related move and signed with the New York Giants.

KYLE RUDOLPH

As the second round went along in the 2011 NFL draft, it looked as if Notre Dame tight end Kyle Rudolph might be bound for Denver. The Broncos had traded down from the No. 36 to the No. 45 overall pick and called Fighting Irish coach Charlie Weis to say they anticipated still getting Rudolph at that spot.

Not so fast. The Vikings, who had interviewed Rudolph at the combine but had not seemed hot on his trail, surprisingly took him at No. 43.

It worked out pretty well. Playing for Minnesota from 2011–2020, Rudolph had 453 receptions for 4,488 yards and a team-record 48 touchdowns for a tight end and made two Pro Bowls.

"Denver was on the clock earlier in the second round and they traded back right behind Minnesota because they didn't think anybody would take me," Rudolph said.

Rudolph made two Pro Bowls and his 48 career touchdown catches are the most by a Vikings tight end.

Rudolph gave the Broncos a taste of what they could have had when he caught the winning 32-yard touchdown pass in the fourth quarter of a November 2019 game in which the Vikings stormed back from a 20–0 deficit to win 27–23. But that hardly was his biggest score of that season.

In a divisional playoff game at New Orleans, Rudolph caught on the first possession of overtime a four-yard touchdown from a pressured Kirk Cousins deep in the left corner of the end zone. That gave the Vikings, who had been 7½-point underdogs, a stunning 26–20 win.

"I knew that if they brought pressure on Kirk that I was the answer," Rudolph said after the upset. "Not many people gave us a chance to go on the road in New Orleans. We knew we had to play near perfect to get a win."

What happened the week after that game summed up the respect Rudolph has had in the Twin Cities for more than just football. Rudolph, who was the Vikings' nominee from 2017–2019 for the Walter Payton NFL Man of the Year Award for his community work, went on Twitter to say he gave his gloves to an alleged media member in the locker room who said they would be used to benefit a charity. Rudolph said he even offered to sign the gloves.

Lo and behold, Rudolph learned a few days later the gloves were sold on eBay for $375, and he was disgusted about being deceived. As it turned out, though, they had been purchased by an avid Vikings fan. When Jason King of Woodbridge Heights, New Jersey, saw Rudolph's tweet, he agreed to donate the gloves to be put on display at Kyle Rudolph's End Zone at the University of Minnesota Masonic Children's Hospital, an area the tight end opened in 2017 with a large donation. King also started an online fund-raising drive that raised more than $20,000 for the hospital.

"That's kind of the good power of social media," Rudolph said. "It was an unfortunate situation with the gloves and sure enough the guy was a huge Vikings fan and reaches out and wants to do good for the hospital."

During his Vikings tenure and beyond, Rudolph has made a big deal out of wanting to do good for the community. Kyle Rudolph's End Zone is an area that provides hospital patients and their families a place to relax.

"It's about leaving a legacy, and I want my legacy to go far beyond what I do in between the lines," Rudolph said.

What the 6-foot-6, 265-pound former basketball player has done between the football lines has helped provide a path to do his community work. He made Pro Bowls after the 2012 and 2017 seasons and in 2016 set a Vikings record for a tight end with 83 catches. He was an iron man, starting 93 straight games until he missed the final four in 2020 due to a foot injury.

"He's got some of the best hands I've ever seen," said cornerback Marcus Sherels, a teammate for all but the last of Rudolph's 10 Minnesota seasons. "He can run really good routes. He's big. He's got a big catch radius."

Later in his career, Rudolph became quite adept at something else: blocking. When Rudolph entered the NFL, he was regarded as more of a receiving tight end and not much of a blocker.

Eventually, though, the Vikings stopped throwing as much to Rudolph. That really began to be the case in 2019, when the Vikings wanted to run the ball more with Dalvin Cook and also drafted tight end Irv Smith Jr. in the second round to share the receiving load.

That year, with Kevin Stefanski in his first full season as offensive coordinator and Gary Kubiak having joined the Vikings as an offensive advisor, Rudolph was targeted 48 times and caught 39 passes for 367 yards. That was down from 82 targets and 64 catches for 634 yards in 2018 and way down from his career highs of 132 targets, 83 catches, and 840 yards in 2016. Then in 2020, with Stefanski having become Cleveland's head coach and Kubiak taking over as offensive coordinator, Rudolph was targeted 37 times and caught 28 passes for 334 yards in the 12 games he played. Kubiak retired after the season, two months before Rudolph was released in a salary-related move and signed with the New York Giants.

"If I was going to (continue to) be a good football player, it meant that I had to be a good blocker," Rudolph said. "I really didn't have any choice. Absolutely, it was frustrating. Catching the ball is what I love to do. But I said that if being more of a blocker is what it takes to win football games, then that's how I can help."

Head coach Mike Zimmer talked plenty late in Rudolph's Minnesota tenure about how much he had improved his blocking.

"I took it as a challenge, something that I hadn't done well earlier in my career," Rudolph said. "So if that's what I'm going to do, I want to do it well."

Put it all together, and Rudolph became an all-around tight end.

"He's a tight end who can do it all," said safety Harrison Smith, who was Rudolph's teammate at Notre Dame and then joined the Vikings in 2012 and spent nine years as his teammate. "He's very big. Even when you have him covered, you don't have him covered. He can go up and catch that ball. He's got huge hands. We've seen that multiple times. And then he's developed a lot, and that was highlighted with how well he blocks."

Smith also lauded the "leadership aspect" of Rudolph, who was long one of the team captains. And Smith said he also was a good landlord when the tight end let him stay at his house throughout the 2012 season in a basement room for minimal rent.

STEVE JORDAN

Not a lot of good things happened during Les Steckel's one season as Vikings coach, when they went 3–13 in 1984. But at least Steve Jordan got a car out of it.

Steckel took over from Bud Grant and ran the team like a military boot camp, alienating many players before he was fired after the season and Grant came back for one more year. One of Steckel's ploys before training camp was an eight-event iron-man competition in which players competed in weightlifting, running, and other drills.

The winner got a new Buick. And the victor was Jordan, entering his third season after having played sparingly in his first two.

"Bud hadn't really cared about weightlifting and all of that," Jordan said. "His thing was you show up in shape and be prepared as a professional. But Les was more along the lines of, 'I want to be ahead of my time.' He brought in an Olympic track coach, and we were doing Jazzercise and aerobics and things like that. Bud had a much less intense workout program, but I always enjoyed working out and really trying to be in top shape, so I really embraced [the ironman competition]. The older guys probably didn't buy into it, but with my strength and my athleticism, I was able to score pretty well on the runs and do pretty well on the weightlifting. It was cool."

The only thing Jordan wasn't cool with was driving a Buick. So he traded it in for a Ford Explorer.

The rest of the season also went quite well for Jordan. He became a starter for the first time in his career and caught 38 passes.

Jordan continued to get better. He caught a career-high 68 passes for 795 yards in 1985. Then, in 1986, he made his first of six straight Pro Bowls.

Jordan played with the Vikings from 1982–1994. Entering 2021, he was Minnesota's career leader among tight ends in catches (498) and yards (6,307).

"He was a heck of a player," said former Vikings linebacker Scott Studwell. "He could run, he could catch, he was a solid blocker. He was kind of an unheralded guy coming into the league, but he bided his time and he found out a way to get on the field because he was just a tireless worker and obviously very intelligent."

Jordan made six
Pro Bowls, and his
6,307 career yards
receiving are the
most for a Vikings
tight end. ST. PAUL
PIONEER PRESS

To say Jordan was unheralded entering the NFL would be an understatement. He had been a seventh-round pick out of Brown of the Ivy League, not exactly a hotbed for pro talent.

Jordan grew up in Phoenix and was a multisport athlete. He said he was initially better at tennis than football and considered going to the Air Force Academy to play tennis. But the 6-foot-3, 236-pound Jordan soon realized he might have trouble fitting in planes.

Jordan chose to attend Brown primarily because of academics. His career goal didn't have anything to do with football.

"I was set on getting an engineering degree and then get into an engineering career," Jordan said. "I didn't pay much attention to being a pro prospect, but then my junior year comes around and I'm first-team All-Ivy League and honorable mention All-American, and I'm like, 'That's cool.' I started to get some feelers from some teams and I'm thinking, 'Maybe this is a possibility.'"

After being selected by the Vikings, Jordan got a two-year contract worth $33,000 the first year and $38,000 the second. He didn't even have a regular agent. A lawyer who was the father of a Brown classmate and represented singer Aretha Franklin handled his contract.

The still-raw Jordan was no lock to make the team. But with his athleticism and work ethic, he soon caught the attention of offensive coordinator Jerry Burns and Steckel, who was then the wide receivers coach and also worked with tight ends.

"I got the nickname 'Ivy' from Les Steckel and [wide receiver] Ahmad Rashad," Jordan said. "So everybody started calling me 'Ivy' and Jerry Burns noticed me and the coaches were like, 'Oh, he's the Ivy Leaguer.' But then what helped me get on Bud's radar was special teams. I did everything on special teams. I was even the wedge buster on kickoffs."

On offense, Jordan caught just three passes as a rookie and 15 his second year. But Joe Senser, who had been named to the Pro Bowl in 1981 when he caught 79 passes for 1,004 yards, had suffered a serious knee injury in 1982 and reinjured it and missed the entire 1983 season. Senser limped through the 1984 season before he was forced to retire.

Bob Bruer at first had taken over as the starter for Senser, but Jordan moved ahead of him. In 1984, the Vikings traded for veteran tight end Don Hasselback because they still weren't sure about Jordan.

"Don never got off the bench and I started for the next 10 years," Jordan said.

In an era when tight ends were starting to put up big receiving numbers, Jordan had good stats although they weren't phenomenal. He had five seasons of 50 or more catches but only once had 800 yards receiving. That was in 1986, when he had 859.

Because Jordan was an adept blocker, that made him a cinch for Pro Bowls. However, he never was named first-team All-Pro, an honor that often went to tight ends with a 1,000-yard season.

"To be honest, I think I was the number one tight end [of the era]," Jordan said. "There weren't people doing what I was doing. Kellen Winslow [of San Diego] was one of the tight ends that was getting down the field and Ozzie Newsome [of Cleveland] worked the middle a lot. I was getting down the field, and I was blocking at a high level. Shannon Sharpe [of Denver] wasn't in there to block anybody. When you look at my total game, I would put myself up against anybody."

Winslow, Newsome, and Sharpe are all in the Hall of Fame, an honor that likely won't come Jordan's way. But in 2019 he was inducted into the Vikings Ring of Honor.

"That was particularly special for me," Jordan said.

His three children were on hand for the induction ceremony, including Cameron Jordan. Cameron, a defensive end for New Orleans, has made six Pro Bowls since entering the NFL in 2011.

When Cameron made his first Pro Bowl in 2013, he had asked for and received Jordan's 1989 Pro Bowl jersey. The 287-pound Cameron Jordan squeezed into it for the event at U.S. Bank Stadium.

"I assumed he was going to frame it," said Steve Jordan. "But he just hung on to it. Then he wore it to the [ceremony]. It couldn't have come at a better time. I was surprised. But it was really cool."

Steve Jordan, who lives in Phoenix, gets to Vikings games when he can. After the 2017 and 2019 seasons, he of course rooted for the Saints in playoff games against Minnesota. The Vikings won both in dramatic fashion, but Jordan figured that at least provided a team to root for later in the playoffs.

Jordan cherished his time in Minnesota. As it turned out, it was simply a detour from what he thought he would do in his career. Since retiring after the 1994 season, he has worked regularly as a civil engineer.

STU VOIGT

Stu Voigt hopes one day to no longer be the answer to a trivia question.

In the final minute of Super Bowl XI in January 1977, the Vikings tight end caught a meaningless 13-yard touchdown pass from backup quarterback Bob Lee in a 32–14 loss to Oakland. He often gets reminded of it since the Vikings haven't been back to the Super Bowl since then.

"People still introduce me as the last Viking to score a touchdown in the Super Bowl," Voigt said. "Well, I guess it's better than a poke in the eye with a sharp stick."

Voigt was a steady tight end for the Vikings from 1970–1980, and their radio analyst for most of the 1980s and 1990s. He was regarded as a ferocious blocker, and despite playing in an era when many teams didn't throw a lot to the tight end, he stepped up as a receiver when needed.

Voigt caught 177 career passes for 1,919 yards, including a career-high 34 for 363 yards in 1975. He was named one of the "50 Greatest Vikings" when the team celebrated its 50th season in 2010.

"Stu was a great tight end," said former Vikings wide receiver Ahmad Rashad. "He could really catch the ball. He wasn't fast, but he never made mistakes, and Bud Grant was all about not making mistakes."

Voigt had some of his better games in the playoffs. He caught four passes for 43 yards in a 14–10 win over the Los Angeles Rams in the 1974 NFC Championship Game. He had four catches for 42 yards in a 35–20 playoff win over the Washington Redskins.

And he is the answer to another Super Bowl trivia question that might not be considered fully flattering. He caught three passes for 46 yards in a 24–7 loss to Miami in Super Bowl VIII, leading all receivers in the game in yardage.

"That was because the Dolphins didn't pass the ball," Voigt said with a laugh. "Bob Griese only threw seven times the whole game."

Voigt joined the Vikings as a 10th-round pick out of Wisconsin in 1970. He had grown up in Madison, Wisconsin, as a huge fan of Vince Lombardi's Packers.

"I lived and died with the Packers," Voigt said. "I can still name every Packers player and their position and their number from the 1960s. They were successful and winning championships, and that motivated me to play football."

Voigt had hoped to be drafted by the Packers but instead went to their rival, which took some getting used to. The Vikings ended up bringing him along slowly.

Voigt didn't have a catch in three games as a rookie in 1970, and had just 21 receptions in his first three seasons. But by 1973, he moved into the starting lineup, and he developed a rapport with quarterback Fran Tarkenton.

"Stu had the surest hands," said former Vikings defensive lineman Bob Lurtsema. "Fran always liked to dump it to him at the end when he went through his progressions. He always knew that Stu was going to be where he was supposed to be. And he was a very good blocker. He could really hit you."

Voigt caught 20 or more passes each season from 1973–1977, including twice having 32 or more. Those were hardly overwhelming numbers, especially considering what today's tight ends put up, but they weren't drastically different from what Charlie Sanders was doing then for NFC Central rival Detroit.

Sanders, who played from 1968–1977, never caught more than 42 passes in a season. But the tight end made seven Pro Bowls and three times was first-team All-Pro and is in the Pro Football Hall of Fame. Sanders once was named All-Pro and to the Pro Bowl during a season in which he had 31 catches.

Voigt, who helped pave the way for Chuck Foreman to have three 1,000-yard rushing seasons, believes he was a better blocker than Sanders and some other tight ends from that era who were making Pro Bowls. But he never got to one.

"Statistics can be a bit misleading," Voigt said. "The tight end position is what the offensive coordinator wants to make it. I was certainly proud and happy with my blocking and catching a few balls here and there and being on winning teams. I was a little disappointed that I didn't get into the Pro Bowl, and I got condolences from teammates that I should have."

One longtime teammate, Hall of Fame safety Paul Krause, said Voigt was underrated.

"He could get open and he could catch the football," Krause said. "We could always count on him, like the time I hit him for a touchdown in overtime on a fake field goal."

That was in 1977. Minnesota and Chicago were tied at 16–16 when the Vikings were at the 11-yard line and Fred Cox lined up for a field-goal attempt on third down.

That was Cox's last NFL season, when he went just 8 of 17 on attempts, so it wasn't exactly a chip shot.

Grant called for a fake, and Krause, the holder, hit Voigt going across the middle for the score. Had the play not worked, the Vikings still could have kicked a field goal on fourth down.

"I was surprised like everybody else that it was called, but it turned out to be a good call," Voigt said. "That was the only pass Krause ever completed."

That's one trivia question Voigt is glad to be associated with.

AND THE WINNER IS . . .
Steve Jordan gets the nod due to being one of the NFL's best tight ends for a prolonged period and making six Pro Bowls. Jordan earned the ultimate Vikings honor when he became in 2019 the first tight end in their Ring of Honor.

Rudolph, 31 entering the 2021 season, looked to potentially have time on his side to catch Jordan in the Vikings' record book. But Rudolph was released by the Vikings in March 2021 in a salary-related move and signed with the New York Giants. So unless Rudolph one day returns to Minnesota, he will finish 45 catches shy of Jordan's team record of 498 for a tight end and 1,819 behind his yardage record. Regardless, Rudolph eventually figures to join Jordan in the Ring of Honor.

TIGHT ENDS WHO DID NOT MAKE THE CUT
Had he not suffered a serious knee injury in 1982, Joe Senser might have gone on to be the top tight end in Vikings history. As a rookie in 1980, he had an impressive 42 catches for 447 yards. In 1981, he broke loose, catching 79 passes for 1,004 yards and becoming the first Minnesota tight end to make the Pro Bowl. He remains the only Vikings tight end with a 1,000-yard season. Senser missed the entire 1983 season after reinjuring his knee and then retired after a 1984 season in which he managed a mere 15 catches. He went on to become a Vikings radio

analyst and successful in the restaurant business before being hampered by strokes suffered in 2016 and 2018.

Byron Chamberlain didn't catch many balls when he played for Denver from 1995–2000, which included winning two Super Bowl rings. That changed in hurry when Chamberlain joined the Vikings in 2001. He had 57 receptions for 666 yards and made the Pro Bowl. Chamberlain slipped in 2002 to 34 catches for 389 yards, and that was it for him in Minnesota. He played sparingly in one final NFL season with Washington.

The Vikings used Jim Kleinsasser in different ways during his 1999–2011 tenure. Some years, Kleinsasser was a valuable target in the passing game, including having 37 catches in 2002 and a career-high 46 in 2003. Other years, he mostly was a blocker. From 2006–2008, he had a 16 combined catches in three seasons while playing in all 48 games.

One reason Kleinsasser was more of a blocker in some seasons was the presence of pass-catching tight end Jermaine Wiggins. He played for the Vikings from 2004–2006, catching 186 passes in those three seasons. Wiggins's most productive season was 2004, when he had 71 catches, the third-most ever by a Minnesota tight end, for 705 yards.

9

WIDE RECEIVERS

Randy Moss
Cris Carter
Anthony Carter
Ahmad Rashad
Jake Reed
Adam Thielen

It used to be no big deal when a Vikings receiver had a 1,000-yard season. After all, from 1979–2009 Minnesota wide receivers 27 different times reached 1,000. Once during that period, even tight end Joe Senser got there.

But then there was a drought. From 2010–2016, the Vikings went seven seasons without a single receiver getting to 1,000 yards.

The dry spell, though, ended with a flurry. Adam Thielen reached 1,000 yards in 2017 and also got there in 2018, when he tied an NFL record with eight straight 100-yard games. Stefon Diggs hit 1,000 in 2018 and duplicated the feat in 2019. And Justin Jefferson blew past the milestone mark with 1,400 yards in 2020, the second-most ever by an NFL rookie.

The drought came during a period in which Minnesota was a run-first team under Adrian Peterson. The Vikings still want to run first with Dalvin Cook, but they at least can fill the air with footballs when necessary.

The Vikings have plenty of history in doing that. They have two wide receivers in the Pro Football Hall of Fame in Randy Moss and Cris Carter. They're among 11 Vikings receivers to have made a combined 30 Pro Bowls.

RANDY MOSS

The first four games of Randy Moss's career were solid, but nobody was wondering then what his bust might look like in the Pro Football Hall of Fame.

Then came October 5, 1998. The Vikings were getting ready to face Green Bay at Lambeau Field on *Monday Night Football* in the rookie's first nationally televised game.

Moss took the NFL by storm as a rookie in 1998, catching 69 passes for 1,313 yards and a league-high 17 touchdowns.
ST. PAUL PIONEER PRESS

"I was standing outside the visitor's locker room about two hours before the game talking with [ABC sideline reporter] Lesley Visser, and then Randy came bopping along," said Hunter Goodwin, then a Vikings tight end. "He basically kind of interjected himself into the conversation, and he said to her, 'My name is Randy Moss and you'll probably be interviewing me later today.' After he walked away, she kind of thought that comment was overconfident and self-serving, and I just remember saying, 'You will be interviewing him.'"

Moss then went out and caught five passes for 190 yards, including touchdown receptions of 52 and 44 yards, in Minnesota's 37–24 win. He was on his way to NFL stardom.

As for that bust in Canton, Ohio, it was unveiled in August 2018 when Moss was enshrined in his first year of eligibility.

"Being first ballot, I mean that's special," Moss said.

Moss, who played in the NFL from 1998–2010 and in 2012, certainly was special. He was with the Vikings from 1998–2004, and had most of his top seasons with them. He did join them again for four games in 2010, although that didn't turn out too well.

Moss had 587 of his 982 career receptions and 92 of his career 156 touchdown grabs with Minnesota. That included his sensational rookie campaign of 1998, when he had 69 catches for 1,313 yards and an NFL-high and rookie record 17 touchdown receptions.

"He took the NFL by storm that year," said former Vikings wide receiver Jake Reed.

You better believe plenty of teams were regretting then not drafting Moss, who had slipped to the No. 21 pick because of off-the-field issues. Moss had originally signed with Notre Dame, but the Fighting Irish backed off after he was charged in a high school fight.

Moss enrolled at Florida State, but never played for the Seminoles after having tested positive for marijuana. He ended up starring at Marshall, then a Division I-AA school.

"He came in with a chip on his shoulder from going in the bottom half of the first round," Goodwin said. "He sure knew everybody who passed on him."

Yes, Moss did.

"I played definitely with a chip on my shoulder throughout my career," said the flamboyant Moss. "Some people I rubbed wrong, some people loved it."

The 6-foot-4, 210-pound Moss was nicknamed "The Freak" for his rare athletic ability. He had tremendous speed, and in his first training camp, offensive coordinator Brian Billick decided to test it out.

"Billick had us three quarterbacks, me, Randall (Cunningham) and Jay Fielder, stay after practice, and he said, 'Let's see if we can overthrow (Moss),'" said then Vikings quarterback Brad Johnson. "He was so fast that we couldn't overthrow him if we were throwing a normal high ball."

Johnson threw Moss his first two career touchdown passes in the first game of the 1998 season, hitting him from 48 and 31 yards out. Moss had four catches against Tampa Bay for 95 yards.

Moss, though, had a lull after that, averaging 59.3 yards in the next three games. But then came his breakout performance against the Packers, a game Moss calls his "favorite Vikings memory." Throwing to him that night was Cunningham, who had taken over as the starter after Johnson suffered a broken ankle in the second game.

"I get a pat on my shoulder and it's [star defensive tackle] Johnny Randle," Moss said of the game. "Johnny Randle telling me as a rookie, 'Man, we're going out and we're going to party tonight.'"

When Moss was a rookie, the Vikings went 15–1 and set an NFL record by scoring 556 points. The season, though, ended with a devastating 30–27 overtime home loss to Atlanta in the NFC Championship Game. Moss was just so-so in the game. He caught six passes for 75 yards and a touchdown but dropped what could have been a second-quarter TD.

The next season, optimism was running high. Season-ticket sales increased from 43,472 to 60,625. But the Vikings lost in the divisional round of the playoffs to St. Louis. They got back to the NFC Championship Game just once with Moss, but were drubbed 41–0 at the New York Giants after the 2000 season.

Moss continued to pile up numbers. He had more than 1,200 yards in each of his first six years. His best Vikings season was 2003, when he caught 111 passes for 1,632 yards and again led the NFL with 17 touchdowns. During that six-season stretch, Moss was three times named first-team All-Pro and five times to the Pro Bowl.

After he entered the NFL in 1998, Moss eventually overtook Jerry Rice, who was starting to slow down and retired after the 2004 season, as the top receiver in football.

"Jerry Rice was good but Jerry Rice couldn't take the top off like Randy Moss," Reed said. "Randall Cunningham would throw the ball as far as he could and Moss would just go up and get it. Defensive backs started playing 12 to 15 yards deep, and then Moss would just come back and get 16 yards on catches."

Moss's Vikings years led him to being named to the 2000s NFL All-Decade Team, and in 2019 he was selected one of the top 100 players in league's first 100 years. But he eventually would wear out his welcome in Minnesota.

Moss slumped in 2004, catching 49 passes for 767 yards, although he did miss three games due to injury. In the regular-season finale at Washington, he walked off the field with two seconds left. The next week, in a 31–17 playoff upset win over

Green Bay, he pretended to moon vocal fans at Lambeau Field after scoring on a 34-yard pass from Daunte Culpepper and was fined $10,000 by the NFL.

"It's not like I pulled my pants down or anything like that," Moss said shortly before his Hall of Fame induction.

Moss also had some brushes with the law in Minnesota, including a 2002 incident in which he was charged for bumping his car into a traffic officer and for marijuana having been in his vehicle. Put it all together, and Moss was traded to Oakland in March 2005.

Moss was just so-so with the Raiders but bounced back with New England in 2007 to set an NFL record with 23 touchdown catches. He was named first-team All-Pro and to the Pro Bowl that season, the only time he had those accolades other than with the Vikings.

Moss returned to Minnesota midway through the 2010 season, but it wasn't the same. Moss, then 33, was released after catching 13 passes for 174 yards.

"I got traded the first time, released the second time," he said. "Let bygones be bygones."

Moss closed out 2010 with Tennessee, retired in 2011, and came back to play in 2012 with San Francisco, his last game a 34–31 loss to Baltimore in Super Bowl XLVII. When he learned at Super Bowl LII in Minnesota in February 2018 he had been elected to the Hall of Fame, Moss said he wished he had never left in the first place.

"I did not want to move out of this state," Moss said. "I wanted to retire here and raise my family."

The Vikings have not retired his No. 84, which has been a source of some controversy. However, he was inducted into the Ring of Honor in 2017, and will live on in team lore.

"It was a pleasure to watch him," said Hall of Fame guard Randall McDaniell. "You knew watching him as a rookie in

1998 that he was going to be something special. You knew he was going to be one of the Vikings greats."

CRIS CARTER

For 16 NFL seasons, Cris Carter never shut up. Not only was he one of the top receivers in league history, he was one of the most legendary trash talkers.

Carter played with the Vikings from 1990–2001. For all but two of those seasons, his teammate was Jake Reed, who saw firsthand how Carter could fluster foes.

Cris Carter, pictured here in training camp with Randy Moss, made eight straight Pro Bowls from 1993–2000 and was inducted into the Pro Football Hall of Fame in 2013.
ST. PAUL PIONEER PRESS

"He could get into an opponent's head," Reed said. "Cris talked a lot of trash on the field. He never shut up. I used to ask him, 'How do you talk so much and continue to stay focused on football.' He just said, 'This is what I do.'"

He sure did it well. When Carter retired, he ranked second in NFL history, behind only Jerry Rice, with 1,101 receptions, and was fourth with 13,899 receiving yards.

Carter, inducted into the Hall of Fame in 2013, holds every single significant Vikings career receiving record. He had 1,004 catches, 12,383 yards, and 110 touchdown catches for Minnesota.

Reed said Carter jabbered after every one of his catches, and then some.

"Whenever they put a rookie or some young guy on him, Cris would be talking so much trash that it would take them off their game," Reed said. "Once we were playing Green Bay and one of their guys had a gap in his teeth and his teeth weren't straight. The whole game Cris was saying, 'Hey, man you really need to take advantage of the NFL dental plan. Until you take advantage of the NFL dental plan, I don't want to see you open your mouth again.' Cris ended up with 100-plus yards on the guy. He would always find out something about the guy covering him and talk about it the whole game."

With the Vikings, Carter played in eight straight Pro Bowls from 1993–2000. He twice was named first-team All-Pro. In 1994, he set a then NFL record by catching 122 passes. In a tribute to his consistency, he also caught 122 in 1995.

Carter's NFL start, though, was rocky. After being taken in the fourth round out of Ohio State in a 1987 supplemental draft, Carter played his first three seasons with Philadelphia. They were plagued by substance abuse issues.

Carter had started drinking at a young age while growing up in Middletown, Ohio. Later, he used marijuana and cocaine.

After his third season with the Eagles, head coach Buddy Ryan had seen enough.

Carter had played sparingly as a rookie and caught just five passes. He showed signs of improvement in 1988, when he caught 39, and in 1989, when he had 45 receptions and scored 11 touchdowns. But then Ryan released him because of his off-the-field issues.

"Buddy Ryan did the best thing that ever happened for me when he cut me and told me I couldn't play for his football team," Carter said in his emotional Hall of Fame speech. "But he told me a story. . . . He asked his wife what he should do, and his wife told him, 'Don't cut Cris Carter. He's going to do something special with his life.'"

The Vikings claimed Carter off waivers for the mere price of $100, and Carter used the experience as a wake-up call to get help. Wheelock Whitney, then one of the team owners, introduced him to Betty Triliegi, a specialist in drug and alcohol treatment. She played a big role in getting him sober.

"She asked me on September 19, she said, 'Cris, can you just not have a drink for one week?'" Carter said in his Hall of Fame speech. "And since September 19, 1990, because of Betty Triliegi, and Wheelock Whitney, I've been able to keep that program."

Carter remains grateful for the help he received in the Twin Cities that turned his career around.

"A lot of people don't realize the state of Minnesota has been at the forefront of recovery," Carter said. "It was for me. Minneapolis is a great place."

When Carter first got to Minnesota, another Carter, Anthony Carter, was the team's primary receiver. But Carter eventually seized that role, and by 1993 had the first of eight straight 1,000-yard receiving seasons.

"When you get a second opportunity, you've got to take advantage of it," said Hall of Fame guard Randall McDaniel, a teammate in Carter's first 10 Minnesota seasons. "He had the opportunity to come in and get a clean slate, and you've got to give Cris credit for taking advantage of it. There were a ton of good receivers back in that era, but I would put him right up there."

Carter worked the sidelines masterfully. He became known for his ability to tap his toes when it appeared there was no way he could stay in bounds.

Carter had his two 122-catch seasons with Warren Moon leading a pass-happy offense. The Vikings later began to run the ball more with Robert Smith, but Carter continued to catch plenty of balls from quarterbacks such as Brad Johnson, Randall Cunningham, and Daunte Culpepper. Overall, he had five seasons with 90 or more receptions and one with 89.

"He understood the game," Reed said. "He wasn't the fastest guy but he knew every position on the field, and when I say every position, he knew what route the tight end ran, each receiver, and where the back was supposed to be. He understood defenses, so he could see the blitz, and he ran really good routes. He was probably the best route runner I've been around."

Jeff Diamond, the general manager during most of Carter's Vikings tenure, remembers how focused Carter was.

"He was as intense as anybody I had seen on game day in terms of getting ready to play and getting in the mode," Diamond said. "You would walk near him before a game and he almost couldn't see you. It was weird. It was almost as if he was in a trance he was so intense and so focused."

Eventually, age began to catch up with Carter. After the 2001 season, when he caught 73 passes for 871 yards and his eight-year streaks of making the Pro Bowl and reaching 1,000 yards came to an end, he retired at age 36.

Carter did end up playing five games for Miami in 2002. However, he always has insisted it was initially not his intention to not finish his career with Minnesota.

"I voided the last year of my contract and I signed with HBO the same day I retired [from the Vikings]," Carter said. "So I thought I was done playing."

Carter's colleague at HBO, former Dolphins star quarterback Dan Marino, had convinced him to come out of retirement to help Miami midway through that season. But he didn't help much, catching just eight passes before retiring for good.

Carter then continued his broadcasting career. Like he was on the field, Carter became known for his trash talking on the air. After running back Adrian Peterson left the Vikings in 2016, Carter got into a feud with him by regularly saying he needed to retire rather than continuing his career with other teams.

ANTHONY CARTER

Anthony Carter was looking forward in 1985 to playing with his hometown team and catching passes from future Hall of Famer Dan Marino.

Well, that didn't happen.

The South Florida native had played from 1983–1985 in the USFL with the Michigan Panthers and Oakland Invaders, and was ready to enter the NFL with Miami. Carter had grown up following the Dolphins, and they were coming off a season in which Marino threw for a then-NFL record 48 touchdown passes.

Suddenly, though, Carter got word that the Dolphins, who held his NFL rights after taking him in the 12th round of the 1983 draft, had shipped him to Minnesota for linebacker Robin Sendlein and a second-round pick.

"I was kind of bummed," Carter said. "Growing up in South Florida, it had been a dream of mine to play for the Miami Dolphins."

So the wide receiver instead headed north to Minnesota. It ended up turning out quite well.

Playing with the Vikings from 1985–1993, the 5-foot-11, 168-pound Carter caught 478 passes for 7,636 yards. He was named three times to the Pro Bowl and had three 1,000-yard seasons.

"I had the opportunity to play in the NFL for 11 years, so I can't be too upset about [not going to Miami]," said Carter, who spent his final two seasons with Detroit. "I felt I had some great years with the Vikings. We didn't get the job done and win Super Bowls but I had some great years."

Carter did what he could to try to put the Vikings over the top, especially during the 1987 playoffs. The Vikings had gone 8–7 during the regular season, which was shortened by one game due to a player strike. They hadn't helped themselves by putting together a lousy strike-replacement team, which went 0–3.

In the playoff opener, Minnesota won 44–10 at New Orleans after being a 6½-point underdog. Carter, who had been a star punt returner in college at Michigan but only had returned three punts during the 1987 regular season, volunteered for return duty and brought back six for 143 yards, including an 84-yard touchdown. He also caught six passes for 79 yards and a touchdown.

"He didn't return punts during the season and then he just came out and he killed it," said former Vikings cornerback Carl Lee. "He just played phenomenal."

Carter was even more amazing the next week. In a shocking 36–24 upset at San Francisco, he caught 10 passes for a then playoff record 227 yards. For good measure, Carter had a 30-yard run and returned two punts for 21 yards. He totaled 278 all-purpose yards.

"I was just on fire that day," said Carter, whose Vikings were an 11-point underdog. "Nobody gave us a chance in that game, and we went out and shocked the world. Things were just going my way that day."

They certainly did.

"He just lifted our team up and put it on his shoulders," said former Vikings tight end Steve Jordan. "He was just jumping up in the air and Wade [Wilson] was just throwing the ball up there. It was awesome to watch."

Carter's record stood until Buffalo's Eric Moulds caught nine passes for 240 yards in the 1998 playoffs against Miami. It remains the second-best performance.

"The amazing thing about A. C.'s game against the 49ers is that there were no touchdowns," said Jeff Diamond. "He was just catching all these intermediate balls or deep balls and then he would get tackled at the 2-yard line. But it was an amazing day."

Minnesota's surprising playoff run came to an end with a 17–10 loss at Washington in the NFC Championship Game. Carter caught seven passes for 85 yards and returned four punts for 57 yards that day, but always will wonder about the Vikings' final offensive play of the game.

Down 17–10, the Vikings faced fourth-and-4 at the Redskins 6 with 1:03 left. A pass by Wilson glanced off the hands of Darrin Nelson at the goal line, but Carter said he might have distracted Nelson since he was the same area.

"I should have probably run a fade and took Darrell Green with me, but unfortunately he had an option," Carter said of the cornerback leaving him to defend Nelson.

Nelson, though, said, "Any time you're out there playing, you should catch it."

It was hard to be critical of anything Carter did in those playoffs. In three games, he caught 23 passes for 391 yards and a touchdown. He added 30 rushing yards and 221 on punt returns for an unbelievable 642 all-purpose yards.

"Anthony Carter was by far the most critical piece to that football team," Lee said.

Carter actually was just getting started in 1987, when during the regular season he caught 38 passes for 922 yards and led the NFL with a staggering average of 24.3 yards per catch. He followed that with seasons of 1,225 yards in 1988, 1,066 in 1989, and 1,008 yards in 1990.

Carter's playoff success continued after 1987. In a 28–17 divisional playoff win over the Los Angeles Rams in 1988, he had four catches for 102 yards.

"He was a really good player," said former Vikings linebacker Scott Studwell. "He had great ball skill and he was fast. He had unbelievable courage for a guy his size. Anthony was a gamer."

Eventually, though, Carter was phased out on the Vikings by another Carter. Cris Carter arrived in Minnesota in 1990 after being waived by Philadelphia, and in 1991 the future Hall of Famer had 72 catches for 962 yards to 51 for 553 yards for Anthony Carter.

"Those things happen," Anthony Carter said of no longer being the No. 1 receiver. "You get different quarterbacks who have different targets they like."

Carter lasted two more seasons with the Vikings but never got close to another 1,000-yard season. He moved on to Detroit at age 34 in 1994 but had just eight catches in two seasons with the Lions before retiring to South Florida.

Carter never did get to play for his hometown Dolphins, but he certainly made an impact in nine Minnesota seasons.

Ahmad Rashad

When Ahmad Rashad was traded from Seattle to the Vikings in 1976, he was thrilled. Rashad long had idolized Minnesota quarterback Fran Tarkenton, and relished the opportunity to play with him.

His hopes, though, almost were dashed.

"The first practice, I caught every pass Fran threw me, and I must have caught 20 or 30 balls," Rashad said. "I was just happy as heck to be there. Then I went to the training room, and they said, 'You know you didn't pass your physical, so we might have to send you back.'"

Rashad was coming off a knee injury that resulted in him missing the 1975 season with Buffalo, but he thought he was

Rashad made four Pro Bowls before going on to a successful broadcasting career.
ST. PAUL PIONEER PRESS

155

fully healed. He was dismayed when he heard the news and remained in the locker room.

"Fran walks up and says, 'What are you still doing here?'" Rashad said. "I said, 'I didn't pass the physical and they're going to send the trade back.' He said, 'Don't move. I'll be right back.' So I sat there for 30 or 40 minutes and finally he came back and says, 'Put your stuff in that locker and let's go.' I later found out Fran had told our general manager, Mike Lynn, that if they sent me back, they might as well cut him because Fran wasn't going to play unless they left me on the team."

It was a good move to keep Rashad, who had been acquired for journeyman defensive lineman Bob Lurtsema and a fourth-round pick. Playing from 1976–1982, Rashad made four Pro Bowls and had two 1,000-yard seasons before going on to a successful sports broadcasting career. He was inducted into the Vikings Ring of Honor in 2017.

Rashad was a valuable weapon for Tarkenton for three seasons before the quarterback retired after the 1978 campaign. Then he became the favorite target for Tarkenton's replacement, Tommy Kramer.

"When somebody came to tackle him, he kind of evaded them or side-slipped them," said former Vikings coach Bud Grant. "He had lot of great instincts. I would say that we got a steal. Rashad worked well into our system, and he became a great player."

Grant had admired Rashad since his name was Bobby Moore and he was a running back at the University of Oregon. As a rookie with the St. Louis Cardinals in 1972, he had caught four passes for 67 yards and scored two touchdowns against Minnesota.

The receiver converted to Islam and changed his name in 1973. He said the transition had its difficulties, including

Cardinals coaches continuing to say to him, "Your name is Bobby Moore."

After spending 1974 with the Bills and being hurt in 1975, Rashad ended up with the Vikings. He never will forget first meeting Grant.

"Bud said, 'This is what I want you to do. I want you tell me what the correct pronunciation is of your name,'" Rashad said. "I told him that the Arabic pronunciation is 'Akmed,' So he always called me 'Akmed.' Bud was the only one to do it. It was a matter of respect."

Grant didn't consider that anything out of the ordinary.

"Well, that was his name," Grant said. "I made a point out of calling people by their right name. If your name is Bill or Billy, whatever you wanted to be called is what I'd call you."

On the field, the Vikings called for Rashad to catch plenty of passes. In his seven Vikings seasons, he had 400 receptions for 5,489 yards. He led the team in receiving in both 1979, when he caught 80 passes for 1,156 yards, and in 1980, when he snared 69 for 1,095 yards.

After the 1978 season, Rashad was MVP of the Pro Bowl in Los Angeles. He caught five passes for 89 yards.

"He was very fluid and a great athlete," said former Vikings linebacker Scott Studwell. "He was deceptive and had great ball skills and was a very intelligent player."

In the next-to-last game of 1980, Rashad had the most dramatic catch in Vikings history until Stefon Diggs scored on the Minneapolis Miracle to win a 2017 divisional playoff game over New Orleans. The Vikings trailed Cleveland 23–22 with five seconds left when Kramer called Squadron Right, their version of a Hail Mary. Rashad hauled in a tipped ball on the right side on the goal line for a 46-yard touchdown grab on the game's final play for a 28–23 win.

"As the ball went up, I think what people don't understand is that I expected to catch the ball," Rashad said. "It wasn't like a crapshoot to me. I was going to make a play. So I never got overwhelmed emotionally or any of that kind of stuff. The ball got tipped, and I saw the ball the entire way and I was just able to reach back and catch it and then fall in the end zone. It wasn't that I was so excited because I expected to do it."

Nevertheless, fans at Metropolitan Stadium went wild and teammates piled on top of Rashad. Not only did the Miracle at the Met win the game, it clinched the NFC Central Division title. Making a reference to a playoff bonus coming, Rashad then said to Vikings receiver Terry LeCount, "Do you like money?"

That play helped make Rashad become more popular on a national basis. Eventually, though, he would become a household name. Rashad, who had worked in television for five years in the Twin Cities while with the Vikings, could have played a few more years but elected to retire after the 1982 season at age 33 to become a broadcaster for NBC.

Rashad became more associated with basketball than with football after NBC acquired the NBA rights in 1990. He became good friends with Michael Jordan while the Chicago Bulls were winning six NBA titles in the 1990s, and the relationship has continued to this day. The two are neighbors in South Florida, and watch football together nearly every Sunday in the fall. Rashad has tried to get Jordan to become a Vikings fan, but he instead is an avid supporter of the New England Patriots.

"Ahmad was a really good guy and a very talented guy who obviously went on to do a lot of good things from a media standpoint with basketball," said former Vikings tight end Steve Jordan. "But before that he was a fantastic receiver."

JAKE REED

At least something good for the Vikings came out of the ill-fated trade for Herschel Walker: Jake Reed.

In October 1989, Minnesota shipped a bevy of draft picks to Dallas for Walker, who flopped with the Vikings. Including Walker, there were 18 players and draft picks involved in the deal.

The Cowboys were fortified with draft picks, and that helped them win three Super Bowls in the 1990s. But Dallas did send a third-round selection in 1991 to Minnesota, and it was used on Reed, taken out of Grambling State.

Reed hears about the trade often since he lives in the Dallas area. He is always ready with a retort.

"I tell them it was a good trade for both teams," he said.

Reed didn't do much in his first three Vikings seasons, catching just 11 passes, but then he erupted. From 1994–1997, he had four straight 1,000-yard seasons. The only other receivers in Minnesota history to have done that were Hall of Famers Cris Carter and Randy Moss.

During that period, the 6-foot-3, 216-pound Reed had 297 receptions for 4,800 yards receiving. The only NFL receivers with more yards during those four years were Herman Moore (5,448), Tim Brown (5,163), Michael Irvin (4,986), and Carter (4,859). Brown and Irvin also are in the Hall of Fame.

"Jake was a terrific player," said Jeff Diamond. "He was a physical player. He was, of course, part of the Herschel Walker debacle, but he was a good part for us."

Reed surprisingly never made the Pro Bowl during his 12-year career, 10 spent with the Vikings. That irked him.

"In those four years, my numbers were better than a lot of the so-called superstars at receiver," said Reed, who had a career-high 85 catches in 1994. "I don't know why I didn't make it. I was a little disappointed."

It didn't help Reed in that four-year stretch that he played in the shadow of Carter, and was regarded as Minnesota's No. 2 receiver. At least Reed gained some consolation from something Carter said in 1996. Reed caught 72 passes that season and was second in the NFL with 1,320 yards. Carter had 96 receptions, but his 1,163 yards were 157 less than what Reed had gained.

"[Vikings coach] Dennis Green brought the team into the indoor practice field and he called out the Pro Bowlers, and I thought, 'I'm in this year,'" Reed said. "But he didn't call my name. And I still remember Cris Carter coming up and saying, 'Dawg, you should have gotten in.' Cris said, 'You should have gotten in before me.' So what Cris did was try to convince the committee that, 'If I don't play, can you bring Jake over?'"

Reed said he wasn't on board with that and the idea soon faded away. Unfortunately for Reed, so eventually did his playing time.

In 1998, the Vikings selected Moss in the first round of the draft, and he had an electrifying rookie year, catching 69 passes for 1,313 yards and NFL-high 17 touchdowns. Reed played 11 games that season, missing five due to a back injury, and caught just 34 passes for 474 yards.

Reed technically was still a starter, getting the nod in all 11 of those games, but was the No. 3 option behind Carter and Moss. The Vikings sometimes started three receivers; when they didn't, Moss, who started 11, was a force off the bench.

Reed said he wasn't frustrated by Moss's arrival since it helped the Vikings win. They went 15–1 in 1998.

What really bothered Reed that season was the lingering back injury that kept him out of the NFC Championship Game, a stunning 30–27 overtime loss at home to Atlanta. Reed had played in the 41–21 win in the playoff opener against Arizona before his back injury flared up.

"If I would have played, I would have really helped the team a lot because with me, Moss, and Cris we would have had triple threats and they couldn't just double Moss and double Cris," Reed said. "Going into the Arizona game, we had thought it was going to be a sweep. You know, 'Let's just get you out there and see how you feel, and then we should beat Atlanta and then you'll be ready for the Super Bowl.' But in hindsight I think I should have not played against Arizona and then played in the NFC Championship Game."

Reed returned to catch 44 passes for 643 yards in 1999 but was surprisingly cut after the season. He ended up with New Orleans in 2000, returned to Minnesota in 2001, and then played a final year with the Saints before retiring. Reed had only 27 catches in his final Vikings season of 2001 but got to play alongside his brother, cornerback Dale Carter.

Entering 2021, Reed was sixth on the Vikings' all-time receiving list with 413 catches and fifth with 6,433 yards, and he remains linked with Moss and Carter. At a 2019 game against Green Bay at U.S. Bank Stadium, the Vikings introduced the three receivers and they walked out together, prompting much applause.

"Absolutely, he was underrated," former Vikings center Jeff Christy said of Reed. "He should have made a Pro Bowl or two."

ADAM THIELEN

When NFL on-field spring drills and preseason games were cancelled in 2020 due to the coronavirus pandemic, Adam Thielen's mind flashed back to when he was trying to make the NFL in 2013.

The wide receiver was undrafted out of Division II Minnesota-Mankato and had to go to a rookie tryout camp before being offered a nonguaranteed contract by the Vikings.

He was able to make the practice squad due to his play in the spring and in preseason games.

"I know that if I was going through (that) offseason as a rookie, I wouldn't be in the NFL," Thielen said of 2020. "There's no chance."

Thielen took advantage of 2013 opportunities to continue to rise through the ranks, and he's become one of the most unexpected success stories in recent NFL history. Thielen made the active roster in 2014 and was a special teams ace for two seasons. He finally moved into the starting lineup at receiver in 2016, and he's made two Pro Bowls since then and had four 900-yard seasons.

"It's almost impossible to believe how that happened with him," said Joe Theismann, a longtime NFL analyst who won Super Bowl XVII in January 1983 as Washington's quarterback and has gotten to know Thielen. "I'm pretty sure that a lot of his inspiration from how he got started helped him get where he is now. He's one of the most intelligent receivers I've ever seen."

Thielen has great hands and is considered one of the best route runners in the NFL. He has an uncanny ability to get open in the end zone.

Thielen's breakout season came in 2016, when he caught 69 passes for 967 yards. He topped that in 2017, when he made his first Pro Bowl during a season in which he caught 91 passes for 1,276 yards.

Thielen then had his best season in 2018, when he had career highs of 113 receptions and 1,373 yards and made his second Pro Bowl. He had 100 or more yards receiving in the first eight games of the season. That broke the NFL record of seven to start a season set by Houston's Charlie Hennigan in 1961 and tied the overall NFL mark set by Detroit's Calvin Johnson in 2012.

"You've got to get better," Thielen said about going through that record stretch. "Teams are just going to have a target on your back."

Teams started to focus more on Thielen after that. He had a frustrating season in 2019, when he caught just 30 passes for 418 yards while missing six games due to hamstring issues.

When Minnesota traded wide receiver Stefon Diggs to Buffalo after the 2019 season, it looked as if teams might focus even more on Thielen. But the Vikings used one of the draft picks acquired in that deal to select wide receiver Justin Jefferson with the No. 22 pick in the 2020 draft.

Jefferson had a spectacular rookie season, catching 88 passes for 1,400 yards and being named to the Pro Bowl. But Thielen also did his part, catching 74 passes for 925 yards and a career-high 14 touchdown passes despite missing one game while on the COVID-19 reserve list.

"That's what you work for," Thielen said of his bounce-back season. "That's why I go back to work right when the season's over."

Thielen, though, got nearly as much praise in 2020 for his work with Jefferson as he did for his own statistics.

"He's been doing a tremendous job on the field and helping me out with the little things that I need help with," Jefferson said. "Just having him on the field and having somebody that I know can go out there and give it their all and make those big plays, it's a joy to watch."

While Jefferson entered the NFL highly publicized after playing on LSU's national championship team, it was the opposite for Thielen, who grew up a big Vikings fan in Detroit Lakes, a small town in northern Minnesota. When he went to Minnesota-Mankato, he got a $500 scholarship and that was it.

Thielen was a complete unknown when he showed up for a rookie tryout camp. But it didn't take him long to turn heads.

"He was relentless," said Zach Line, an undrafted rookie at that camp who went on to be an NFL fullback from 2013–2019 with Minnesota and New Orleans. "He had a mission in mind. And then he finally got on special teams with the Vikings, and you couldn't keep him off the field because he was making so many plays. Then he ran routes so well that you had to start him at receiver, and he hasn't let off the gas since."

After his banner 2018 season, Thielen was rewarded with a four-year, $64 million contract extension. And by 2020, he was the Vikings' second-highest paid player behind quarterback Kirk Cousins.

Thielen entered 2021 eighth on both the Vikings' all-time receiving list with 397 catches and on their all-time yardage list with 5,240. Not bad for a player who came out of nowhere.

"It's a great story, and you don't get there without believing in yourself and working hard," said Kyle Rudolph, a Vikings tight end from 2011–2020.

AND THE WINNERS ARE . . .

Two of three receivers on the all-time team are no-brainers. Randy Moss and Cris Carter are two of the best ever and are both in the Hall of Fame.

Moss and Carter were teammates from 1998–2001. During that period, they comprised one of the great receiving duos in NFL history.

For the third wide receiver spot, Ahmad Rashad gets the nod in a close decision over Anthony Carter. Rashad made four Pro Bowls to three for Carter. Carter had three 1,000-yard seasons to two for Rashad, but Carter played in a more pass-happy era. Rashad is the only receiver in the Vikings Ring of Honor other than Moss and Carter.

WIDE RECEIVERS WHO DID NOT MAKE THE CUT

Gene Washington was the Vikings' first great deep threat. A first-round pick out of Michigan State in 1967, Washington helped shake up the three-yards-and-a-cloud-of-dust NFL. He caught just 13 passes as a rookie but had a staggering average of 29.5 yards per catch. In 1969, Washington was named first-team All-Pro and to the Pro Bowl by catching 39 passes for 821 yards and a 21.1 average. Washington added another Pro Bowl berth in 1970. Washington played just seven NFL seasons, six with Minnesota, but left an impact.

John Gilliam took over from Washington as Minnesota's deep threat. He played for the Vikings from 1972–1975, making the Pro Bowl in each of his four seasons. The speedy Gilliam became the Vikings' first 1,000-yard receiver in 1972, catching 47 balls for 1,035 yards and leading the NFL with an average of 22.0 yards per catch. He had another strong season in 1973, catching 42 balls for 907 yards and a 21.6 average. But Gilliam made the Pro Bowl simply on reputation in 1974, when he slumped to 578 yards receiving. He had 777 yards receiving in his final Minnesota season of 1975, when he had slowed down a bit at age 30 and averaged just 15.5 yards a catch.

Sammy White made an immediate impact after being a second-round pick in 1976 out of Grambling State. He made the Pro Bowl in each of his first two seasons, catching 51 passes for 906 yards in 1976 and 41 for 760 yards in 1977, the last two years the NFL had 14-game seasons. Helped by a 16-game season, White reached 1,000 yards for the only time in his career in 1981, getting 1,001. White played for Minnesota from 1976–1985, and had 393 catches for 6,400 yards.

Stefon Diggs always will be known for the greatest play in Vikings history, the Minneapolis Miracle. His 61-yard touchdown reception from Case Keenum on the final play gave the Vikings a 29–24 win over New Orleans in the 2017 playoffs.

After being a fifth-round pick in 2015 out of Maryland, Diggs didn't play in the first three games before finally being activated and finishing the season with 52 catches for 720 yards. By 2018, Diggs had 102 catches for 1,021 yards. He caught 63 passes for 1,130 yards in 2019 but became disgruntled that Minnesota was running too much. He then was traded to Buffalo, and led the NFL in 2020 with 127 catches and 1,535 yards while being named All-Pro.

While Randy Moss and Cris Carter figure to be locks for a long time on the all-time team, Justin Jefferson is off to a good start to perhaps one day join them. In 2020, Jefferson followed Moss in 1998 and Percy Harvin in 2009 to become just the third Vikings rookie receiver to make the Pro Bowl, and he also was second-team All-Pro. He broke Moss's rookie team record of 69 catches in a season with 88 and topped his yardage mark of 1,313 with 1,400. Jefferson's yardage figure was the second most in NFL history, trailing only the 1,473 by Houston's Bill Groman in 1960.

10

KICKER

THE CANDIDATES

Fred Cox
Gary Anderson
Ryan Longwell

The Vikings developed one star kicker in Fred Cox, who manned the position from 1963–1977. Most of their top kickers, though, reached career heights elsewhere before eventually showing up in Minnesota.

In 1984, the Vikings picked up future Hall of Famer Jan Stenerud, who had starred with the Kansas City Chiefs and won a Super Bowl with them 15 years earlier, when they beat Minnesota. At 42, Stenerud made the Pro Bowl that season before retiring after the following year.

In 1989, the Vikings brought in Rick Karlis, who had kicked for Denver in two Super Bowls. He spent just one season with the Vikings but was around long enough to tie a then NFL record with seven field goals in a game.

In 1997, Eddie Murray was the kicker for one season at age 41 after he had sat out in 1996. Before that, he kicked for 16 seasons, including making two Pro Bowls with Detroit.

In 1998, Gary Anderson arrived after having been a star kicker for 16 seasons. He stuck around for five in Minnesota. Not long after that, future Hall of Famer Morten Andersen kicked for the Vikings in 2004, his 23rd of 25 NFL seasons.

In 2006, Ryan Longwell arrived after he had kicked for Green Bay for nine seasons and played in a Super Bowl. He lasted for six Minnesota seasons.

The trend continued up to recent seasons. In 2018, the Vikings signed Dan Bailey, who had kicked for Dallas for seven years, including making a Pro Bowl. He was Minnesota's kicker for three seasons before being released in March 2021 after a shaky finish in 2020.

FRED COX

Fred Cox was an All-Pro kicker for the Vikings. That was his low-paying job.

Cox also was a successful chiropractor, and built up a lucrative practice in Minnesota. He was one of the inventors of the Nerf football, which made him millions.

"You don't see too many people excel in so many walks of life that Fred did," said former Vikings halfback Dave Osborn.

Cox, who died in 2019, played for the Vikings from 1963–1977, and remains their all-time leading scorer with 1,365 points. When he retired, he was second in NFL history in scoring and with 282 field goals.

In 1972, after taking classes during off seasons, Cox earned a chiropractic degree. He could have made more money then as a chiropractor than a kicker, and eventually had a practice for 16 years after he retired as a player. He also continued to earn money from his association with the Nerf football, one that began when he signed a contract with Parker Brothers in 1972.

Cox was a star running back and kicker at the University of Pittsburgh, and was selected in the eighth round of the 1961

Cox is the all-time leading scorer in Vikings history with 1,365 points.
ST. PAUL PIONEER PRESS

draft by Cleveland. But the Browns didn't want Cox as a position player, and they already had future Hall of Famer Lou Groza at kicker.

"They needed me like a used shoe," Cox said in 2019.

After being let go, Cox worked as a school teacher in Pittsburgh. He tried to make the Vikings in 1962, but was unsuccessful.

Finally, Cox in 1963 earned a roster spot with Minnesota, serving as both the kicker and punter. The Vikings brought in Bobby Walden to handle the punting in 1964, and Cox continued what would be a 15-year run at kicker. But Norm Van

Brocklin, a gruff old-school coach, wouldn't even let him wear a special shoe for kicking.

That changed when Bud Grant arrived as the coach in 1967, and Cox developed into one of the NFL's top kickers. He was named first-team All-Pro in 1969 when he led the NFL in points (121), field goals (26), and field-goal percentage (70.3). He was chosen to the Pro Bowl in 1970 when he led the NFL with career-high totals of 30 field goals and 125 points.

"I look at it and say, 'You know, actually I did pretty good,'" Cox had said. "I scored a lot and everything that goes with it."

Nicknamed "Freddie the Foot," Cox was one of the NFL's last straight-on kickers. He had a career-field goal percentage of 62.0, which would be awful by today's standards, but he played in an era when kickers were regarded differently.

Grant considered it important when Cox kicked off to get down the field and help break up the wedge. And his percentage wasn't helped by kicking at often-frigid Metropolitan Stadium, known for having some of the most adverse weather in NFL history.

"You'd get up and hear the wind whistling outside the stadium and you'd cringe," Cox had said. "Then sometimes it was like kicking ice chunks. The ball would be as hard as a rock."

Cox wanted to retire after the 1974 season for a more lucrative job as a chiropractor. But Grant convinced him to sign a three-year contract and spend his final years grooming replacement Rick Danmeier, another straight-on kicker.

"Fred was very consistent," said former Vikings linebacker Jeff Siemon. "He wasn't the longest kicker in the world, and he lost some distance as the years went on. But he remained consistent, and Bud really respected that. So that's why he was able to hang on for so many years."

When he finally did retire from the Vikings, Cox opened a chiropractor office in Buffalo, Minnesota, 30 miles west of the Twin Cities. He also continued to bring in checks related to the Nerf football.

In 1972, a man named John Mattox approached Cox with a miniature goalpost, and they discussed needing a ball that kids could kick through it without difficulty. The two went to an injection molder, who came up with a lightweight ball. They then went to pitch it to Parker Brothers officials.

"They brought out a box full of footballs and said, 'We've been trying to make a ball like this for two years, and I think this is it,'" Cox said in 2019. "They wanted us to sign a contract right there. I almost fainted. We had this massive contract, but it's endless. That was a major mistake on their part."

The contract with Parker Brothers had no expiration date, and that continued when Hasbro took over the company in 1991. Cox often had checks of more than $400,000 come in annually, and even late in his life the checks were for more than $200,000 a year.

Cox was known for giving a lot of money to charity. When he died at age 80 due to heart and kidney issues, there were plenty of tributes about Cox as a player as a person.

"I was his holder for most of his kicking," said Paul Krause, a Vikings safety from 1968–1979. "He still holds the all-time scoring record with the Vikings, and that says it all. He was a great kicker, but he also was a great person. He was just a perfect gentleman."

Shortly before his death in November 2019, Cox reflected upon all the things he had done in his life.

"Nobody's going to live forever and nobody's going to live more than I did," he had said.

GARY ANDERSON

As the 1998 regular season wound down, Vikings general manager Jeff Diamond was secretly hoping Gary Anderson would miss one meaningless attempt.

Anderson ended up making all 35 of his field-goal tries and all 59 of his extra points to become the first kicker in NFL history to have a perfect regular season. When the Vikings, who went 15–1, were in the playoffs, it was brought up each time Anderson was set to kick that he had been flawless.

"He was phenomenal that season," Diamond said. "But I would watch these games and I would be like, 'Gary, go ahead and miss one,' because we were beating everybody by two or three touchdowns. So I would be like, 'You don't have to go into the playoffs with a perfect record.'"

The perfection continued in the playoff opener against Arizona, a 41–21 win, and for much of the NFC Championship Game against Atlanta. When Anderson lined up for a 39-yard attempt with 2:11 left in regulation, he had overall on the season been 39 of 39 on field goals and 63 of 63 on extra points.

The Vikings were leading the Falcons 27–20, so another successful kick likely would clinch the game and send them to the Super Bowl. But Anderson stunningly pulled the ball a few feet to the left. Atlanta came back and won 30–27 in overtime. He was devastated by the miss.

"It certainly was difficult," he said. "I took tremendous pride throughout my career about being the one guy on the team that everyone could count on in a critical situation and that time, that particular kick, I missed the kick. So yeah, that was certainly a difficult thing to deal with."

Vikings fans have moaned about the miss for more than two decades, but teammates haven't. Many say it's unfair it cast a pall over the career of one of the best kickers ever.

The native of South Africa played in the NFL from 1982–2004, and retired as the all-time leading scorer with 2,434 points. Entering 2021, he was ranked third behind Adam Vinatieri and Morten Andersen.

Anderson made the Pro Bowl four times, including 1998, when he also was first-team All-Pro. Anderson played for the Vikings from 1998–2002 and made 109 of 129 field-goal attempts for 84.5 percent.

"He was probably the best kicker I've ever seen," said Mitch Berger, a longtime punter who was the holder on Anderson's infamous miss against the Falcons. "He wasn't the strongest, by any means, but he was the most consistent and the most naturally gifted. [The miss is] something that will be on him the rest of his life. He had an amazing career and should be in the Hall of Fame, but I haven't heard his name at all about being a Hall of Famer because that kick is what he mostly is known for, and that stinks."

There were no issues with the snap or the hold. It just surprisingly drifted left.

"If he hadn't had that perfect season, we wouldn't have been where we were that year," said Mike Morris, then the long snapper. "Fans are allowed to think what they want to think because they pay enormous prices to attend the games. But from the players, there is no blame to be cast."

Anderson's miss perhaps affected him mentally the next season, when he made just 19 of 30 field-goal attempts. But he bounced back in 2000, making 22 of 23 field-goal attempts and going 45 of 45 on extra points.

"The only one he missed was blocked," Berger said. "He got it back together and nearly had another perfect year again."

After leaving the Vikings, Anderson finished his career by kicking for Tennessee from 2003–2004. He then finally retired at age 45.

Anderson became a fly fishing guide in Canmore, Alberta, a picturesque town of 12,000 in Canada's Rocky Mountains. He dubbed it the "most beautiful place on the planet."

High in the mountains and in another country, Anderson is mostly spared from revisiting the 1998 NFC Championship Game. But when asked, he's willing to talk about what was one of the biggest downers in Vikings history.

"It's certainly not a fond memory, but you have to move on," he said. "That's part of being a field-goal kicker and it's reality, and you have to learn in life how to deal with adversity."

Overall, Anderson speaks with fondness about his Vikings seasons and his career. He has a website on fly fishing and his NFL career. It can be found at www.garyandersonperfectseason .com.

Ryan Longwell

The first time Ryan Longwell kicked for the Vikings in a pre-season game at the Metrodome, he couldn't believe what he was hearing. Or actually what he wasn't hearing.

Longwell had spent the previous nine seasons with Green Bay, Minnesota's hated rival. So the atmosphere when he lined up to kick against Oakland in 2006 was a lot different than what he had previously experienced at the Metrodome.

"It was one of the weirdest field goals I ever had, that first home preseason game," Longwell said. "When I was a Packer, every time I stepped on the field everybody was screaming and yelling at me and all that stuff. Then we line up for a 42-yarder and all of a sudden it's dead silent in the Metrodome. That's because I'm the home guy and that kind of threw me off."

Longwell still made the kick, and he ended up making a lot more for the Vikings. Longwell, who played from 2006–2011, still has the highest field-goal percentage in Minnesota history at 86.0. He made 135 field goals, the second-most in team history, and tacked on 228 extra points.

"Ryan was a former Packer, and it was crazy when he came in," said former Vikings cornerback Antoine Winfield. "They were our rival and he was Mr. Clutch for the Packers, and he beat us a couple times on game-winning field goals. But we were excited to have him, and he did a great job."

Longwell had kicked for some strong Green Bay teams, and as a rookie played in Super Bowl XXXII, a 31–24 loss to Denver in January 1998. But when 2006 rolled around, the Packers cast their eyes elsewhere.

"They were looking to go younger at the position, so I hit the open market," Longwell said. "It came down to Minnesota and Tampa Bay, but I really hit it off with [head coach] Brad Childress and obviously the prospect of kicking in the dome for me was good."

Signing with Minnesota ensured that Longwell would make one return trip each year to Green Bay. And while Longwell had some great years there, they were quickly forgotten by Packers fans.

"I was the Packers' all-time leading scorer at the time and had most of their kicking records, but I was booed," Longwell said. "There wasn't one person cheering. The P.A. announcer announced me like 30 seconds early, and everybody booed."

The Packers won in five of Longwell's six return trips to Green Bay, but the one Minnesota victory was a memorable one. It featured former Packers star quarterback Brett Favre leading the Vikings to a 38–26 win in 2009.

Longwell had played with Favre throughout his Packers tenure, so he was excited to be reunited with him in 2009, when the Vikings made it to the NFC Championship Game. After training camp had started in 2010, Longwell played a role in convincing Favre to return to the team for one final season after he had contemplated retirement at his home in Kiln, Mississippi.

"Me, Jared Allen, and Steve Hutchinson went down to Mississippi to try to convince him to come back and we told him how much fun it was, and he did come back," Longwell said. "We had seen some of the news reports, but we didn't think anybody knew we were coming back with him. But after we flew into [a suburban Twin Cities airport], there were news media there and there were helicopters following us. It was surreal."

Longwell had the task of driving Favre to the team's practice facility. Chris Kluwe, then Minnesota's punter and holder, likened it to the slow chase involving O. J. Simpson in 1994.

"It was nuts," Kluwe said. "It was like O. J. in the white Bronco with all those helicopters following him."

Favre's final season wasn't nearly as good, and the Vikings faltered to a 6–10 record. After a 3–13 season in 2011, Minnesota let Longwell go in favor of rookie Blair Walsh. He was signed for one playoff game with Seattle in 2012, but his career then was over at age 38.

And the Winner Is . . .

If a kicker in today's NFL had statistics similar to Fred Cox's, he wouldn't last more than a few games. But it must be understood that Cox played in an entirely different era. And when that is taken into account, he is the greatest kicker in team history.

Cox was a reliable specialist for 15 Minnesota seasons. No other kicker has been with the team for more than six years.

Cox is the only kicker in Vikings history to have been named first-team All-Pro and to the Pro Bowl in different seasons. Gary Anderson and Blair Walsh also achieved that double, but each did it in the same season.

KICKERS WHO DID NOT MAKE THE CUT . . .

Jan Stenerud was one of the greatest kickers in NFL history. He was the first player inducted into the Hall of Fame who exclusively played that position. He was named to six Pro Bowls, five while with Kansas City from 1967–1979. Stenerud's sixth career Pro Bowl came when he was 42 and playing his first season for the Vikings in 1984. He made 20 of 23 field-goal attempts, including 3 or 4 from 50 yards or longer. Stenerud played one more season with Minnesota in 1985 before retiring.

Fuad Reveiz was a mostly reliable Vikings kicker from 1991–1995. He made the Pro Bowl in 1994 when he led the NFL in field goals with 34 (in 39 attempts). The next season, though, Reveiz's field-goal percentage slipped from 87.2 to 72.2 (26 of 36), and he never kicked again in the NFL.

Blair Walsh wasn't perfect, like Gary Anderson in 1998, but he had perhaps the greatest kicking regular season in team history. Walsh was 35 of 38 on field-goal attempts, including making all 10 tries from 50 or more yards. In 1998, Anderson was just 2 of 2 from 50 and beyond. Walsh, named first-team All-Pro and to the Pro Bowl in 2012, ended up making his first 12 career attempts from 50 yards or longer, an NFL record. But he eventually slipped. He missed a 27-yarder wide left in the waning seconds in the 2015 playoffs against Seattle, and the Vikings lost 10–9. Walsh was cut after going 12 of 16 on field goals and 15 of 19 on extra points in the first nine games of 2016.

11

KICK RETURNER

THE CANDIDATES

Cordarrelle Patterson
Marcus Sherels

The excitement of kickoff and punt returns has diminished over the past decade in the NFL due to rule and strategy changes, but that wasn't always the case with the Vikings.

During a four-season stretch from 2013–2016, Minnesota had the most electrifying return game in the NFL. Cordarrelle Patterson brought back five kickoffs for touchdowns during that period, and Marcus Sherels returned four punts for scores.

Patterson eventually moved on to Oakland, New England, Chicago, and Atlanta, and Sherels began to show signs of age and was out of the NFL. But memories of many impressive returns continue to linger in Minnesota.

CORDARRELLE PATTERSON
The Vikings were so intrigued by the athleticism of Cordarrelle Patterson that they traded second-, third-, fourth-, and seventh-round draft picks to New England to move up to take him with the No. 29 overall pick in the 2013 draft.

Patterson, nicknamed "Flash," did not disappoint as a rookie. He opened his second NFL game by returning a kickoff 105 yards for a touchdown at Chicago. In his seventh game, he returned one 109 yards for a score against Green Bay to tie an NFL record that never can be broken.

Patterson that season averaged an NFL-best 32.4 yards per kickoff return, and was named All-Pro and to the Pro Bowl. For good measure, he caught 45 passes for 469 yards.

"At first you didn't know what to expect," then Vikings cornerback Xavier Rhodes said of his rookie year. "But he was very electrifying. It got to be that once he got the ball in his hands, it was over. There was always a chance he was going to take it to the 50 or past."

Patterson had a lull in his second season of 2014, when his return average slipped to 25.6 yards and he didn't have a touchdown. But he soon returned to his previous form, leading the NFL with a 31.8-yard average in 2015 and with a 31.7-yard average in 2016. He had a touchdown in each of those seasons, and in 2016 was again named All-Pro and to the Pro Bowl.

While with the Vikings, Patterson led the NFL three times in kickoff return average.
ST. PAUL PIONEER PRESS

179

"He was awesome," said Vikings safety Harrison Smith. "It was like any time he touched the ball it was thought he was going to score. He was explosive."

What didn't go as well for Patterson was his attempt to establish himself as an NFL receiver. In 2014, he slipped to 33 catches and in 2015 had a meager two. The Vikings made a point of trying to get him the ball in 2016, and he had a career-high 52 catches. But he only gained 453 yards for an 8.7 average.

"I thought he was going to have a great career [in Minnesota] but it didn't go quite the way he expected as a receiver, and that made it tough on him," said former Vikings defensive tackle Kevin Williams. "But he was a dynamic player on kickoff returns."

After being unable to distinguish himself in Minnesota as a receiver, Patterson moved on as a free agent to Oakland in 2017. He left the Vikings with a 30.4-yard kickoff return average over his four seasons.

Patterson was traded to New England in 2018, and won a Super Bowl that season with the Patriots. Then he spent 2019 and 2020 with Chicago before signing with Atlanta in 2021.

At his stops after Minnesota, Patterson was unable to become a starting receiver, catching 84 balls over four seasons. He was at least used more in the running game, including gaining 228 yards for the Patriots in 2018 and 232 for the Bears in 2020.

As a kickoff returner, though, Patterson continued to excel. He ran back kicks for touchdowns in 2018, 2019, and 2020, giving him an NFL record-tying eight for his career. He was named All-Pro for the third time and made his third Pro Bowl with the Bears in 2019, when he averaged 29.5 yards per return. Then in 2020, he earned his fourth All-Pro nod and made his fourth Pro Bowl when he averaged 29.1 yards per return, and brought back one 104 yards for a touchdown against the Vikings.

That return enabled Patterson to tie the NFL career record originally set by Josh Cribbs and Leon Washington for most kickoff returns for a touchdown. Patterson is also in rare company when it comes to his career kickoff return average of 29.8. The only player in history with a higher average was Bears legend Gale Sayers, who averaged 30.6 from 1965–1971.

"He's the best special teams player in the league," Vikings wide receiver Adam Thielen said about Patterson.

Marcus Sherels
Marcus Sherels had a long road to the NFL even though he came from just down the road.

Sherels grew up in Rochester, Minnesota, 80 miles south of the Twin Cities. And he attended the University of Minnesota, just two miles from where the Vikings played in 2010 at the Metrodome.

The 5-foot-10, 175-pound Sherels, a cornerback, wasn't drafted after his senior season of 2009 and wasn't even immediately signed as a free agent. He went to a Vikings tryout camp in the spring of 2010, got a contract offer, and then spent most of that season on the practice squad. He was activated and got into the season finale against Detroit, but didn't accumulate any statistics.

By the next year, though, Sherels began to show a knack on special teams, and became Minnesota's primary kickoff and punt returner. He soon distinguished himself more as a punt returner, and that became his primary role on the Vikings in a tenure that stretched through 2019.

"He always made the first guy miss, and that's what always stuck out to me," said cornerback Xavier Rhodes, Sherels's teammate for seven seasons. "The first guy was never going to tackle him."

In 10 Minnesota seasons, Sherels had 2,480 yards on punt returns, the most in team history, and his 10.5-yard average also ranks as the best in Vikings history. His top seasons were 2013, when he averaged a career-high 15.2 yards per return and scored a touchdown, and 2015, when he averaged 13.9 yards and tied for the NFL lead with two brought back for scores.

"Just being consistent," the modest Sherels said of what made him a good returner. "I've had great coaching. I've had the benefit of really good blockers and good schemes and just consistency and working on my craft each and every day."

Entering 2021, Sherels was 14th on the all-time NFL list with five career touchdowns on punt returns. There was no hesitation when asked to name his favorite.

On September 30, 2012, Sherels's 25th birthday, the Vikings played at Detroit. Minnesota's Percy Harvin opened the game with a 105-yard kickoff return for a touchdown. In the third quarter, Sherels scored his first career touchdown on a 77-yard punt return, and the Vikings went on to win 20–13.

"To get my first NFL touchdown on my birthday, that was pretty cool," Sherels said. "I remember Percy getting the kickoff return before that and he said, 'Now, it's your turn.' So it was a good birthday present."

Sherels played sporadically on defense with Minnesota and eventually slowed down as a punt returner. After he averaged 9.5 yards in 2017 and 12.0 in 2018, without scoring a touchdown in either season, the Vikings elected not to bring him back when he became a free agent.

Sherels signed with New Orleans and didn't make the team. The Vikings brought him back for three games early in 2019, and then he was cut. He joined Miami for five games, and was released again. He was signed for Minnesota's two playoff games, but in a 27–10 loss at San Francisco in the divisional round lost a fumble on his final Vikings play.

During a season in which he turned 32, Sherels averaged just 4.7 yards per return in 2019, a far cry from what he used to do. And he was out of the NFL in 2020. Overall, though, former Vikings cornerback Antoine Winfield said it was quite a ride for Sherels.

"He was undrafted and when he got his opportunity, he took advantage of it," Winfield said. "He was a Minnesota product and I'm sure that was a dream come true for him to get a chance to play with the Vikings."

AND THE WINNER IS . . .

Cordarrelle Patterson is one of the best kickoff returners in NFL history, and he gets the nod hands down.

Had Patterson not become frustrated by his inability to become an impact receiver, he might have stuck around Minnesota. Instead, he ended up facing the Vikings five times in his first four seasons after leaving, and he had some good moments.

RETURNERS WHO DID NOT MAKE THE CUT

Had wide receiver Percy Harvin not missed seven games due to injury in 2012, he might have had one of the greatest kickoff return seasons in NFL history. Harvin returned 16 kickoffs for a 35.9-yard average but didn't have enough attempts to qualify for the league lead. Playing for the Vikings from 2009–2012, Harvin averaged 27.9 yards per return and scored five touchdowns, getting at least one each season. In 2009, when Harvin averaged 27.5 yards and scored two touchdowns, he made the Pro Bowl as a returner.

Wide receiver David Palmer was equally adept as a kick and punt returner while with the Vikings from 1994–2000. He averaged 22.6 yards while scoring one touchdown on kickoff returns and 9.9 yards while scoring two TDs on punt returns.

Palmer's best season came when he led the NFL in 1995 with a punt-return average of 13.2.

Wide receiver Leo Lewis was a valuable punt returner during his 1981–1991 tenure with the Vikings. In 1988, he returned a whopping 58 punts, tied for the third-most in NFL history. Lewis averaged 9.4 yards per return with Minnesota and scored one touchdown, a 78-yard runback against Atlanta in 1987.

12

DEFENSIVE ENDS

THE CANDIDATES

Jim Marshall
Carl Eller
Chris Doleman
Jared Allen

During the days of the Purple People Eaters defensive line, the motto was, "Meet at the quarterback."

The Purple People Eaters terrorized opposing quarterbacks in the late 1960s and during the 1970s. The members were defensive ends Carl Eller and Jim Marshall and defensive tackles Alan Page and Gary Larsen, with Doug Sutherland replacing the retired Larsen in 1975.

The guys getting the most sacks then were Eller and Marshall. Sacks didn't become an official NFL statistic until 1982, but the Vikings always have kept them. They list Eller as their career leader with 130 and Marshall right behind at 127.

Some of the biggest stars in Vikings history have been defensive ends. In their history, six ends have combined to be named first-team All-Pro 10 times and to be selected for 23 Pro Bowls.

The first two stars at the position were Eller and Marshall. After the Purple People Eaters were done, the Vikings continued to have sack specialists at defensive end such as Chris Doleman, Jared Allen, Everson Griffen, and Danielle Hunter.

JIM MARSHALL

For 20 straight seasons, Jim Marshall never missed an NFL game. But don't think there weren't some close calls.

Marshall played in the NFL from 1960–1979, including 1961–1979 with the Vikings. The stories are legendary about how Marshall always showed up for games even if injured or ill.

"Once, Jim came to the stadium in an ambulance," said safety Paul Krause. "He had been in the hospital all week and he came up in the ambulance and played in the game and played well."

Okay, so Marshall didn't always get the ambulance service.

"Sometimes he was in the hospital and they would go get him the morning of the game and bring him to the game," said running back Chuck Foreman. "He had this ability to overcome pain mentally that most guys couldn't."

When Marshall retired, he held NFL records for most consecutive games played (282) and most consecutive starts (270). The marks are now held by punter Jeff Feagles for most games in a row (352) and quarterback Brett Favre for most consecutive starts (297).

As for the stories about going from the hospital to games, Marshall speaks as if it was simply business as usual.

"Once I had acute asthmatic bronchitis," he said, "Another time it was pneumonia. The way I was taught was you work to find something you like and are successful at, and you stick to it. It was a lot of fun that I got to play this little kid's game that I started playing back in the alleys and I made a living playing the game."

After playing with Cleveland as a rookie in 1960, the Danville, Kentucky, native was taken in the expansion draft by Minnesota. For 19 seasons, Marshall was the heart and soul of the Vikings.

Marshall, whose listed playing weight was 248 pounds, arrived in Minnesota weighing less than 200. He had been bitten by a mosquito while on Army duty, contracting encephalitis and losing 50 pounds.

"It left me very weak," Marshall said. "There was a chance of me not surviving."

Marshall eventually regained his strength and became the Vikings' first key defensive building block. He was a constant as the roster was built up and they played in four Super Bowls.

"It was great for us to be able to experience what it was like always being the underdog and then getting to be the dog," Marshall said. "We worked our way up from a team that was a bunch of mavericks from all over the league and we turned it into what became winning football."

Marshall became the team captain. His longtime coach, Bud Grant, put him in charge of policing players.

"Jim was a true team leader," Krause said. "Guys knew what they could do and what they couldn't do. Jim would keep them in line."

Marshall had responsibilities beyond football. With players getting ready to drive from training camp in Mankato, Minnesota, the 90 minutes to Bloomington for a preseason game at Metropolitan Stadium, Marshall would fire a pistol in the air to start the procession.

Marshall was often performing pranks. He liked to fire homemade rockets, and once concocted an elaborate plan with defensive linemen Carl Eller and Bob Lurtsema.

"We caught a frog and put him in a parachute," Lurtsema said. "We named him Freddie after [athletic trainer] Fred

Zamberletti. We got the whole team together and we shot the rocket off the top of the dorm [at training camp]. We were all waiting for Freddie to parachute out but then the thing exploded. Nobody found Freddie ever again."

Ever the adventurist, Marshall almost died when he was among a party of 16 lost in a blizzard while snowmobiling in Wyoming in 1971. The party burned money and credit cards to keep a fire going during the night, and one ended up dying from exposure.

Marshall was an avid skydiver. That was before teams put in contracts language banning activities deemed dangerous.

On the field, Marshall was a hazard to quarterbacks. He played before sacks became an official statistic in 1982, but the Vikings list him with 127, second in team history behind Eller's 130.

Marshall had great speed that enabled him to get to the ball. He set an NFL record by recovering 30 opponent fumbles, and that remains second in league history behind Rod Woodson's 32.

Unfortunately for Marshall, some remember him most for what he did after one fumble recovery. In the fourth quarter of a 1964 game at San Francisco, he scooped up a loose ball and ran 66 yards in the wrong direction to score a safety for the 49ers. The play long has been a staple on blooper reels.

"That was unfortunate because the league itself kept replaying it," Eller said.

Marshall doesn't like to talk about the play.

"I was ashamed of it then, and it's been talked about for 50 years," he said. "Don't you think that's enough?"

Marshall noted that the Vikings won the game 27–22, and he had a key forced fumble. Early in the fourth quarter, before the safety, Marshall knocked a ball loose that Eller returned 45 yards for a touchdown and a 27–17 lead.

Another subject Marshall doesn't like to discuss much is the Hall of Fame. Many consider it a travesty Marshall hasn't been inducted into the Canton, Ohio, shrine, but he has been hampered by making only two Pro Bowls in his 20 seasons.

"If I had the credentials to get in the Hall of Fame, then I should be in there," he said. "If somehow they deem that I don't have the criteria, that I don't meet the criteria that the Hall of Fame has set, then I don't belong."

Eller, who was inducted into the Hall in 2004, long has campaigned for Marshall to join him.

"Jim should be in the Hall of Fame because he was a really good example of being a team player, a great player," Eller said. "He has the records for being ready for every game. That's important because he always answered the call. He was a great teammate and a great captain."

Marshall's No. 70 was never worn again for Minnesota after he played his last game on December 16, 1979, and it was officially retired in 1999. Other team captains followed, but it wasn't always the same.

"Jim Marshall was our leader, our captain," said Ahmad Rashad, a Vikings receiver from 1976–1982. "Bud made me the captain my last two years there and I was proud. But when you say, 'captain of the Vikings,' there's no question, it's Jim Marshall."

Carl Eller

Carl Eller doesn't care that sacks didn't become an official NFL statistic until 1982. He doesn't care that the term sack wasn't widely used when he played. All he asks for is he be known as the all-time Minnesota leader in that category.

The Vikings consider him that. They list their career sack leader as Eller, who had 130 while playing from 1964–1978.

"Whether the words are sack, quarterback tackles, it doesn't matter," he said. "I'm still the sack leader no matter what they call it."

Officially, the Vikings sack leader is defensive tackle John Randle, who had 114 while playing from 1990–2000. But some might not want to mention that to the 6-foot-6, 247-pound Eller, who used to terrorize foes with Minnesota.

The defensive end was named first-team All-Pro five times and selected to six Pro Bowls with the Vikings. He was inducted into the Hall of Fame in 2004.

"He was a physical specimen," said Chuck Foreman. "He played the game at such a high level that you couldn't help but be impressed. He certainly was one of the best that played."

Eller is listed by the Vikings as their all-time sack leader.
ST. PAUL PIONEER PRESS

Eller was known as "Moose" because of his size and quickness. He used his quickness to run down ball carriers and to get to the quarterback.

"He was magnificent," said Ahmad Rashad. "Sometimes I couldn't wait to get off the field so I could watch him play."

Eller joined the Vikings in their fourth season after having been a standout at the University of Minnesota. The North Carolina native enrolled in 1960 after he was unable to attend a major Southern school in an era of segregation and Wake Forest's coach recommended the Gophers.

In college, Eller teamed with Bobby Bell, who would go on to become a Hall of Fame linebacker with Kansas City. The Vikings had selected Bell in the second round of the NFL draft, but he spurned them for the Chiefs, who had taken him in the AFL draft.

When the 1964 NFL draft came around, the Vikings were taking no chances. Buffalo had selected Eller two days earlier with the fifth overall pick in the AFL draft, and the Vikings had planned to take him No. 6 in the NFL draft in Chicago.

"I was in Chicago and one of the Vikings assistants was there," Eller said. "He was staying at the same hotel and he had to watch my every move. He was thinking that the Bills were snooping around and he didn't want me to make any funny moves with the Bills before the Vikings drafted me."

The Vikings indeed drafted Eller, and they were able to stave off Buffalo and sign him. It turned out to be a great choice. In his rookie season, Eller recovered four fumbles, including returning one 45 yards for a touchdown in the fourth quarter that gave the Vikings 27–17 lead at San Francisco in an eventual 27–22 win.

Jim Marshall forced that fumble, but it was understandable the play got lost in the next day's paper. Later in the quarter,

Marshall scooped up another 49ers fumble but ran 66 yards the wrong way to score a safety for San Francisco.

Between 1968–1974, with Deacon Jones starting to slow down, Eller was the NFL's most dominant defensive end. He had all of his All-Pro and Pro Bowl selections during that period.

Helping Eller was the arrival in 1967 of defensive tackle and eventual Hall of Famer Alan Page. That's when the Purple People Eaters line, which also featured Marshall and defensive tackle Gary Larsen, was born.

"We were one of the best [defensive lines ever], if not the best," Eller said. "I know for many years, we gave up the lowest points in the NFL and we took a lot of pride in that."

The Vikings were No. 1 in the NFL in scoring defense in 1969 and 1970 and second in 1971. In 1969, when they went to their first Super Bowl, they gave up a meager 9.5 points per game, then a record for a 14-game season.

Eller made a key play in the postseason opener against the Los Angeles Rams. With the Vikings clinging to a 21–20 lead late in the fourth quarter, Eller dumped quarterback Roman Gabriel in the end zone for a safety to extend the advantage to 23–20, which would be the final score. Minnesota got the ball back and ran down the clock to secure the team's first playoff win.

"That was a big play for me and it was a big day for us," said Eller, who had two sacks that afternoon.

The Vikings the next week defeated Cleveland 27–7 in the NFL Championship Game to advance to Super Bowl IV. But they were walloped 23–7 by the Chiefs, who featured Bell, Eller's old college teammate.

Eller was mostly a nice guy off the field, although sometimes he could boil over. The Vikings always were served steak for their pregame meal at 9 a.m. before a noon game. Once, Eller, tired of having steak, demanded pancakes. When he was told that wasn't possible, he knocked over an entire tray of steaks and stormed out of the room.

"He didn't just turn it over," Page said. "He essentially drop-kicked it and made it explode. A whole tray. Jim Marshall and I were sitting there at that table, and it was like a bomb went off in the room. It scared the living daylights out of me."

During halftime of a 1973 playoff game against Washington, the Vikings trailed 7–3 and Eller was dismayed that they were playing so poorly. So he smashed a blackboard. That spurred Minnesota on to a 27–20 win.

While there is no official record of it, Eller claims to have had as many as 19 sacks in a season when teams played 14 games. Projected over a 16-game season, that would be roughly 22. The NFL record is 22½ by Michael Strahan of the New York Giants in 2001.

Despite all his accolades, it took some time for Eller to get into the Hall of Fame. He finished his career by playing with Seattle in 1979, and was first eligible in 1985. Finally, after 19 years he got the call.

"That was kind of the icing on the cake for my career, and I guess I deserved to be in there," Eller said. "I didn't start out with the idea, but as my career went on, I felt I certainly could compete against anybody I faced, and I felt I had a Hall of Fame career."

CHRIS DOLEMAN

Late in the 1986 season, right defensive end Mark Mullaney went down with an injury and the Vikings needed help. Where would they turn?

After some deliberation, defensive coordinator Floyd Peters suggested moving linebacker Chris Doleman to the spot even though he had never played it before. Doleman had been the

No. 4 pick in the 1985 draft out of Pittsburgh but hadn't been too impressive in his first two seasons.

The Vikings, though, were fighting to get into the playoffs. So it was decided to give Doleman a try at defensive end.

"I didn't like it," Doleman, who died in January 2020 from complications from brain cancer, said in 2019.

Doleman didn't like putting his hand on the ground after he had played upright as a linebacker. Nevertheless, Doleman agreed to give it a try. So what did he find out?

"I was a natural," he had said.

Doleman had a sack in three of the final four games and the Vikings won three. They just missed the playoffs with a 9–7 mark, but a valuable move had been made for the future.

The 6-foot-5, 289-pound Doleman ended up being a fixture at defensive end the rest of his career and was inducted into the Hall of Fame in 2012. He played for the Vikings from

Doleman moved from linebacker to defensive end in 1986 and his career took off.
ST. PAUL PIONEER PRESS

1985–1993 and in 1999. He also had stints with Atlanta from 1994–1995 and San Francisco from 1996–1998.

Doleman was diagnosed in January 2018 with glioblastoma, the same cancer that late Arizona Sen. John McCain had, and underwent surgery. In an interview with the *St. Paul Pioneer Press* in March 2018, Doleman said he "cried like a baby" when he heard the news.

"When a doctor tells you that you have brain cancer, it changes your whole world," he had said. "Those are the scariest words that you'll ever hear in your life."

With the support of many teammates, Doleman's spirits improved. He was able to attend several Vikings functions in the final two years of his life, including a ceremony in which his late coach, Dennis Green, was inducted in September 2018 into the Vikings Ring of Honor at U.S. Bank Stadium.

Doleman had been hoping to attend Super Bowl LIV in February 2020 in Miami to visit with some fellow members of the Hall of Fame. However, the trip was cancelled when his health took a turn for the worse and he died at age 58 five days before the game. He was honored before the game with a moment of silence.

Doleman had both of his first-team All-Pro selections and made six of his eight Pro Bowls with the Vikings. He ranks fifth in NFL history with 150½ sacks, including 96½ with Minnesota. He had all but a half sack playing defensive end.

"He whined about [moving to defensive end] but frankly it saved his career," said former Vikings tight end Steve Jordan. "I think he would have had a good career at linebacker but he wouldn't have had a great career. He wouldn't have been a Hall of Famer. I remember him bitching and moaning and finally they said to him, 'Hey, Dole, You'll make a lot more money if you're a D-lineman than an outside linebacker,' and that helped bridge the gap for him."

Doleman broke loose in 1987 by having 11 sacks, leading the league with six forced fumbles, and making his first Pro Bowl. By 1989, he was one of the most dominant defensive ends in the NFL.

Entering the 1989 regular-season finale against Cincinnati, Doleman had 17 sacks, five shy of the NFL record then held by Mark Gastineau. On *Monday Night Football*, Doleman had one of the top defensive showings in Vikings history, getting four sacks to finish with 21.

"I knew about the record," Doleman said in 2018. "[Defensive tackle] Keith Millard was my statistician out there, so he was telling me about it. I could have tied the record but I hit [quarterback] Boomer Esiason on the sideline and they took it away from me [with a penalty]. But 21 is still pretty good. That was a great game because I was playing against a great player."

That player was Bengals left tackle Anthony Munoz, considered by many the greatest offensive lineman in NFL history.

"He had an unbelievable skill set when it came to beating guys, no matter who they were," Millard said. "To get four sacks on Anthony Munoz when he was in his prime was unbelievable. He terrified offensive linemen, even the best ones."

The sacks continued to pile up for Doleman. He had 14½ in 1992, the other season in which he made first-team All-Pro.

After the 1993 season, with Doleman seeking a big raise, he was traded to Atlanta for first- and second-round picks. He did return to Minnesota for one final NFL season in 1999, and had an impressive eight sacks at the age of 38.

Jordan called Doleman a "freak athlete." Cornerback Carl Lee called him "essentially unblockable." Defensive tackle and fellow Hall of Famer John Randle said he "was the same as Bruce Smith," the NFL's all-time sack leader with 200.

"In my opinion, as a pure pass rusher, he was one of the top two or three ever to play in the NFL," Millard said. "He had incredible athleticism and speed, an incredible competitive spirit. He was going to do whatever he had to beat you."

Gary Zimmerman, who went on to make the Hall of Fame, can attest to how good Doleman was. Zimmerman, Minnesota's left tackle from 1986–1992, went against him regularly in practice.

"The reason I'm in the Hall of Fame is because of Doleman," Zimmerman said. "The game became the easy part after the two days of practice every Wednesday and Thursday against Doleman. The way it usually went is one of us would win on Wednesday and then the other would win on Thursday. If I won on Wednesday, he would come out Thursday ready to go. But it made me a better player."

There were some legendary battles in practice in the early 1990s when the Vikings had Doleman at right defensive end, Randle at right defensive tackle, Zimmerman at left tackle, and Randall McDaniel at left guard. That was four Hall of Famers battling on that side.

"Doleman was all business," McDaniel said. "He used to come to practice with a briefcase and everybody thought it was it was funny. It was like, 'What the heck are you doing bringing a briefcase into a football locker room?' But he had his playbook in there and he treated it like a business. So he was prepared."

JARED ALLEN

Jared Allen used to keep a running tally in his locker on where he stood on the NFL's all-time sack list. He needed a good eraser for continuous updates.

Allen had 136 sacks, including 85½ in his six Vikings seasons. When he retired after his 12th NFL season in 2015, he was tied for ninth in league history. He had dropped to 12th entering 2021.

In terms of production, the defensive end was the best sacker of quarterbacks the Vikings ever had. Playing from 2008–2013, he averaged 14.25 sacks per season, which worked out to .89 per game.

"To me, it was an art form," Allen said of getting to the quarterback. "It was technique, it was attention to detail, and then there was a willingness to get the job done."

Allen reached double figures in sacks in each of his Minnesota seasons. He had 22 in 2011, tied for second in NFL history.

With the Vikings, Allen earned three of his four first-team All-Pro selections and four of his five Pro Bowl berths.

"He just worked at his craft," said former Vikings defensive tackle Kevin Williams. "He had this move that was almost impossible to stop. He'd stick his arm out and then he'd let (the left tackle) grab him and then he'd pull his arm down."

Williams was a perennial All-Pro selection, and the Vikings also had Pro Bowl nose tackle Pat Williams when they acquired Allen from Kansas City in 2008. There was plenty of euphoria when it was announced another star would join the line.

Allen had played his first four seasons with the Chiefs, and in 2007 was named first-team All-Pro and to the Pro Bowl. But he had been plagued by off-the-field issues. Allen had been charged with three DUIs and served a two-game NFL suspension to start the 2007 season.

Because of those issues, the Chiefs had not signed Allen to a long-term contract extension and were shopping him. The Vikings, trading a first-round pick and two third-round selections, took a chance in acquiring Allen and then signed him to a six-year, $73.5 million deal, the richest at the time for a defensive player.

"I always tell people it was a maturity issue," Allen said. "You can't go running around having fun with no consequences. It leads you to make dumb decisions. For me, it was a matter of growing up and maturing and figuring out what I wanted out of my life."

Allen vowed not to get in trouble again and never did. As for showing up in Minnesota with the huge new contract, Allen said there "absolutely" was plenty of pressure.

"But I put more pressure on myself," he said. "I always put pressure on myself to be great throughout my career. My expectations were always higher than anybody else's expectations."

Allen getting 14½ sacks in both 2008 and 2009 quieted those who thought the Vikings had overpaid for him. And in 2009 the Vikings, with quarterback Brett Favre the big star on offense, went 12–4 and advanced to the NFC Championship Game at New Orleans. But the Vikings lost 31–28 in overtime, and Allen was devastated.

"It was heartbreaking," Allen said. "Everything up to that point had been magical that season. We had so many great moments but we didn't accomplish the ultimate goal."

Two years later, the Vikings slipped to 3–13, but Allen had the best individual season of his career. He challenged the record of 22½ sacks Michael Strahan of the New York Giants set in 2001.

Entering the finale against Chicago, Allen had an outside shot at the mark with 18½ sacks. The way he started out, though, he soon looked to have a good shot. Allen had 3½ sacks on Josh McCown by the 5:27 mark of the third quarter, and set his sights on the record.

"I had some opportunities but on one I slipped and there were two times that I hit McCown when he was outside the pocket just as he released the ball," Allen said. "It was a special year but unfortunately we were 3–11. I feel like if we had put a better record together I probably would have won Defensive Player of the Year."

Allen finished a half sack short of the record. He remains miffed about a sack of Aaron Rodgers that was rescinded after a November 14, 2011, Monday night game at Green Bay.

"I still joke with Aaron Rodgers that I should have gotten the record," Allen said. "I had two sacks of him [that night]. But on Wednesday, [the NFL] took one away from me, saying it was a team sack because he muffed it."

Two years later, Allen was gone from Minnesota. The Vikings had improved to 10–6 in 2012 and earned a wild-card playoff berth but fell back to 5–10–1 in 2013.

Leslie Frazier was fired as coach and replaced by Mike Zimmer. There were discussions about re-signing Allen, then 32, but he didn't feel the Vikings were close enough to get to the Super Bowl.

"I wanted to stay with the Vikings for the rest of my career but we didn't have a quarterback at the time," said Allen, who departed before the Vikings drafted eventual starter Teddy Bridgewater in May 2014. "So I wanted to go try to find a quarterback that might be able to get me to the Super Bowl. I obviously took a longer route than I expected."

Allen signed with Chicago, but the Bears went just 5–11 in 2014. Allen was traded midway through the 2015 season to Carolina, and the Panthers, with quarterback Cam Newton named NFL MVP, made it to Super Bowl 50. Alas, they lost 24–10 to Denver.

"The agony of defeat at the end was a lot like 2009," Allen said.

Allen retired after an injury-riddled season in which he had a career-low two sacks. Allen, always one to keep track of his sack totals, did note what 2015 did to his final numbers.

"I always wanted to average 12 sacks a year and in my first 11 years, I was just over that," said Allen, who averaged 12.2 during that period. "But then after that last year I ended up at (11.3)."

Will his numbers end up being good enough to land him in the Hall of Fame? He was a finalist in 2021, his first year of eligibility, but wasn't selected.

"The way I look at it, I'm not arrogant in saying I deserve to be in the Hall of Fame," Allen said. "I think my numbers match up well with everyone that ever played. I qualify for the Hall of Fame, absolutely."

AND THE WINNERS ARE . . .

Carl Eller is a lock. He played 15 years with the Vikings, and was a dominant defensive end. He terrorized quarterbacks on a regular basis and was one of 10 players to appear in all four of Minnesota's Super Bowls.

For the second spot, it's close. Marshall was the consummate leader and became the first defensive player to be active for 20 NFL seasons. Marshall, though, was named to just two Pro Bowls and has been regarded more for his longevity than for being dominant at his position. He has been a finalist just once for the Hall of Fame. So the nod for the second spot goes to Doleman, chosen for the Pro Bowl in six of his 10 Minnesota seasons and enshrined in Canton, Ohio.

Doleman played during a golden era for defensive ends, one that included Reggie White and Bruce Smith. Doleman at times was mentioned in the same sentence with them.

Allen could end up joining Eller and Doleman in Canton, but his Vikings career was much shorter. While Allen doesn't make the all-time team, he certainly goes down as one of the greatest Minnesota pass rushers ever.

DEFENSIVE ENDS WHO DID NOT MAKE THE CUT

The NFL made sacks an official statistic in 1982, and the initial leader was Doug Martin. He had 11½ sacks during a season shortened to nine games because of a player strike. That pace over a 16-game season would have resulted in about 20½ sacks. Martin played for the Vikings from 1980–1989, rolling up 50½ sacks. He had a career-high 13 in 1983.

Brian Robison was a steady Vikings performer from 2007–2017, which included six seasons as a starter. He had 60 sacks, including a career-high nine in 2013. An avid fisherman, Robison celebrated them with a sack dance in which he pretended to reel in a big fish. Robison was a team captain during his later years in Minnesota.

The Vikings didn't go hard after free agent Jared Allen after the 2013 season, deciding instead to re-sign free agent Everson Griffen to a five-year, $42.5 million contract. It was a bit risky since Griffen had started just one game in his first four seasons. But he had shown some flashes of brilliance, including getting eight sacks in 2012. Griffen took off as a starter. He had 57 sacks from 2014–2019, and made the Pro Bowl in four of those five seasons before leaving as a free agent and spending 2020 with Dallas and Detroit.

Danielle Hunter, taken in the third round of the 2015 draft, turned out to be a steal. Hunter, six months shy of his 21st birthday when drafted, had a strong rookie season with six sacks and then broke loose in 2016, getting 12½ despite not starting a single game. Hunter moved into the starting lineup in 2017. He had 14½ sacks in both the 2018 and 2019 seasons and each time made the Pro Bowl. In 2019, shortly after turning 25, he became the youngest NFL player ever with 50 sacks and finished the season with 54½. However, he missed the 2020 season due to a neck injury that required surgery.

13

DEFENSIVE TACKLES

THE CANDIDATES

Alan Page
Keith Millard
John Randle
Kevin Williams

The Vikings have had plenty of top defenders and seven times have led the NFL in total defense. But only two Minnesota players ever have been named NFL Defensive Player of the Year.

Both were defensive tackles. Alan Page won the award in 1971, the first year it was handed out. Then Keith Millard claimed it in 1989.

The Vikings have had a rich tradition of defensive tackles, one that has continued in recent years. When Linval Joseph was chosen for Pro Bowls in 2016 and 2017, he became the eighth different Minnesota defensive tackle to make the game multiple times.

Page and Millard are in that group. So are Gary Larsen, John Randle, Henry Thomas, Kevin Williams, and Pat Williams.

On five occasions, the Vikings have had both their defensive tackles in the same Pro Bowl. That was the case with Page and Larsen in 1969 and 1970 and with the "Williams Wall" in 2006, 2007, and 2008.

ALAN PAGE

Since 1961, the Associated Press has been handing out the official award for NFL Most Valuable Player. Only twice has the award gone to a defensive player.

The first to win it was Vikings defensive tackle Alan Page in 1971. The only other defender to claim it was New York Giants linebacker Lawrence Taylor in 1986.

"It was quite the honor to be in the league for five years and to be recognized at that level," said Page, also named NFL Defensive Player of the Year in 1971. "Up to that point, defensive players just weren't recognized for their overall contributions."

The honors have continued to pour in for Page, who was with the Vikings from 1967–1978 and is perhaps the greatest player to ever wear purple. In 1988, he was inducted into the Pro Football Hall of Fame. In 2019, he was named to the NFL's All-Time 100 Team on its 100th anniversary.

And that's just what he did in football. Page, who earned his law degree while still playing in 1978, went on to become an associate justice of the Minnesota Supreme Court. He and his wife Diane, who died in 2018, founded the Page Education Foundation, which has raised more than $15 million for college scholarships for students of color. And in 2018, Page was presented the Presidential Medal of Freedom, the nation's highest honor for a civilian, by President Donald Trump in a White House ceremony.

"Don't misunderstand me when I say this, all of my teammates I have great respect for, but I think the world of Alan Page," said former Vikings running back Chuck Foreman. "He is the only player that I played with that I truly admired. He has accomplished so much in his life."

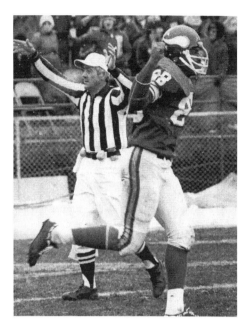

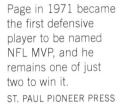

Page in 1971 became the first defensive player to be named NFL MVP, and he remains one of just two to win it.

ST. PAUL PIONEER PRESS

Page didn't waste any time asserting himself in the NFL. After being taken with the No. 15 pick by the Vikings in the 1967 draft out of Notre Dame, he quickly moved into the starting lineup. By 1968, he made his first of nine career Pro Bowls. By 1969, he was named first-team All-Pro the first of six times.

That was the season the Vikings made it to the Super Bowl for the first time. And their amazing defensive line, also featuring defensive tackle Gary Larsen and defensive ends Carl Eller and Jim Marshall, was dubbed the Purple People Eaters. The name came from a 1958 hit song by Sheb Wooley.

"I didn't much care for [the nickname], but I didn't have much choice in it," Page said. "There was that song of the 'One-eyed, one-horned, flying purple people eater,' and at least in my view of the world at that time it didn't exactly inspire much in terms of anything other than a humorous song. But it stuck with people."

One reason was because Page was so good. He threw fear into quarterbacks. Although sacks didn't become an official NFL statistic until 1982, Page is credited by the Vikings with having 108.

"That's when we really got the notoriety and of all of that with the Purple People Eaters," Eller, named to the Hall of Fame in 2004, said of Page's arrival. "That's when people really noticed us. Alan was very, very quick. He would line up next to the ball and read his keys really well. Alan was a great, great student of the game."

Page had an uncanny ability to know when the snap was coming.

"What made me effective was the ability to focus on the task at hand and be able to see and sense what was going on around me," Page said. "I was able to see and sense when the ball was going to be snapped, and given that the offensive player had to sit and wait for the ball to be snapped, it was, at least I thought, an advantage."

It certainly was. Page played a pivotal role in the Vikings having the best defense in the NFL. They were No. 1 in the league in scoring defense in each season from 1969–1971 and in the top three in seven of eight seasons between 1969–1976.

Super Bowls, though, did not go well for the Vikings. As for being on the wrong side in four of them, Page said, "Well, I never was a very good loser."

Most shocking was how Page's Vikings tenure ended. He had missed portions of training camp in 1975, 1976, and 1977 while attending the University of Minnesota Law School, but that didn't seemingly affect his play. He made the Pro Bowl in 1975 and 1976.

By 1978, Page had been getting into long-distance running. After playing at 245 pounds for much of his career, his weight had dropped to 222. That played a role in head coach

Bud Grant's decision to first reduce his playing time and then to cut him midway through the 1978 season.

"He just can't make the plays anymore," Grant said at the time. "Here is a man we had to take out in short-yardage situations, who was not strong enough to rush the passer."

Being cut, and hearing those comments from Grant, stung Page, a man of great pride.

"After 12 years they fired me over the phone," Page told *Sports Illustrated* in 1979. "That hurt a little bit."

The stubborn Page had a frosty relationship with Grant. Page was an active, outspoken officer for the NFL Players Association, and played a significant role in a strike by veteran players during the 1974 preseason. Page once was fined $50 by Grant for being late for a meeting, and then filed a grievance with the union regarding rules on time off for players.

Four decades after his release, Page doesn't have a lot to say about his unexpected release.

"It was disappointing, but that was the nature of the game back then, and it turned out well," Page said.

That's because Page was picked up by the Chicago Bears for the mere $100 waiver price. It turned out to be quite a bargain as Page started 58 straight games for the Bears before retiring after the 1981 season.

"He was still dominant, it's as simple as that," Foreman said of Page's Chicago years. "When I came into the locker room the day Alan Page was cut, in my opinion, I thought, 'None of us are protected in this game. No matter what you do, you're just a commodity.'"

Also stunned by the move was wide receiver Ahmad Rashad, who had joined the Vikings in 1976 after stints with St. Louis, Buffalo, and Seattle.

"When something like that happens, you realize it's a business," Rashad said. "Somebody gets fired and the beat goes on.

But we missed him. I missed him. I learned so much from him. Alan Page inspired me. When I came to the Vikings, we hit it off right away. I had problems on some of the other teams that I was with. If you were reading a book other than your playbook, it was considered odd. But I had conversations with Alan about everything, about life, about politics."

Page wasted no time moving on to the next phase of his life. He became a lawyer and in 1992 was elected to an open seat on the Minnesota Supreme Court, becoming the first African American on the court. Page served until he reached the mandatory retirement age of 70 in 2015.

Page and his wife had formed the Page Education Foundation in 1988. Page, who slowly mended fences with Grant and the Vikings after his retirement, praised the team for financial assistance provided over the years to the foundation.

"Life is a journey and all of those things are part of the journey," Page said about all he has accomplished. "At the end of the day, I tried to do as well as I could whatever I was doing. At the end of the day, I hope I did."

When Page looks at all of his lifetime honors, there is one that stands out. And, no, it's not winning NFL MVP or being inducted into the Hall of Fame.

In 2017, students at Alexander Ramsey Middle School in Minneapolis initiated a campaign to change the name to Justice Page Middle School after studying the career of Ramsey, a former Minnesota governor, and learning he had called in 1862 for Native Americans to be "exterminated" or driven out of the state.

"I've received a lot of honors and that one is singular because it was student driven and the students were not happy with the image created by its namesake at that time," Page said. "What they were seeking in their view was justice, so they in fact named the school Justice Page Middle School, not Alan

Page Middle School. It thrills me to no end to be a part of their vision of trying to endorse justice."

KEITH MILLARD

Entering a September 30, 1990, game at the Metrodome against Tampa Bay, Keith Millard was the best defensive tackle in the league. He was coming off a season in which he had been named NFL Defensive Player of the Year and had 18 sacks, a league record for a defensive tackle that would stand for 29 years.

Then it all came crashing down.

Millard thought he had beaten Buccaneers center Randy Grimes as he moved in to sack Vinny Testaverde. Suddenly, Millard saw Grimes come back around and he leaped over him. When Millard landed, his right foot got caught in a seam on the often-criticized Metrodome turf.

"There was this explosion of my knee," Millard said. "It was just, 'pop, pop, pop,' and the next thing I know I'm in major pain rolling around on the carpet. I knew something was pretty bad when it happened. It was a nightmare. Here I was at the top of my game, and at that point I thought my career was over."

It wasn't technically over, but Millard never would be the same player. He had torn his anterior cruciate and medial collateral ligaments, ensuring that he was out for the rest of the 1990 season.

Millard tried to come back in 1991, but the knee hadn't healed and he needed another surgery. He missed that season and never played for the Vikings again. He did get into 18 games with Seattle, Green Bay, and Philadelphia in 1992 and 1993 and had four sacks, but was a shell of his former self. Millard then retired at 31, and doesn't deny there was a period of depression.

"No doubt about it," he said. "I hate to use the word depressed, but that's probably what it was."

Millard eventually got over that after he had left the game. He came back a decade later and was a successful defensive line coach for four NFL teams.

To this day, though, the question remains: How would Keith Millard rate had he not hurt his knee?

"He definitely would have been a Hall of Famer," said Hall of Fame defensive tackle John Randle. "To me, Keith was along the same lines as [Raiders Hall of Fame defensive end] Howie Long, and I think Keith was faster."

If it hadn't been for Millard's injury, Randle might not have emerged the way he did in the NFL. Randle was an undrafted rookie free agent in 1990 who first played defensive end before eventually taking over Millard's former defensive tackle spot in 1992.

"Millard was the first version of John Randle," said Vikings Hall of Fame guard Randall McDaniel. "He was not as full go as Johnny at times, but he had that nastiness. He could take on double teams. Millard was John Randle before John Randle. If he hadn't have gotten hurt, he would have been with us [in the Hall of Fame]."

Millard joined the Vikings in 1985 after a season in the USFL with the Jacksonville Bulls. Millard had been selected out of Washington State with the No. 13 pick in the NFL 1984 draft but joined the USFL when offered a lucrative three-year, $1.5 million contract, including a $500,000 signing bonus.

"My dream was always to play in the NFL but I could not pass up the money the USFL offered me compared to what Minnesota did," Millard said.

After a year, the struggling USFL let Millard out of his contract to join the Vikings, who signed him to a deal similar to what had been offered before. But at least Millard got a second signing bonus of $300,000 included in his three-year, $825,000 deal.

Millard's impact was immediate. He had 11 sacks in 1985 and 10½ in 1986. By 1988, when Millard had eight sacks while facing constant double teams, he was named first-team All-Pro and to the Pro Bowl for the first time.

He duplicated those honors in his epic 1989 season. With defensive end Chris Doleman getting 21 sacks, one shy of the NFL record at the time, Millard had more room to operate. He rolled up 18 sacks, a record for a defensive tackle that stood until Aaron Donald of the Los Angeles Rams had 20½ in 2018.

"I just got in a zone," Millard said. "I couldn't do any wrong. Everything just clicked. I was healthy. I didn't think that anybody could stop me. I knew what I had to do to beat guys."

After the regular season, Millard was in the locker room preparing for Minnesota's playoff opener at San Francisco. He was told he had been named NFL Defensive Player of the Year.

"I didn't even know there was an award for NFL Defensive Player of the Year," Millard said. "A reporter came up to me and said, 'You're the NFL Defensive Player of the Year.' I was like, 'What?' Because, remember. Chris Doleman had 21 sacks that year. But Chris was proud of me and so were all my teammates."

Millard remains just one of two Minnesota players to win the award since it was first handed out in 1971. The only other one was defensive tackle Alan Page in 1971, the same year he was named NFL MVP.

"I'm proud of that but it really surprises me there's just two of us," Millard said. "Think of all the other great defensive players we've had in Minnesota, especially on the D-line, guys like John Randle, Kevin Williams, Chris Doleman."

In 75 Vikings games over six seasons, Millard had 53 sacks, which translates to .71 per game. That's a higher career figure than Randle, who averaged .63 sacks per game in his career and is tied for 10th in NFL history with 137½.

"His knee injury was extremely hard on him because I think he realized how great he was," said former Vikings cornerback Carl Lee. "His future looked bright at the pace he was going and then all of a sudden you have an injury and you just can't find your way back."

Millard eventually did come to terms with his career ending prematurely. He doesn't get caught up in speculation he could have ended up in the Hall of Fame had he not suffered a serious injury.

"Looking back now, I never dwell on it," he said. "I accomplished what I wanted to accomplish. I played in the NFL with the best of the best, and I did all right."

JOHN RANDLE

When John Randle sees highlights from his days with the Vikings, he often wonders if he's looking at the same person.

When Randle starred for the Vikings from 1990–2000, he disrupted opponents with his nonstop trash talking. He played with his face covered in black paint.

"I don't really like watching myself because I'm embarrassed," Randle said. "That person who I was when I played is the opposite of how I am off the field. So it's kind of unique. It's like you're a different person."

Randle's antics, though, certainly worked. With the Vikings, he was six times named first-team All-Pro and six times to the Pro Bowl. He added one Pro Bowl appearance while finishing his career with Seattle from 2001–2003.

The honors continued to come in after Randle retired. Randle, the leading sacker in NFL history among defensive tackles with 137½, was inducted into the Hall of Fame in 2010 and was named to the NFL 100 All-Time Team in 2019 in conjunction with the league's 100-year anniversary.

Randle went from being an undrafted free agent to being inducted in 2010 into the Pro Football Hall of Fame.
ST. PAUL PIONEER PRESS

Not bad for a guy who grew up dirt poor in a shack in Mumford, Texas (population 170), and entered the NFL as a 240-pound defensive end undrafted out of Division II Texas A&I (now known as Texas A&M–Kingsville).

"You couldn't write this stuff," Randle said. "Where are you going to start? You're an undersized free agent and you're going to a team that nobody really expects you to make, and then you're playing special teams [at the start]. I was a Division II guy that nobody believed in. I was given a chance, so I took full advantage of it. I didn't take a play off."

The stories about Randle's first training camp in 1990 remain legendary. He was inked to a $5,000 signing bonus, which Jeff Diamond, then Minnesota's assistant general manager and later the general manager, called "one of the greatest bargains of all-time."

His teammates initially knew nothing about Randle, with left tackle Gary Zimmerman saying, "He came out of nowhere." But they started to learn about him in a hurry.

"We were at practice one day when he was at D-end on the scout team, and I heard Gary Zimmerman and [right tackle] Tim Irwin complaining about this kid," said Randall McDaniel. "They told me to come out there and slow him down. I said, 'That's your problem.' Two years later, they moved him inside, and I saw what they were complaining about. He was going all out on every single play in practice. He was hands down the best lineman I ever played against."

As a rookie in 1990, Randle played mostly on special teams, and didn't start a single game. In 1991, he got eight starts at defensive end.

By 1992, the Vikings were looking for a long-term solution at defensive tackle. Former All-Pro Keith Millard had suffered a serious knee injury in 1990 and missed the entire 1991 season. He was gone when 1992 began.

"They really didn't know where to play me, but when Tony Dungy came in as defensive coordinator in 1992 along with Dennis Green [as head coach], Tony was like, 'Let's give him a shot at defensive tackle,'" said the 6-foot-1 Randle, who eventually would beef up to 290 pounds. "It was the right place for me because it kind of hid my size inside and it allowed me to just take advantage of my speed and my strength. It was the perfect position."

By 1993, when Randle began a streak of six straight All-Pro nods, he was the best defensive tackle in football. He had as many as 15½ sacks in 1997. One of those quarterbacks often in his line of sight was Green Bay's Brett Favre. Randle shot a Nike commercial in which he made a miniature Favre jersey and put it on a chicken, and then chased the chicken around before placing it on a grill.

Randle also became well known for his wild antics. He wore black paint on most of his face, including all around his eyes. He once was fined $7,500 for pretending to relieve himself on the field.

Randle screamed throughout the game, yelling things like, "Regulators, mount up," and "It's Johnny's time," and making up nicknames to get under the skin of foes. Highlights of Randle's boisterous behavior remain a staple on the NFL Network.

"If you didn't know John, you would say he was a little off in the head," said former Vikings receiver Jake Reed. "He had that wrestler mentality. Before games, he walked around with all that black stuff around his eyes, and he was like a wrestler, like he was about to go crazy."

Randle said the decision to paint his face and go through his antics stemmed from having been such an underdog when he entered the NFL.

"Me and some of my Vikings teammates who came in were branded as like misfits or undersized or too small or troublesome guys, so we just kind of started calling us, 'The Misfits,'" Randle said. "We said, 'We might as well put on some face paint.' It was like it was us against the world."

Randle said other "Misfits" during the 1990s were defensive linemen Roy Barker, Fernando Smith, Tony Williams, Stalin Colinet, and Duane Clemons. As for individual nicknames for Randle, he had at least two.

"When he first came in, we called him 'Little Muscle,'" said former Vikings tight end Steve Jordan. "His brother Erwin was an outside linebacker for the Tampa Bay Buccaneers, and he was 'Muscle.' So his little brother was 'Little Muscle.' John Randle just came in as a rookie and he had a motor that ran nonstop. I just remember having conversations about his background that he came from and he didn't ever want to be poor again."

Speaking of Randle's nonstop motor, that led to a nickname that stuck after he had developed into a star.

"His nickname became 'Motor,'" McDaniel said. "He never turned it off. He would be walking in the mall and he would be working on his pass-rush moves. People would walk up to him and would want to shake his hand and he would slap it away or do a spin because he was always thinking of a better move."

At least Randle didn't run over anybody at the mall. On the football field, it was far different. McDaniel remembers Randle bull rushing Oakland's 6–7, 317-pound star guard Kevin Gogan and "putting him on his butt" in a 1996 game.

Randle eventually slowed down a bit. Or at least that's what the Vikings thought. About to turn 33 in 2000, Randle became a free agent and signed with Seattle.

"Dennis Green at the time wanted me to take a pay cut and I just didn't feel like that was right for me to do," Randle said. "So I went to Seattle, where Mike Holmgren was and he was a coach who still believed in me. So going to the Pro Bowl [in 2001] and proving to them I could still do it was special to me."

There was plenty special about Randle's career. When he retired after the 2003 season, he was fourth in the NFL in sacks behind only Bruce Smith, Reggie White, and Kevin Greene. Not bad for an undrafted guy who got a $5,000 signing bonus.

KEVIN WILLIAMS

The Vikings went from laughing stocks in the first round of the 2003 draft to having the last laugh.

The Vikings had the No. 7 pick and were trying to make a trade when the clock ran out and they were pushed down to No. 8. Then they still couldn't make their pick in time and were shoved down to No. 9.

Finally, NFL commissioner Paul Tagliabue was able to announce the Vikings had selected defensive tackle Kevin Williams out of Oklahoma State at No. 9.

"We were having a cookout, and I didn't even know the Vikings had missed their pick a couple of times," said Williams, who was in his native Arkansas. "I kind of was paying attention, but I wasn't paying attention. I remember getting picked and my brother's girlfriend just screaming, 'Kevin got picked by Minnesota.' And I got a call from [head coach] Mike Tice. Usually, you get the call beforehand."

Williams said he was told he was the player Minnesota wanted all along. Whether that was truly accurate remains uncertain, but the Vikings sure ended up looking good.

Jacksonville, which had moved up to No. 7, took quarterback Byron Leftwich, who had some solid seasons but was hardly great. Carolina, which had moved up to No. 8, took tackle Jordan Gross, who did make three Pro Bowls. But Williams, who played for Minnesota from 2003–2013, ended up playing in six Pro Bowls and five times was named first-team All-Pro.

"He was like a dancing bear," said Jared Allen, a star defensive end who joined forces with Williams in 2008 to give the Vikings one of the NFL's best lines. "He was so smooth and so powerful and his technique was dang near flawless. And he was as smart as a whip."

During the first decade of the 21st century, Minnesota had "The Big Ticket" starring for the NBA Timberwolves in Kevin Garnett. Down the street, there was the 6-foot-5, 311-pound Williams.

"We called him 'Ticket,'" said former Vikings cornerback Antoine Winfield. "That was my guy. Kevin was an athlete. As big as he was, he could really run. He had great technique, great leverage."

Williams burst on the scene as a rookie, getting 10½ sacks. He was even better in 2004, piling up 11½ sacks while making All-Pro and being named to the Pro Bowl for the first time.

Williams's sack totals decreased (his seasonal best the rest of his career was 8½), but that didn't diminish his reputation. Teams had begun to pay more attention to Williams, and that helped open up things for other defensive linemen, including Allen, who played for the Vikings from 2008–2013.

"Teams find out about you," said Williams, who had 60 sacks with the Vikings and added three more while finishing his career with Seattle in 2014 and New Orleans in 2015. "I got my fair amount of double teams. But we had Jared and [nose tackle] Pat Williams and [defensive end] Brian Robison and they came in and reaped the benefits. It's easier to double team the inside guy than one of those guys on the edge."

From 2005–2010, Kevin Williams, who played three-technique defensive tackle, lined up next to Pat Williams, a three-time Pro Bowl selection. They were known as the "Williams Wall."

"We did things as far as shutting down people's run game completely," Kevin Williams said of the pair.

While Allen and Pat Williams were both big talkers, Kevin Williams didn't say much. He simply came in every day and got the job done.

"He was very quiet off the field, very humble, but on the field he was a problem, and no offensive lineman wanted to play against him," Winfield said.

Williams has been described as a hardworking guy who showed up with his lunch pail and gave an honest day's work.

"I wasn't the most flamboyant player," Williams said. "I wasn't out there talking a bunch of trash. I just did my job, and I kind of whistled while I worked. One of the veterans told me when I was a youngster that 'the best ability is availability,' so I always tried to grind every day."

Williams missed just five games in his 11 Minnesota seasons. Two came in 2008 when he and Pat Williams both were suspended for the first two games for taking a performance-enhancing substance both claimed they did not know was banned.

When Mike Zimmer replaced Leslie Frazier as Vikings coach in 2014 and Williams became a free agent, there was interest in bringing him back. But Williams said he wasn't ready for a possible reserve role.

"They wanted me to come back and kind of back up maybe Sharrif Floyd at the time, and nothing against Sharrif, but I kind of felt that I was still better than Sharrif," Williams said of Floyd, a first-round draft pick in 2013. "Good kid, but I just didn't think it was time to pass the torch to him if I was going to stay."

Williams signed with Seattle and almost won a Super Bowl ring. However, the Seahawks were doomed by New England cornerback Malcolm Butler's interception at the goal line in the waning seconds, and lost Super Bowl XLIX 28–24.

"It was tough and I was kind of bummed out, but the disappointment went away because I had the gratification at that point in my career to have a chance," Williams said.

Williams first became eligible for the Hall of Fame in 2021 but wasn't even named a semifinalist for induction. He believes, though, he did enough to one day get a bust in Canton, Ohio.

"I have a good resume," Williams said. "If you look at the D-tackles still out there throughout the years, I don't think too many did the things that I did. But I'll leave that up to the people that decide that. Would I love be in the Hall of Fame? Yes. I think I did enough."

He certainly did enough for the Vikings to bounce back from whiffing twice in the 2003 draft.

AND THE WINNERS ARE . . .

No debate here. When the league unveiled the NFL 100 All-Time Team in 2019, two of the seven defensive tackles selected were Alan Page and John Randle. The two were introduced in February 2020 at Super Bowl LIV.

Interestingly, neither finished his career with the Vikings. Page was cut in 1978 when Bud Grant believed his skills had diminished, and Randle was lowballed with a 2000 contract offer when Dennis Green believed he had slipped. Both, though, played three more full seasons with other teams and were effective.

For both, bygones have been bygones. They both live in the Twin Cities and regularly attend team functions.

DEFENSIVE TACKLES WHO DID NOT MAKE THE CUT

Gary Larsen was the other guy on the Purple People Eaters. He wasn't as heralded as Alan Page, Carl Eller, and Jim Marshall, but still made Pro Bowls after the 1969 and 1970 seasons. Larsen was a rookie with the Los Angeles Rams in 1964 before going to Minnesota, where he played from 1965–1974. After he retired, Doug Sutherland replaced him as the fourth member of the Purple People Eaters.

Aggressive Henry Thomas, whose nickname was "Hardware Hank," was underrated as a nose tackle. That can happen when you play alongside Keith Millard and then John Randle. But Thomas, who played for the Vikings from 1987–1994, did get into Pro Bowls after the 1991 and 1992 seasons. He was one of the top pass-rushing nose tackles ever. He had 56 sacks for the Vikings, including nine in a season twice. Thomas, who closed out his career with Detroit and New England from 1995–2000, had a career-high 10½ sacks with the Lions in 1995.

On the "Williams Wall," Kevin Williams, listed at 311 pounds, was the skinny one. The other member was nose tackle Pat Williams, who was listed at 317 pounds but acknowledged playing at 340. He played for the Vikings from 2005–2010, and made Pro Bowls after the 2006, 2007, and 2008 seasons. He played for Buffalo 1997–2004 and then flourished in Minnesota even though he didn't arrive until he was about to turn 33. He was a terrific run stopper.

Minnesota's latest decorated run stopper was Linval Joseph. He began his career with the New York Giants from 2010–2013, which included winning a Super Bowl after his second season. After Mike Zimmer took over as Minnesota's coach in 2014, Joseph was his first marquee free-agent signee. He became a fixture on the line, and made Pro Bowls after the 2016 and 2017 seasons before being released after the 2019 season in a salary-related move and signing with the Los Angeles Chargers. Despite his massive 6-foot-4, 329-pound frame, Joseph showed his athleticism when he scooped up a fumble against Philadelphia in 2018 and sprinted 64 yards down the sideline for a touchdown.

14

LINEBACKERS

THE CANDIDATES

Jeff Siemon
Matt Blair
Scott Studwell
Eric Kendricks
Anthony Barr

Vikings linebackers often have been overshadowed by the many great defensive linemen the team has had.

During the early days of the fabled Purple People Eaters defensive line, steady linebackers Wally Hilgenberg, Lonnie Warwick, and Roy Winston didn't get their full due. In the later years of the Purple People Eaters, at least Jeff Siemon and Matt Blair began to get more recognition. Siemon made four Pro Bowls and Blair six. They were teammates in the Pro Bowl in 1977.

Scott Studwell was selected to two Pro Bowls in the late 1980s but often was overshadowed by top-notch defensive linemen Chris Doleman and Keith Millard. Anthony Barr made four straight Pro Bowls from 2015–2018 but often had to take a backseat when it came to publicity to defensive ends Everson Griffen and Danielle Hunter.

The Vikings' linebackers haven't earned cool nicknames or piled up a bunch of sacks, but they still have had plenty of good ones over the years.

JEFF SIEMON
With his father being a doctor at the Mayo Clinic, Jeff Siemon was born in Rochester, Minnesota, 80 miles south of the Twin Cities. His family moved to California when he was two, so Siemon left with no childhood memories of Minnesota.

When Siemon was growing up, he thought about one day returning to the area where he was born. It ended up happening sooner than expected. After a standout career at Stanford, the linebacker was selected by the Vikings with the No. 10 pick in the 1972 NFL draft.

"When I learned the Vikings took me, I was quite surprised and also a little bit amused," Siemon said. "Minnesota was where my whole life began and I always had a secret interest in coming back and visiting my birthplace and, lo and behold, it would happen at age 22."

Some 50 years later, Siemon hasn't left Minnesota. After playing for the Vikings from 1972–1982, he remained in the Twin Cities while working for a Christian ministry.

Siemon joined the Vikings after having played on two Rose Bowl–winning teams at Stanford and winning the Butkus Award as a senior for being the nation's top linebacker. He wasted little time in establishing himself.

Lonnie Warwick, who had been Minnesota's starting middle linebacker since 1965, suffered a leg injury, and Siemon ended up starting eight games. Siemon looked so good that by the next season he was still in the lineup and Warwick, then 31, was playing for Atlanta.

"I was thrust into the middle linebacker role, and I had a pretty good year," Siemon said. "I think the Vikings had their eye on the future, and I guess I was the future at that position." The Vikings made the right decision. Siemon went on to play in four Pro Bowls and was equally adept against the run and pass. Siemon had 11 career interceptions, including a career-high three in 1973, and recovered 11 fumbles.

"Jeff Siemon never made a mistake," said former Vikings safety Paul Krause. "He was a very smart football player. He called the defenses for the line and the linebackers."

The deeply religious Siemon was mild mannered before he underwent a transformation on the field. He crunched his share of opponents.

"I was a little bit of a Jekyll and Hyde, although I will say that hopefully I played within the rules and regarded opposing players with respect," Siemon said. "But I did play with a measure of intensity. When the ball was snapped, I was able to do that. I played for a long time, and I was able to turn up the temperature when the situation called for it."

Indeed Siemon did.

"He was deeply religious, but I can tell you on Sundays I'm sure he said a lot of prayers before he brought a lot of heat to a lot of people," said former Vikings running back Chuck Foreman. "He came to play."

Siemon was on three of the four Minnesota teams that lost Super Bowls. He said that was frustrating but it shouldn't take away from what the Vikings did.

"It would be foolish to discount the success we had," he said. "You lost the last game and it tends to put a black mark on everything, but I refused to say that the whole season was a disaster. There was some dignity to being one of the two teams out there before the season ended."

Siemon was solid in the playoffs. In his first two postseason games in 1973, he returned a fumble 16 yards in a 27–20 win over Washington and then had an interception in a 27–10 win at Dallas in the NFC Championship Game.

Siemon was extremely durable. After missing the fifth game of his rookie season, he played in 152 straight games to conclude his career.

By 1980, just as Warwick had once gotten old, so did Siemon. At the age of 30, he lost his starting middle linebacker job that season to Scott Studwell. He returned as a starter in 1981 as a left inside linebacker, when the Vikings shifted from a 4–3 to a 3–4 scheme. But he was back on the bench in 1982, and then decided to retire.

"It was pretty clear that [Studwell] was the heir apparent," Siemon said. "I could see the end coming. My last year wasn't a stellar year for me and I didn't play as much as I was accustomed to, so the writing was on the wall and it was a pretty easy decision."

Studwell, who entered the NFL in 1977 and played sparingly early in his career, was appreciative of Siemon showing him the ropes.

"He was a fixture for a number of years with the Vikings," Studwell said. "He was probably somebody underrated as a pro but he really had a heck of a career."

While Siemon never had the satisfaction of winning a Super Bowl, he was able to see his daughter, Kelley Siemon [now Deyo], win a national championship in 2001 for the Notre Dame women's basketball team. She was a four-year starter and wore No. 50 just like her dad.

MATT BLAIR

Matt Blair was exciting to watch during the football season and in the offseason.

The 6-foot-5 Blair starred at linebacker for the Vikings from 1974–1985. He put his height to good use on defense and on special teams, where he was adept at blocking kicks. And during the offseason one still could buy at ticket to watch Blair play.

"We had a Vikings basketball team and he was the best player we ever had on it," said former cornerback Bobby Bryant. "He was slam-dunking back then like the guys in the NBA and he was doing it much better than most of those guys were."

Blair had played basketball at Colonel White High School in Dayton, Ohio, and at Northeastern Oklahoma A&M, a junior college. He didn't turn exclusively to football until he went to Iowa State.

Blair was taken in the second round of the draft by Minnesota. He didn't become a full-time starter until his third season, but after that emerged as the best linebacker in team history.

Blair was named to six Pro Bowls, and his 20 blocked kicks are third in NFL history.
ST. PAUL PIONEER PRESS

Blair, who died in 2020 at age 70, made six Pro Bowls, the most ever for a Vikings linebacker. He was the only Minnesota linebacker to be named first team All-Pro, getting the nod in 1980, until Eric Kendricks duplicated the feat in 2019.

"Matt was such a great athlete," said former Vikings cornerback Carl Lee. "He was slim and trim and tall and when he played outside linebacker he looked more like a basketball player than a football player. But he was so smart and he understood the dynamics of the game. He was one of those guys that was in the next wave after the Purple People Eaters."

Not long after Blair arrived, the Vikings' defense began to show age. Blair got into Super Bowls in two of his first three seasons, but Minnesota fell off after that. Longtime linebackers Roy Winston and Wally Hilgenberg were gone after the 1976 and 1979 seasons, respectively. But Blair was able to help provide some youth at the position.

"Matt was a great talent," Siemon said. "He could run like the wind. He had long arms."

Blair had 16 career interceptions and 20 fumble recoveries. He ranks second in team history with 1,404 tackles. Sacks didn't become an official statistic until 1982, and Blair had 4½ in 1983.

On special teams, Barr could change a game. He had 20 blocked kicks in his career, third in NFL history.

"He was strong and could get through the little cracks in the line," Bryant said. "And he was so tall, and in those days they would allow guys to jump over the linemen. He was really good at using his height."

As a rookie, Blair blocked a punt in Super Bowl IX by Pittsburgh's Bobby Walden. It was recovered in the end zone by Terry Brown for Minnesota's only points in a 16–6 loss.

"He blocked a ton of kicks," said former Vikings wide receiver Ahmad Rashad. "He was always where the action was."

Another sort of action also appealed to Blair. After joining the Vikings, he took up photography and made a point of capturing shots of teammates behind the scenes. During one training camp, Blair shot photos for the *St. Paul Pioneer Press*. He had a field day taking photos in London when the Vikings played a preseason game there in 1983.

When U.S. Bank Stadium opened in 2016, the Vikings set aside an area to show art work by some former Vikings greats. Put on display were ceramics by Carl Eller, drawings by Jim Marshall, and photographs by Blair.

"I was a rookie, and I was able to buy a camera," Blair said then about how it started. "I flew to Europe and I took pictures, and when I came back, people said, 'Man, those are good.' I said, 'Really?'"

A year after the stadium opened, Blair stopped giving interviews due to health issues, and soon after that he was placed in a memory care facility after having been diagnosed with dementia. Blair gave one of his last interviews in July 2017 to KMSP-TV in the Twin Cities. He said then that doctors had told him he had frontal lobe damage in his brain, likely from all the hits he took as a player.

"I got hit, and I got hit, but then again I hit so many people myself," Blair said in the interview.

Concussions weren't looked at when Blair played the same way they are now, but Blair did suffer a significant one in the fourth quarter of a 1976 playoff game against Washington on a hit on running back Calvin Hill that knocked the linebacker's helmet off. Blair was carried off the field and hospitalized during the week. But he returned to play the next week in Minnesota's 24–13 win over the Los Angeles Rams in the NFC Championship Game.

Years after he retired, Blair had two knees and two hips replaced, another consequence of his dozen years in the NFL. When he died, there was an outpouring of support.

"He embodied the best of what it means to be a Viking," said team president Mark Wilf.

Blair remains one of just two linebackers to have been inducted into the Vikings Ring of Honor. He was enshrined in 2012 following Scott Studwell, who had gotten the nod in 2009.

"The Ring of Honor, I think, is something that is very special," Blair said prior to being honored in 2012. "[Was getting in] on my mind? Oh yeah, it's on your mind and I knew that there [would] be a time, when there's a chance, and this is my chance. I'm honored to be a part of it."

Studwell, who played for the Vikings from 1977–1990, was thrilled to have Blair join him in the Ring of Honor. The two started alongside each other at linebacker from 1979 until Blair was forced to retire after the 1985 season due to knee issues.

"You could see his athleticism," Studwell said. "He could run, he was mobile, he was productive. He had all the physical tools to be a great player and he was a great player. It was just unfortunate he got the injury bug late in his career and he had some knee problems, but he had a great career. I was very fortunate to be able to play with him."

Scott Studwell

Scott Studwell had the easiest nickname anyone ever came up with. He was called "Stud."

Yes, it was a play on his last name, but that's exactly what Studwell was when playing for the Vikings from 1977–1990. He was aggressive and hardnosed and piled up tackles like nobody in team history ever has. He had an unofficial 1,928 in his career, an NFL record that stood for 20 years until it was broken by Ray Lewis.

"I inherited it, so I guess I can credit my parents for it," the middle linebacker said of his nickname. "But it's just one of those things; if the shoe fits."

It certainly did. Studwell's rugged play earned him Pro Bowl nods in 1987 and 1988, and he should have made more. It didn't help him that the Vikings failed to make the playoffs from 1983–1986. That four-season postseason drought is the longest in team history since Minnesota made the playoffs for the first time in 1968.

After Studwell retired as a player, he was a longtime Vikings scout and front-office official before he stepped down in 2019. In 2009, he was the first linebacker inducted into the Vikings Ring of Honor.

Studwell holds the Vikings record with 1,928 tackles and was the unofficial all-time NFL record holder when he retired after the 1990 season.
ST. PAUL PIONEER PRESS

"Studwell was our Dick Butkus," said Ahmad Rashad. "I mean, Studwell would knock you out."

Sometimes that was the case with his own teammates before a game even started. Rashad recalled making the mistake of once standing next to Studwell before the kickoff.

"I'm on the sideline and Studwell walks by me and he's all fired up and he's ready to play," Rashad said. "He yells, 'Let's go Ahmad,' and he swings his arm and hits me in the side of the head and cracks me in the head. He almost broke my neck. I felt the pain and the game hadn't even started. And then he pounds me on the shoulder pads, and I think he broke my shoulders. From that day on, I never got near him before a game. That's the hardest I ever got hit in my entire career."

Thankfully for the Vikings, the 6-foot-2, 228-pound Studwell saved most of his hard hits for opponents.

"Studwell was as good of a middle linebacker as I ever saw play," said Bobby Bryant. "He was big and muscular but he also was very smart. He just played hard. He loved the game. It never got too tough for him."

Some of Studwell's intensity was fueled by having had to work so hard just to make the team. After playing at Illinois a decade after Butkus did, Studwell wasn't taken until the ninth round of the 1977 NFL draft. Studwell signed a two-year contract worth $22,000 the first season and $24,000 the second. He got a $4,000 signing bonus.

"We didn't even know if he'd make the team," said Chuck Foreman.

Studwell, though, impressed Vikings coach Bud Grant with his tenacity.

"It was certainly very paramount that I do everything I could to make an impression and make either the Minnesota Vikings or some other team in the league," Studwell said. "The timing for me was actually ideal since Roy Winston had just retired the year before that draft and there was kind of an opening there."

Studwell didn't play much in his first three seasons. From 1977–1979, he started just four times.

By 1980, Studwell was too good to keep off the field. The Vikings benched Jeff Siemon, who had made four Pro Bowls in the 1970s, and inserted Studwell as the starting middle linebacker.

"Jeff Siemon was a phenomenal mentor," Studwell said. "I was able to sit back and learn and listen and bide my time until I got the opportunity to play. Jeff was a great guy. It was probably a hell of a lot more exciting for me [to become a starter] than it was disappointing for him. Any time I had a question, he would tell me the answer."

Siemon was glad to help in any way he could.

"He was a very dedicated middle linebacker," Siemon said. "He had the skills and the smarts, and it was good to see him mature over the years and have some really good success."

Studwell led the Vikings in tackles eight times, the most by any player in team history. His 230 tackles in 1981 remains a team record.

While tackles always have been an unofficial NFL statistic, Studwell retired as the NFL record holder. His mark finally was broken by Lewis, the Hall of Fame linebacker who had an unofficial 2,061 while playing for the Baltimore Ravens from 1996–2012.

"I don't think it's that widely recognized," Studwell said of his tackle statistics. "I mean, it's not going to put food on my table and it's not going to put me in the Hall of Fame, but it's something that I'm proud of. I think my instincts served me well. It was my job to make plays and make tackles."

After he retired, Studwell took a football job of another kind by joining Minnesota's front office. And just as Studwell had made the team as a late-round pick in 1977, he played a key role for years in the drafting of some late-round prospects who went on to have success with Minnesota.

"I've been very fortunate to have had my career kind of fall in place like it did," Studwell said. "To be able to play 14 years and then be able to stay at the same place, the timing was impeccable. My wife [Jenny] came up to me one day and asked me what I was going to do for the rest of my life and I told her I didn't want to coach, and I didn't want to put my family through the coaching syndrome of moving every four or five years. So it just kind of fell into my lap, and it just worked out."

It worked out for 42 years before Studwell finally retired from the Vikings after the 2019 draft.

Eric Kendricks

Quarterback Kirk Cousins meant no offense to running back Dalvin Cook, wide receiver Adam Thielen, or any of the other notable players on Minnesota's offense when he talked during the 2020 season about a special place that linebacker Eric Kendricks holds in his heart.

"He's one of my favorite players," Cousins said. "I say that when my boys, Cooper and Turner, are old enough, I'm going to get them Eric Kendricks jerseys because he's the player I want my kids to wear the jersey of. I just think he's as good of a linebacker as there is in the league."

Cousins is hardly alone in having a soft spot for Kendricks. While Vikings coach Mike Zimmer wouldn't name a favorite player he has, he pointed to his mentor, Hall of Fame coach Bill Parcells.

"I know Parcells told me he's his favorite player," Zimmer said.

What's there not to like about Kendricks, who in 2021 will enter his seventh season as Minnesota's middle linebacker? In

2019, he became just the second linebacker in team history to be named first-team All-Pro, following Matt Blair in 1980. He is a tackling machine, having led the Vikings five straight years in that category until he missed the final five games in 2020 with a calf injury and the streak was snapped. He is considered by many the leader of the defense.

And then there is Kendricks off the field. He has become a prominent NFL voice for social justice, gaining a national profile after the May 2020 killing of George Floyd while he was in the custody of Minneapolis police. He has been heavily involved in the community in the Twin Cities, and was the Vikings' 2020 nominee for the Walter Payton NFL Man of the Year Award.

"Eric has grown tremendously as a leader for this football team, and now he's become a leader in the community," said Vikings co-defensive coordinator and linebackers coach Adam Zimmer. "I'm extremely proud of him for standing up for what he believes in and trying to make a difference in the community."

Adam Zimmer, the son of the head coach, has been Kendricks's position coach since he was selected in the second round of the 2015 NFL draft, a year after linebacker Anthony Barr, taken in the first round by Minnesota, had been his UCLA teammate and roommate. Kendricks was inserted into the starting lineup in the fourth game of his rookie year and hasn't looked back.

Kendricks led the team in tackles as a rookie and by his third season had a career-high 136 as the Vikings in 2017 advanced to the NFC Championship Game. Still, Kendricks couldn't land a spot in the Pro Bowl.

The snubs continued through the 2018 season. While other Minnesota defensive players, such as Barr, defensive ends Everson Griffen and Danielle Hunter, nose tackle Linval Joseph, safety Harrison Smith, and cornerback Xavier Rhodes, were earning selections to the game, Kendricks continued to have to stay home.

"I just feel like that's kind of how it's been throughout my career," Kendricks said of the snubs. "As I came from high school to college and college to pro, I've just been a little under the radar. When the timing is right, the timing is right. I just do what I do and keep stacking the years and show how consistent I am and go from there. I'm trying to be the best."

Kendricks began to live up to that billing from a national perspective when he made All-Pro in 2019 and was selected to his first Pro Bowl. The reaction from those on the Vikings was along the lines of, why did take so long?

"I say that every year (that) it's the best he's ever played," said Adam Zimmer. "He's constantly improving. He just knows where things are going to be because of experience and the more he's played. He wants to be the best linebacker in the NFL. He wants to win a Super Bowl with us. He's going to keep striving to get better."

Kendricks also is never satisfied when it comes to work in the community. He has worked with All Square, an organization designed to help those who have been convicted of a crime get another opportunity in life; Every Meal, which works with children's hunger issues; and Project Success, an organization that inspires young people to plan for the future.

When Floyd, a Black man, was killed, sparking protests around the country, Kendricks sprung into action. He gained national notice when he called out the NFL in a tweet for not doing enough to "support the fight for justice and system reform," and saying that an initial statement by commissioner Roger Goodell "said nothing."

Kendricks later joined with a number of other prominent NFL Black players, including Barr, to put out a video calling on the league to do more. Goodell soon followed by releasing a video in which he said the NFL was "wrong for not listening to NFL players and earlier and encourage all to speak out and peacefully protest."

"I'm very proud for Eric taking that stance," said his brother, longtime NFL linebacker Mychal Kendricks. "I think that it takes a brave soul to do righteous acts."

For Kendricks, he simply considered it his obligation.

"I realized that my platform is larger than most and I actually do have an influence, so maybe I need to be speaking up a little more about these issues," Kendricks said of his decision to become more outspoken.

On the field, Kendricks's play has been speaking volumes. In 2019, the analytics site Pro Football Focus ranked him as the second-best linebacker in the NFL after New Orleans's Demario Davis. In 2020, before he missed the final five games with an injury that likely cost him at least a second straight Pro Bowl berth, he was ranked second behind Seattle's Bobby Wagner.

Then again, No. 2 isn't No. 1. So Kendricks will have more to strive for in 2021.

"I wanted to be the best linebacker there was in the NFL even when I was in college," he said.

ANTHONY BARR

In March 2019, it looked as if linebacker Anthony Barr would be gone from the Vikings. The New York Jets had offered the free agent a lucrative contact, and he told them he would accept it. Headlines blared that the Vikings had lost a team captain and player who had made four straight Pro Bowls.

Suddenly, though, Barr had a change of heart. Even if it meant taking less money, he began to think it might be worth sticking around Minnesota, which had for three straight years finished in the top four in the NFL in total defense, rather than join the rebuilding Jets.

Barr was Mike Zimmer's first draft pick as Vikings coach in 2014 and
has made four Pro Bowls.
ST. PAUL PIONEER PRESS

"I talked to my agent and within minutes, it was like, 'I think
we should maybe revisit,'" Barr said. "An epiphany happened."

After a night of negotiations, the Vikings raised their offer
to $67.5 million over five years. The average of $13.5 million
per year was still less than the Jets' offer of more than $15 mil-
lion annually, but it was good enough for Barr.

"Happiness, peace of mind, being somewhere you want, I
think that's all priceless," Barr said of his decision then to stay
in Minnesota. "It's all invaluable. You can't put a number on
being in the place you want to be."

Flash forward two years later and the Vikings had salary-
cap issues. Barr had missed the last 14 games of the 2020 season after undergoing shoulder surgery following his suffering
a right torn pectoral muscle in Week 2 at Indianapolis. The
Vikings requested he cut his base salary in 2021 from $12.9
million to $10 million or be released.

Barr contemplated whether he wanted to remain with the
only team he had played for the NFL. He agreed to the pay

cut under the stipulation that the last two years of his contract would be voided and he could become a free agent in 2022.

"I kind of didn't want to go out like that," Barr said about being injured in Week 2. "I didn't want my last game being the one in which I got hurt and then missing an entire year. I didn't want that to be my last memory as a Minnesota Viking, so that played a big factor in returning and taking the pay cut to be back with this organization."

So back for an eighth season was the athletic Barr, who was head coach Mike Zimmer's first draft pick for the Vikings, being taken No. 9 overall in 2014 out of UCLA. He had developed into a top linebacker despite having played the position just two years in college after entering UCLA as a running back.

The 6-foot-5, 255-pound Barr has made Zimmer proud during his Vikings tenure. He had a solid rookie season, which included being given the responsibility of wearing the headset and calling defensive signals. Then in 2015 he began his streak of four straight Pro Bowls. The streak ended in 2019 and his season was cut short in 2020, but Barr entered 2021 still believed to be in his prime at age 29.

"He's a good leader on the defense," Zimmer said. "He does his job. We ask him to do a lot of different things. We ask him to do a lot of communication type of things with the front guys and the back-end guys. He plays hard. He's a good tackler. He's physical. He's a good rusher."

Barr isn't the most vocal guy. But in 2018, Zimmer named him one of the team captains for the first time. After that, he developed into even more of a leader.

In 2019, Barr took a liking to then rookie cornerback Kris Boyd and took him under his wing. Boyd moved to a locker next to Barr's in order to get regular advice and the veteran gave him a nifty Louis Vuitton bag for Christmas.

"I see him as a big brother to me," Boyd said.

On the field, Adam Zimmer, the Vikings co-defensive coordinator and son of the head coach, considers the rangy Barr one of the NFL's top linebackers.

"He's up there," said Adam Zimmer, who has been Barr's position coach since he was drafted. "There's few linebackers that can do the physical things he does and lot of it gets unnoticed because they don't throw to his guy when he's covering him because he's covering him so good."

Barr also is an adept pass rusher. And putting pressure on the quarterback once led to the most controversial moment of his career.

In a Week 6 game at U.S. Bank Stadium in 2017, Barr hit Green Bay star quarterback Aaron Rodgers just after he had rolled to his right and threw an incompletion. Rodgers suffered a broken collarbone, missed nine of the final 10 games, and the Packers failed to make the playoffs. Meanwhile, the Vikings went 13–3 and advanced to the NFC Championship Game.

Barr was not penalized or fined for the hit, but that didn't stop Packers fans from calling it a cheap shot. Rodgers added fuel by claiming on the TBS show Conan that Barr gave him the "finger [and] suck-it sign" after the hit. Barr took to Twitter to say Barr didn't retaliate until after Rodgers was "calling me all kinds of names, F you this, F you that."

After the hit, Barr was bombarded with hate messages either in the mail or on the Internet. One apparent Packers fan mailed a card with a message saying it was hoped Barr would end up like Darryl Stingley, the New England receiver who was paralyzed by a hit in a 1978 preseason game and died in 2007.

"I don't feel it's going to stop," Barr told the *St. Paul Pioneer Press* in 2017 about the hate messages. "I don't really care. It doesn't really affect me or this football team in any way."

The controversy eventually died down. However, Rodgers did bring it up after the Packers won 23–10 at U.S. Bank Stadium in December 2019 to clinch the NFC North.

"It feels great to win [the division] in this stadium where a couple of years ago I was jeered leaving the field after breaking my collarbone," Rodgers said.

Barr's injury hampered Minnesota's chances in 2020 to challenge Green Bay in the NFC North. But he entered 2021 with plenty more years left to potentially climb the charts when it comes to linebackers with the most Pro Bowl appearances in team history. Barr came in tied with Jeff Siemon for second place, two behind Matt Blair, who made it six straight times from 1977–1982.

"I was very proud of him for coming back to us and turning down the money to stay and play here," Scott Studwell said about Barr not bolting to the Jets in 2019. "To me, that shows the type of character that we want and the kind of loyalty."

Barr showed even more loyalty to the Vikings when he agreed to a pay cut to return in 2021.

AND THE WINNERS ARE . . .

Matt Blair is hands down the best linebacker in Vikings history. He was tall and athletic and provided a much-needed youthful infusion when many of Minnesota's defensive players began to show age during the 1970s. He was one of the most effective special teams players in the NFL due to his ability to block kicks.

Anthony Barr, the highest-paid linebacker in Vikings history, also gets a spot. Barr plays the run and the pass equally well, and it was a boost for the future of Minnesota's defense when he reneged on an oral commitment to join the New York Jets in 2019 to stay with the Vikings.

At middle linebacker, just as Scott Studwell replaced Jeff Seimon as the starter in 1980, he beats him out here. Studwell was a tackling machine who commanded plenty of respect. For 14 years, from the days of the Purple People Eaters to a more high-tech era, he was a fixture.

LINEBACKERS WHO DID NOT MAKE THE CUT

Rip Hawkins was the first elite Vikings linebacker, playing for them from 1961–1965. In 1963, he became the first Minnesota linebacker named to a Pro Bowl. In 1964, Hawkins returned two interceptions for touchdowns, one a 56-yard jaunt and the other from 29 yards out. On his 12 career interceptions, he averaged an impressive 19.3 yards per return.

Wally Hilgenberg, Lonnie Warwick, and Roy Winston are forever linked. From 1968–1972, when the Vikings had a dominant defense, they were the three starting linebackers. Winston played the left side from 1962–1976, Hilgenberg the right side from 1968–1979, and Warwick manned the middle from 1965–1972. None ever made a Pro Bowl, but with the three playing together, the Vikings had a top-notch group.

With his tackling prowess, Chad Greenway conjured up some memories of Scott Studwell. Playing from 2006–2016, Greenway had 1,334 tackles, fourth in team history. From 2018–2013, Greenway led the Vikings each season in tackles. That six-year run tied Studwell for the longest such streak in Minnesota history. Greenway was named to Pro Bowls in 2010 and 2011 and was well regarded as a team leader. He was active in the community and four times was nominated for the NFL Walter Payton Man of the Year Award.

15

CORNERBACKS

THE CANDIDATES

Bobby Bryant
Carl Lee
Antoine Winfield

Vikings coach Mike Zimmer likes to say, "You can never have too many cornerbacks." No wonder his team between 2015–2020 drafted three players at that position in the first round, one in the second, and one in the third round.

It didn't used to be like that with the Vikings. After entering the NFL in 1961, they selected no cornerbacks in the first three rounds in any of their first seven drafts.

In 1967, the Vikings took Bobby Bryant, a skinny cornerback from South Carolina, in the seventh round. The pick seemed so insignificant that equipment manager Stubby Eason was the one to call Bryant and tell him he had been selected.

Well, that pick worked out pretty well. Bryant became a starter for 10 seasons until retiring after the 1980 campaign, and made two Pro Bowls. And plenty of good cornerbacks have followed.

BOBBY BRYANT

Being mostly an afterthought in the 1967 draft, Bobby Bryant still remembers his miniscule first-year salary of $12,000 with a signing bonus of $7,500. Nevertheless, he decided to splurge when his name was called in the seventh round.

"I bought a 1967 Pontiac Bonneville that was gold and white," he said. "It was a really nice car that was the first car I ever owned. I paid $3,500 for it, so I had $4,000 left after my bonus."

As it turned out, Bryant eventually was driving more snazzy cars during his impressive career. At one point, he had a Jaguar but found out that wasn't ideal in Minnesota due to the car's crummy heater.

Bryant is second in Vikings history with 51 interceptions.
ST. PAUL PIONEER PRESS

The 6-foot-1, 170-pound Bryant retired after the 1980 season with 51 interceptions, 32nd in NFL history. That ranks just two picks behind the team record of 53 set by safety and former teammate Paul Krause, who also played with Washington and holds the NFL mark with 81.

Bryant made Pro Bowls in 1974 and 1975. But former running back Chuck Foreman believes he should have been selected for more.

"Bobby Bryant I think has been shortchanged," said Foreman, a Vikings star from 1973–1979. "He was one of the best to play the game in my time. When you talk about the best guys at that position then, Bobby never gets mentioned. But he rarely got beat. He was scrappy and aggressive and smart, all of that."

It did take awhile, though, for Bryant to become a stalwart at right cornerback. He missed his entire rookie season because of a left knee injury and didn't start a single game in 1968 until moving into the starting lineup in 1969.

The knee injury wasn't as bad luck as one might think.

"I had been drafted by the Army, and I was supposed to be inducted into the Army in December 1967 but I had surgery to repair torn cartilage, so I flunked my physical," Bryant said. "I was not unhappy about that. It was near the end of the Vietnam War and a lot of soldiers were being sent over there, and I really had no desire to go into the Army in Vietnam."

The Army's loss became the Vikings' gain. Playing in just 10 games in his first season as a starter, Bryant had a career-high eight interceptions in 1969. That included three against Cleveland, which remains tied for the team record. The negative that year was Bryant suffering a knee injury late in the regular season that kept him out of the playoffs, including Super Bowl IV.

Bryant was a player who earned the respect of many. He was good in coverage and a rugged tackler.

"Bobby Bryant was a tough guy," said former Vikings receiver Ahmad Rashad. "He was like a cowboy. He would take no crap. In practice you'd catch a pass on him and he almost wanted to fight you."

Despite his scrawny build and having the nickname "Bones," Bryant would take on much bigger running backs and drop them.

"He would come up against these big backs, guys that really outweighed him, and he would bring them down," said former Vikings defensive end Carl Eller. "He was a great part of our defense. He would do whatever he was asked to do."

That included being adept on special teams. Bryant was used on punt returns for much of his career. His career average of 5.9 yards was modest, but he did what head coach Bud Grant told him to do and rarely made a mistake.

"Bud had a philosophy that he didn't want to return kicks a whole lot because he didn't want us to be called for clipping or holding or something," Bryant said. "And he wanted us to put pressure on the punter, so the shorter his kicks were in the long run we were going to get better field position."

The most memorable touchdown of Bryant's career came on special teams. In the first quarter of the 1976 NFC Championship Game against the Los Angeles Rams at Metropolitan Stadium, Bryant scooped up the ball after a blocked field goal by Nate Allen and ran 90 yards for a 7–0 lead.

The Vikings went on to win 24–13 before losing 32–14 to the Oakland Raiders two weeks later in Super Bowl XI. That was the last touchdown Bryant scored in an NFL regular-season or playoff game.

"I was getting near the end of my career, and I had told my wife, Stephanie, that the next touchdown I scored I was going to throw her a kiss from the end zone," Bryant said. "So I got down to the end zone at the far end and the wives were seated in the corner behind home plate [of the stadium also used by the Minnesota Twins]. She never saw the kiss I threw to her, but she did see it later on TV."

That was perhaps the greatest game of Bryant's career. He also had two interceptions.

Bryant was at his best in the playoffs. In 14 career games, he had six interceptions, including four in four NFC championship games. Bryant also had two picks in the 1973 NFC Championship Game at Dallas, returning one 63 yards for a touchdown. That locked up the game for the Vikings, giving them a 24–10 lead in the fourth quarter on their way to a 27–10 win.

After the 1980 season, Bryant retired just shy of his 37th birthday. He stepped away a year after Krause had retired.

"Bobby Bryant was a true athlete," Krause said. "He was one of the best I ever played with."

After he retired, Bryant turned his attention to another sport. For a while, he took over ownership of the Vikings' off-season basketball team, which included setting up games in small towns around Minnesota and neighboring states.

CARL LEE

When Carl Lee was at Aloha Stadium in Honolulu following the 1988 season, it suddenly hit him.

Lee, a seventh-round pick by the Vikings in 1983 who had been cut prior to his rookie season before being re-signed, was about to be introduced at the Pro Bowl. It was then he realized he had arrived as an NFL player.

"I was standing at the 50-yard line listening to the names that they were announcing of everybody in the Pro Bowl," Lee said. "They would call the names out and you would step up to the next yard line. I'm hearing all these names being called out like Reggie White, and this phenomenal group of names. And

I'm standing there at the far end, and it's like, 'Are they really going to call my name with this group of guys?'"

Lee's name indeed was heard. And it was announced again at the two Pro Bowls that followed. That was during a three-year stretch when Lee, also named first-team All-Pro after the 1988 season, was regarded as one of the best cornerbacks in the NFL.

Lee was a shutdown corner during a time when Deion Sanders, who entered the NFL in 1989, was popularizing the term. He was extremely fast, having run a 40-yard dash in 4.28 seconds during an eight-event ironman competition that Les Steckel had instituted during training camp in 1984, his only season as Vikings coach.

Lee was named to three Pro Bowls and was first-team All-Pro in 1988.
ST. PAUL PIONEER PRESS

"I remember all of the coaches looking at each other and saying, 'That must be wrong,'" tight end Steve Jordan, who ended up winning the overall ironman competition, remembers about Lee's 40. "They made him run it again. Then he runs it again, and it was the same, in the high 4.2's, low 4.3's on grass. It was like, 'You've got to be kidding me.'"

Once Lee got on the carpet at the Metrodome, it seemed as if he was even faster.

"Carl was an exceptional press corner, and he could run all day," said former Vikings linebacker Scott Studwell. "He had great play speed and he could run with anybody in the league. And he was physical enough that as a press corner he could reroute receivers, and he could play the run."

It took awhile, though, for the Vikings to realize what they had in Lee. After he was selected out of Marshall in the 1983 draft, he ended up being released by coach Bud Grant.

"I was cut for four days," he said. "I remember Bud telling me when I was cut, 'Your best football is ahead of you.' I couldn't understand then why they would cut me if my best football was ahead of me. I was going to Pittsburgh for a workout but they brought me back."

As a rookie, Lee played mostly on special teams. The next season, with Steckel as the coach, he was a starter but at free safety.

"I was playing safety and Joey Browner was playing corner-back," said Lee, referring to Browner, who later was an All-Pro safety. "When you look back on it, how would anybody think that made sense?"

That didn't last long. Grant returned as coach in 1985, and Lee was moved back to cornerback and Browner to safety. Those positions didn't change when Jerry Burns took over as coach in 1986.

One of Lee's top games came in a 1987 divisional playoff at San Francisco, an 11-point favorite. But the Vikings stunned the 49ers 36–24.

The legendary Jerry Rice was coming off an All-Pro season in which he caught a then NFL record 22 touchdown passes in just 12 games. But Rice that afternoon, with Lee on him plenty, caught just three balls for 28 yards.

"All week long, going into that game, all you heard was, 'How do you cover Jerry Rice?'" Lee said. "One of the things is we didn't disguise our coverages because [quarterback Joe] Montana would see it. We just lined up and we played. People would say, 'How will you stop Rice, how will you stop [running back] Roger Craig, how will you stop Joe Montana?' But we were good, too."

Najee Mustafaa returned a Montana interception 45 yards for a touchdown late in the second quarter to make the score 20–3 at halftime. Montana was benched and replaced in the second half by Steve Young. Lee added an interception of Young.

"People still talk about that game with me to this day," Lee said. "It's one of those big wins in Vikings history."

Lee had his share of top moments while playing for the Vikings from 1983–1993. He had 29 of his 31 career interceptions with them. In 1988, he had eight interceptions, second in the NFL, and ran back two for touchdowns.

"Carl Lee was a speedy guy and he was a very intelligent player," said Hall of Fame guard Randall McDaniel. "He seemed to know what was going to happen before it was to happen. He was in the right position."

Lee ended up in the wrong spot, though, at a 1993 Christmas party. That led to Lee, then about to turn 33, being surprisingly released.

"That was the first year they were starting to make pay cuts," Lee said. "To make a long story short, we were at a Christmas party and [team president] Roger Headrick asked me my thoughts about taking a pay cut. I was going into Year 12, and I thought that I could speak my mind comfortably and I said that I already put in the work to earn this contract and it would be hard for me to take a pay cut. Unbeknownst to me, I didn't know that would come back to haunt me."

Lee wasn't done, though, with his NFL career. He played a final season with New Orleans in 1994, and had two interceptions at Denver in the last game of his NFL career.

ANTOINE WINFIELD

Cornerbacks are often regarded as being ultraconfident. Antoine Winfield was no exception.

Winfield signed as a free agent with the Vikings in 2004 after five years with Buffalo. He played with the Vikings for nine seasons, and showed plenty of pizzazz.

The feisty 5-foot-9, 180-pound Winfield was adept in coverage. But he is not shy to discuss the skill he believed really set him apart.

"I was the best tackler period in the league," he said. "No one could tackle like me in the open field. I put my numbers up against Ray Lewis, anybody."

While tackle figures always have been unofficial, Lewis became the league's career leader with 2,061 while playing for Baltimore from 1996–2012. He broke the mark held by linebacker Scott Studwell, who had 1,928 tackles with the Vikings from 1977–1990.

Winfield had an unofficial 1,057 tackles in his 14-year NFL career, which ran through 2012. He said he was "absolutely" the best tackler in Vikings history and that includes Studwell.

"I've watched film on him and seen the stats," Winfield said. "I know he was a great player but he's in the box, he's not in that open space like a corner."

Told Winfield said he was the better tackler, Studwell was diplomatic.

"Well, I think I had more, so I'll lean my way," Studwell said. "But if you're tackling in the box as opposed to tackling in space, then I would certainly give him the nod, but I'll let the numbers stand for themselves."

Studwell, who was in the front office when Winfield played for Minnesota, called him "pound for pound" the better tackler. Plenty of his teammates agree Winfield was a tackling machine.

"He was undersized but you would never have known it as hard as he played," said defensive tackle Kevin Williams. "I loved it when he was playing on my side because the running back wouldn't want to run around the edge."

A year after Williams arrived in Minnesota as a rookie, Winfield joined the Vikings as a free agent in 2004. But he almost ended up with the New York Jets.

After playing in the AFC East for five seasons with Buffalo, Winfield thought he might remain in the division with the Jets. They got his first visit in free agency.

"We had a verbal agreement," Winfield said. "I didn't sign, but we were supposed to go to dinner that night, but then my agent got a phone call from [Vikings coach] Mike Tice. And I knew the defensive coordinator, Ted Cottrell. He had been at Buffalo. They had a better offer, and I knew the defensive scheme he was going to run. So off to Minnesota I went."

The Jets offered a five-year, $24 million contract before Winfield turned it down to sign a six-year, $36 million deal with Minnesota.

"The Jets were upset," Winfield said. "They thought we had a deal done, and they announced it. I was in my room getting dressed for dinner and it came across my screen I had signed with Jets, and I said, 'No, that didn't happen.' And right then my agent called and we got the Vikings on the phone, and made our way downstairs and out."

It turned out to be a good move. Winfield fit well in Cottrell's scheme and became an immediate force.

Still, it took a while for Winfield to make his first Pro Bowl. That happened in 2008 when he was 31 and in his 10th season.

Being on teams that weren't winning much didn't help Winfield's cause. In Winfield's first four Vikings seasons, they had just one playoff appearance and just one winning record.

When he did finally make his first Pro Bowl and had his three-year run, Winfield called it "the highlight of my career." He ended up with 27 interceptions in his 14-year career, 21 with Minnesota.

Winfield had a knack for making big plays. With Minnesota, he scored five touchdowns, two on interception returns, two on fumble recoveries, and one on a blocked field goal. On *Monday Night Football* in 2008, Winfield returned the blocked field goal 59 yards at New Orleans.

That was the first season star defensive end Jared Allen had joined the Vikings in a trade from Kansas City. The Chiefs had played Minnesota in 2007, but Allen didn't really learn about Winfield until he became his teammate.

"I didn't respect his game at such a high level until I got to Minnesota and understood what he was doing, and it was special," Allen said. "That dude was insane. I don't think he gets enough credit for what he did in the run game. He was one of the hardest-hitting corners and one of the most intelligent corners I had had ever seen. He was a lockdown corner."

With Winfield, Allen, and Williams being Pro Bowl selections on defense, the Vikings in 2009 went 12–4 and made the NFC Championship Game. An indication of how much respect Winfield had earned came when he made the Pro Bowl despite missing six games due to injury.

But it didn't end well for Winfield in Minnesota. He was asked to take a pay cut after the 2012 season and declined. He signed with Seattle but was cut before the season.

The Vikings offered to re-sign Winfield early in the 2013 season when they had injuries at cornerback. But he declined and retired.

"I didn't consider it at all," he said. "Once they broke up with me, I couldn't see myself going out and fighting for a team that didn't have interest in me a couple of months ago."

At least Winfield, who lives in the Houston area, eventually had reason to return to Minnesota on a regular basis. His son, Antoine Winfield Jr., was an All-American safety at the University of Minnesota before he was taken in the second round of the 2020 draft by Tampa Bay and became an immediate starter as a rookie. He then won a Super Bowl with the Buccaneers with his proud father in attendance.

AND THE WINNERS ARE . . .

It's a close race between all three. Bobby Bryant was a key and versatile performer during the greatest seasons in Vikings history, so that helps him get the nod at one spot.

For the other spot, Carl Lee wins out over Antoine Winfield. Lee's notable 1987 playoff game against Jerry Rice and his 1988 All-Pro selection help his cause. Also, he played 11 Minnesota seasons, two more than Winfield.

CORNERBACKS WHO DID NOT MAKE THE CUT

Ed Sharockman, who died in 2017, was the first cornerback to enjoy long-term success with the Vikings. He arrived as a fifth-round pick in their first season of 1961 and played 12 years for them. He remains third in Vikings history with 40 interceptions.

Nate Wright was a steady Minnesota performer from 1971–1980. Unfortunately for Wright, he is best known for being the guy Dallas wide receiver Drew Pearson allegedly pushed off on before Pearson caught a 50-yard Hail Mary pass from Roger Staubach to win a 1975 playoff game.

Audray McMillian followed Carl Lee in 1992 as the second Vikings cornerback named All-Pro, a season in which he tied for the NFL lead with eight interceptions. But McMillian, who played with the Vikings from 1989–1993, was out of the NFL after the next season.

Xavier Rhodes was selected in the first round of the 2013 draft by the Vikings and initially made Pro Bowls in 2016 and 2017. He was named first-team All-Pro in 2017, and looked well on his way to being one of the top cornerbacks in the NFL. Rhodes slipped significantly in 2018, some of it due to injuries. In 2019, he was healthy but ranked just No. 108 out of 114 cornerbacks by Pro Football Focus. Surprisingly, Rhodes, who had been an alternate, was named to his third career Pro Bowl. But that didn't mean much to the Vikings, who released him after that season, and he signed with Indianapolis.

16

SAFETIES

THE CANDIDATES

Paul Krause
Joey Browner
Harrison Smith

When Vikings safety Brian Russell had a chance in 2003 to tie safety Paul Krause's team record of having an interception in six straight games, Krause was invited to the game at the Metrodome. In a protest move, he declined.

Krause, the NFL career record holder for interceptions, long has believed his No. 22 should be retired. That has fallen on deaf ears with the Vikings.

Krause, who had 53 of his 81 interceptions while playing for Minnesota from 1968–1979, returned to attending Vikings games after Russell tied his record before failing to break it. But in the back of his mind, Krause, who was inducted into the Pro Football Hall of Fame in 1998, still believes his number should be hanging from the rafters.

"I just feel like I've broken an NFL record and it's going to be tough for somebody to break, and they treat me just like I'm another guy," Krause said.

At least there is one thing about No. 22 that has made Krause feel better in recent years. After eight different players wore the number following Krause's retirement, it has been donned since 2012 by Harrison Smith.

Smith has become one of the NFL's best safeties, and has developed a relationship with Krause. In 2016, when a company formed a partnership with the Vikings and unveiled a plan to feature Smith and five other Vikings players on six different drinking cups to be used at U.S. Bank Stadium, Smith had a request.

While Adrian Peterson, Teddy Bridgewater, Chad Greenway, Kyle Rudolph, and Linval Joseph were depicted on cups, Smith insisted Krause's picture also be on his. On the cup, a Smith quote read, "It's an honor to share #22."

"Whenever I see him, I try to tell him that I try to do the number proud," Smith said.

Krause certainly appreciates it, saying, "There's kind of a bond" between the two and that he's "still got a couple of those cups." But that doesn't mean he still doesn't believe his number should retired.

"I own the all-time interception record, and I think it should be retired, but that's not Smith's fault," Krause said. "He's a very, very good safety."

PAUL KRAUSE

Baseball has Cy Young's 511 career wins. Basketball has Wilt Chamberlain's 50.4 seasonal scoring average. Football has Paul Krause's 81 career interceptions. All are records that look to be unbreakable.

Krause played in the NFL from 1964–1979, including 1968–1979 with the Vikings. Since he retired more than 40 years ago, nobody has come closer than 10 interceptions from the record.

Among players to have entered the league this century, the closest to have come to the mark has been Hall of Fame safety Ed Reed, who had 64 from 2002–2013.

"I look at Paul Krause's numbers and I'm just thinking that they were silly," said Brian Russell, a Vikings safety from 2002–2004. "Nobody has done that since and I'm guessing nobody ever will do it."

That's because it has become a different game. Quarterbacks throw the ball more now but they don't go downfield nearly as much, instead opting for shorter, less risky passes. And

Krause is the NFL's all-time leader with 81 interceptions, including having 53 with the Vikings.
ST. PAUL PIONEER PRESS

rule changes prevent defensive backs from being as physical as they once were with receivers.

In 2019, Vikings safety Anthony Harris tied for the NFL lead with a modest six interceptions. Krause actually led the league just once in interceptions, but he had twice that number, getting 12 as a rookie with Washington in 1994. Krause's high with Minnesota was a team-record 10 interceptions in 1975, which led the NFC but was one behind Pittsburgh's Mel Blount for the NFL lead.

"You always hear records are made to be broken but I've had that [career] record for more than 40 years," Krause said. "It's something I'm very proud of. I don't want it to be broken. It's something I've done and nobody else has done it."

During his illustrious career, Krause made eight Pro Bowls, six with Minnesota. He was inducted into the Hall of Fame in 1998.

Had it not been for a college injury, though, perhaps Krause might instead have ended up playing Major League Baseball. He was a baseball star at Iowa, and hit .386 as a center fielder. Krause also played football for the Hawkeyes, and he tore up his shoulder his junior year.

"I had a tough time throwing the baseball, so that really ended my baseball career," Krause said.

So Krause focused on becoming a center fielder of another kind. In football, his job often was to play deep to intercept or break up downfield passes.

After being selected in the second round of the 1964 NFL draft, Krause did that quite well for the Redskins. In addition to leading the league in interceptions as a rookie, he earned two of his three career first-team All-Pro selections with them in 1964 and 1965.

Nevertheless, Krause said the Redskins weren't overjoyed with his play.

"I had 28 interceptions in four years there, which isn't bad, but the defensive backfield coach just didn't like how I played, and I decided I was not going to go back there," Krause said. "I just said that I'm not happy there and they should trade me."

Two connections led to Krause being dealt to the Vikings for linebacker Marlin McKeever and a seventh-round draft pick. His former college coach, Jerry Burns, was Minnesota's offensive coordinator. And Jimmy Carr, who had been a linebacker in Krause's first two Washington seasons, was defensive backs coach.

As it turned out, the Vikings got a steal.

"Krause roamed back there in that zone and of course got the record for interceptions," said then Vikings coach Bud Grant. "We were one of the first teams to use almost exclusively a zone defense because we had four guys who could rush and we did not have to blitz."

Those four guys were the legendary Purple People Eaters line of Alan Page, Carl Eller, Jim Marshall, and Gary Larsen, with Doug Sutherland later replacing Larsen. They pressured the quarterback, and Krause often would take advantage of the mistakes created.

"Bud wanted him to play center field and to help on deep passes down the middle and deep on the outside, too, but he could read the quarterback, and he got all those interceptions," said former Vikings cornerback Bobby Bryant. "He was a great ball hawk, the best in the history of the league."

Krause said his baseball ability came into play in football. Think of Willie Mays running down Vic Wertz's long drive in the 1954 World Series, and then translate that to football.

"I remember my high school coaches and even my college coaches tried to hit the ball over my head with fungo bats with me being way out in the field and they couldn't do it," Krause said. "I could run down all of that. I could figure out real quick the flight of the ball whether it was a football or a baseball and how far it was going to go and what angles I had to take to get to it."

Krause was extremely durable, playing in all 172 games during his 12 years with the Vikings. He broke Emlen Tunnell's interception record of 79 when he snared his 80th on December 2, 1979, at the Los Angeles Rams, his first of two that day in the third from last game of his career.

The perception was Krause wasn't the most physical player, but Bryant said he was underrated as a tackler. Perhaps because of that perception, Krause wasn't inducted into the Hall of Fame until 13 years after he was first eligible.

"It was very frustrating," Krause said. "I waited a long time to get in the Hall of Fame but then I got in and everything is good."

As for another frustration in Krause's career, it can't be fixed. The Vikings lost all four Super Bowls they played in from 1969–1976.

Some say the Vikings had their best team in 1975, when they went 12–2. But the Vikings were stunned 17–14 in a divisional playoff at Metropolitan Stadium on Roger Staubach's 50-yard Hail Mary touchdown pass to Drew Pearson in the waning seconds. It long has been contended in Minnesota that Pearson should have been called for offensive interference on cornerback Nate Wright at the Vikings 5 before Krause arrived at the play a split second late and Pearson scored.

"Well, I could have run faster if I could but that was a situation that he pushed off on Nate Wright," Krause said. "We should have won the game."

Although it ended on a sour note, that 1975 season was the best individual one Krause had with the Vikings. It was the only time he was named first-team All-Pro for Minnesota and he led the NFL with 201 yards on interception returns.

Krause had 10 interceptions that season. When Miami cornerback Xavien Howard had 10 in 2020, he became the first player to have that many in 13 years. So you better believe it will be difficult for someone to break Krause's career mark.

JOEY BROWNER

Joey Browner played mostly in the 1980s, but he would have been more comfortable in the 1950s.

Browner was perhaps the most physical defensive back in Vikings history. He was a throwback who would have thrived in the days when players took vicious shots with little concern of a penalty being called.

When Browner entered the NFL in 1983, the horse-collar tackle, one of Browner's specialties, was at least still allowed. But the strong safety's presence played a role in it eventually being outlawed.

In a 1987 Minnesota game against Denver on *Monday Night Football*, Browner chased down Broncos running back Gerald Willhite after a 29-yard run. He grabbed him from behind with a horse-collar tackle, and Willhite hit the hard Metrodome turf in a heap. He was carted off the field in agony, and was out for the season with a multiple fracture in his right leg.

That played a key role in the horse-collar tackle being banned. Not that Browner didn't stop doing it.

"Now, there's a rule for everything," Browner complained in 2013 when it was announced he would be inducted that year into the Vikings Ring of Honor. "The horse-collar was my signature tackle. I'd get fined every time I'd do it, but I'd still do it."

Browner played for the Vikings from 1983–1991 before finishing up with one season for Tampa Bay. He was named three times first-team All-Pro and six times to the Pro Bowl, with all of those honors coming for Minnesota.

Browner was named to six Pro Bowls and holds the Pro Bowl record with three fumble returns for touchdowns.
ST. PAUL PIONEER PRESS

"There was no tougher guy in our locker room than him and no one wanted to find out if they were tougher than him," said Vikings Hall of Fame guard Randall McDaniel. "He was into martial arts and all that stuff."

Browner had earned a black belt in Kenpo Karate. He used the tactics he learned on the football field.

"We would call him 'The Claw,'" said former Vikings tight end Steve Jordan. "He would put that claw on the back of your shoulder pad and it was game over. He was going to drop you."

Former Vikings cornerback Carl Lee said Browner wasn't a dirty player and never meant to hurt anybody. But Lee said Browner often was in sort of a trance when he played.

"He got a personal foul once in a game at Tampa Bay in which he literally picked the receiver up and dropped him," Lee said. "We're sitting on the bench after that and I'm thinking,

'I'm going to ask him why he did it.' So I looked at him and said, 'Joe B., why did you pick him up and throw him down like that?' He said, 'I didn't.' I'm like, 'Okay, he didn't even know that he did that.'"

The 6-foot-2, 221-pound Browner was extremely strong, but sometimes Lee said he didn't even know his own strength.

Browner could do more than just hit. He was adept in coverage. He had 37 career interceptions, all with Minnesota. In a dominant performance in a 28–17 playoff win over the Los Angeles Rams in 1988, Browner had two interceptions, returning them for 40 yards, and a sack.

Browner also was valuable on special teams. His first Pro Bowl selection in 1985 came for special teams and was followed by five straight selections at safety.

Browner was selected with the No. 19 pick in the 1983 draft after starring at USC. The Warren, Ohio, native and son of a steelworker came from one of most notable families of football.

The Browner family has produced six NFL players. Browner's brothers, defensive end Ross Browner, defensive back Jim Browner, and defensive end Keith Browner all played. So did Ross's son, tackle Max Starks, and Keith's son, defensive end Keith Browner Jr.

Family members always have been close. Once when Browner was asked to name the greatest thrills in his NFL career, he pointed to two games in 1986. One was against Cincinnati, which had his brother Ross, and the other against Tampa Bay, which featured brother Keith.

"My mother got a chance to see me play against my brothers in the same season," Browner said.

Browner's mother, Julie Geraldine Browner, died in 1990. His father, Jimmy Browner Sr., had died in 1976 of lung cancer.

After Browner retired from the NFL, he settled in the Twin Cities. Browner, who described himself as three-fourths indigenous, with Polynesian and Cherokee on his mother's side and Seminole and Blackfeet on his father's, became involved in Native American causes. He protested at least twice outside Vikings games in Minnesota against Washington, calling for the Redskins to change their name. The team finally did drop it in 2020.

Browner, named to the 1980s NFL All-Decade second team, has said he believes he is worthy of induction into the Pro Football Hall of Fame. Many of his teammates have agreed.

"I don't know why Joe B. is not in the Hall of Fame," Jordan said. "He was a big guy as a DB. He had long legs and he was deceptively fast and could cover so much ground. He was a phenomenal athlete and he was a great leader on the team."

Browner had 18 forced fumbles and 16 fumble recoveries in his career. He holds the Pro Bowl record with three fumble returns for touchdowns.

Browner had 987 career tackles, the second most by a Vikings defensive back, and he twice led the team in tackles. And, yes, some were of the horse-collar variety.

"I've had some people kid that they should have called it the Browner Rule," he told *Viking Update* in 2013. "There were some other guys who did [the horse-collar tackle] often, but I got associated with it and, when it was banned, some people blamed me. . . . I guess I just did it too well."

HARRISON SMITH

Harrison Smith wasn't always tough, and he doesn't deny it.

In his hometown of Knoxville, Tennessee, when Smith was in the third grade in 1997, he was a running back for the Bearden Bulldogs. It didn't always go well.

"I would put my hands out and always get them stepped on, so I was kind of always like crying," Smith said.

Smith eventually realized he needed to toughen up, and then opponents were crying. By the time he was in the eighth grade, his youth coach was former Vikings tackle Tim Irwin, and Smith got his first nickname.

"They called him 'Bonecrusher,'" Irwin said. "He was like a heat-seeking missile."

The hits have continued for Smith for going on two decades. And for the much of the past one, he's been churning them out as a safety for Irwin's old team. Smith in 2021 was in line to enter his 10th Minnesota season.

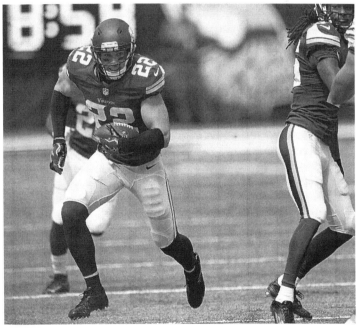

Smith has been named to five Pro Bowls and holds the Vikings career record with four interception returns for touchdowns.
ST. PAUL PIONEER PRESS

"Bonecrusher" has faded away, but Smith still has a nickname. He is known on the Vikings as "Harry the Hit Man."

"That's pretty good," Smith said. "It sounds good with the alliteration."

Cornerback Captain Munnerlyn tried calling him "Dirty Harry" when he was Smith's teammate from 2014–2016, but it never really caught on.

"That one's all right, too," Smith said. "A little Clint Eastwood action but I don't think many kids would get that these days."

Whatever he is called, opposing ball carriers know the 6-foot-2, 214-pound strong safety could be coming their way. And that's not a good thing.

"I think it's good to have that reputation or respect or whatever you want to call it," Smith said of being known as a hard hitter. "Maybe that affects a play here or there. Anything you can have, that kind of elevates that persona to help you play successful."

Smith does plenty more for the Vikings than make highlight-tape hits. He's a top-notch cover guy, gets in good position to stop the run, and can blitz the quarterback.

"I like to be able to do everything, and I think that's what I'm best at is that versatility," Smith said. "Maybe I'm not the best in the league at one specific thing but I'm pretty darn good at everything."

After being taken by Minnesota with the No. 29 pick in the 2012 NFL draft out of Notre Dame, Smith wasted no time in asserting himself. He started all 16 games, returned two interceptions for touchdowns, and was named Vikings Rookie of the Year.

Smith was selected to his first Pro Bowl in 2015 and didn't slow down. He made his fifth straight in 2019, which tied him with Joey Browner for the second most in Vikings history for a safety (Browner made six, but one was on special teams). Smith's streak was snapped in 2020, and he entered 2021 one behind Hall of Famer Paul Krause, who was selected for six Pro Bowls with Minnesota from 1968–1979 after having made two earlier ones with Washington.

Smith was named first-team All-Pro in 2017. He entered 2021 with 28 career interceptions, the most for any NFL safety during a nine-year span, while holding the Vikings record of returning four for touchdowns. Smith, though, has wanted to extend that mark. He hadn't scored a touchdown since 2015, getting 15 interceptions since then.

"It's been too long since I've been back in there," he said.

Nevertheless, Smith still has made plenty of big plays in recent years. From 2017–2020, he had 16 interceptions, 43 passes broken up, and 28 tackles for loss. In a 2019 game at Green Bay, Smith became the first Vikings player in 11 years to have a pass broken up, forced fumble, fumble recovery, and a tackle for loss, and he did it all in the first half.

"He's pretty smart," said cornerback Xavier Rhodes, a former Vikings teammate. "He puts himself in great situations. He watches film regularly. He's a great, great, great safety. He's everywhere on the field. He never stops. His motor never stops."

The gritty Smith is an old-school guy. He would have fit in well in the days of leather helmets or at least back when the Vikings played their home games outdoors at Metropolitan Stadium, often in snow or mud.

"You have to adapt to the new rules and they are constantly changing," Smith said. "But I try to keep as much of that old-school toughness or whatever you want to call it. And I'm not the kind who's making a tackle after a three-yard gain and celebrating like you just won the Super Bowl. That's not my thing. You just go on to the next play."

Smith entered 2021 first in Vikings history among defensive backs with 13½ sacks and third with 867 tackles. In 2020, he was fourth on the team with 89 tackles.

"He thinks he's a linebacker," Krause said. "He loves playing up there."

Told what Krause said, Vikings coach Mike Zimmer didn't disagree.

"He could probably play linebacker if we asked him to," Zimmer said. "He does a lot of different things. He plays in coverage, he plays in the box, he blitzes. He does a lot of different things, so I would never disagree with Paul Krause."

Smith wears No. 22 just as Krause once did. While some say Smith is challenging Krause to be the best safety in team history, Krause looks at it diplomatically.

"Harrison Smith can be the best strong safety [in Vikings history], but he has not passed me at free safety," Krause said.

Pro Football Focus has rated Smith highly since he had a breakout season in 2014, when many thought he was snubbed for the Pro Bowl. The analytics site named Smith first-team All-Pro in 2014, 2015, and 2017. It ranked him as the NFL's top safety in 2017 and No. 3 in 2015 and 2019.

"We practice against each other all the time," tight end Kyle Rudolph, who played for the Vikings from 2011–2020 and also was Smith's teammate at Notre Dame, once said. "It's always a great gauge going against Harrison because I know if I can beat him and defeat him in coverage, I like my chances against any safety in this game because in my opinion he's the best in the NFL."

AND THE WINNERS ARE . . .

Hall of Famer Paul Krause considers himself the best free safety in Vikings history and Harrison Smith the best at strong safety.

With that in mind, consider them the top two safeties in team history.

Browner could have an argument to get the nod over Smith. He made the official NFL All-Pro team three times to once for Smith, but the latter has three overall career Pro Football Focus All-Pro selections. Smith often has changed games with big plays. Smith, 32 entering the 2021 season, needs just one Pro Bowl selection to tie Krause for the most ever by a Vikings safety.

Krause was the first safety inducted into the Vikings Ring of Honor in 2005, and Browner became the second in 2013. Look for Smith eventually to be the third.

SAFETIES WHO DID NOT MAKE THE CUT

Karl Kassulke was a reliable Vikings defender from 1963–1972, and made the Pro Bowl in 1970. He had 19 career interceptions and nine fumble recoveries. Kassulke's career ended when he was involved in a motorcycle accident while on his way to training camp in 1973 and was paralyzed from the waist down. He died in 2008.

Robert Griffith played for the Vikings from 1994–2001, and made the Pro Bowl in 2000. Griffith, who finished his career with Cleveland and Arizona from 2002–2006, had 27 career interceptions, 17 with Minnesota. He was a hard hitter at strong safety, and had four sacks in 1999.

Orlando Thomas burst upon the scene by intercepting an NFL-high nine passes as a rookie in 1995, returning them for 108 yards with a touchdown. He played for the Vikings through 2001. He was strong in coverage, intercepting 22 passes in his career. He died in 2014 after a long battle with amyotrophic lateral sclerosis (Lou Gehrig's Disease).

Darren Sharper played for the Vikings from 2005–2008, and made two Pro Bowls. Overall, he made five Pro Bowls while playing in the NFL from 1997–2010. In 2005, Sharper intercepted nine passes for Minnesota with an NFL-most 276 yards return yards and two touchdowns. In 2016, Sharper pleaded guilty to multiple rape and drug-related charges and was sentenced to 20 years in prison.

17

PUNTER

THE CANDIDATES

Greg Coleman
Mitch Berger
Chris Kluwe

When the Vikings began play in 1961, roster spots were precious. That meant it was impractical to exclusively have a punter on the team.

In their first two years, when the roster limit was 36, the Vikings had kicker Mike Mercer also serve as the punter and then backup quarterback John McCormick do the job. In their third season of 1963, the roster limit was expanded to 37, but the Vikings had kicker Fred Cox also punt.

"Not very well," Cox once said about his performance.

Cox, who died in 2019, averaged 38.7 yards in the only one of his 15 seasons in which he also punted. But by 1964, when the roster was expanded to 40, the Vikings had room for their first player who was exclusively a punter. That was Bobby Walden, who led the league with an average of 46.4 yards per boot in 1964 and played for Minnesota for four seasons before moving on to Pittsburgh for 10.

GREG COLEMAN

They called him "Touch."

Greg Coleman didn't have the biggest leg but, boy, was he accurate. Well before it was fashionable to do so, Coleman specialized in pinning opponents deep in their own territory. That included trying to punt the ball out of bounds inside the 5-yard line, known as the coffin corner.

After spending 1977 as a rookie with Cleveland, Coleman played for the Vikings from 1978–1987, making him the longest tenured punter in team history. He finished his career with Washington in 1988 and then returned to Minnesota, where he long has worked with the team in radio and television.

If it wasn't for an impressive tryout in 1978, Coleman might never have made the Vikings. Entering the eighth game that season, coach Bud Grant wasn't happy with punter Mike

Coleman played for the Vikings from 1978–1987, his 10 years being the longest stint for any punter in team history.
ST. PAUL PIONEER PRESS

Wood, so he brought in Coleman, who had been released by the Browns at the end of the preseason.

"Those were the days when they could stash you and I was [in Minnesota] for about three days for my tryout, and Bud would always go in after practice," Coleman said. "So that Friday, I said, 'Heck, I've got to get Bud's attention.' So I put a trash can on the goal line, one on the 5 and one on the 10 and I took a bag of balls."

Coleman then began to land some of the balls inside the trash can with his tremendous accuracy.

"A couple of guys, Ahmad Rashad and Rickey Young, saw it and they were saying, 'Dang, you got some special touch.'" Coleman said. "So that's how I got that nickname."

Grant got wind of what was going on and had Coleman sign a contract the next day. He was in uniform for that Sunday's game against Green Bay.

Coleman punted well in his Vikings debut, having six boots for a 42.0-yard average. He's fortunate, though, he lasted for another game.

"Bud hadn't said anything to me all game long and at one point he comes up to me and says, 'Whatever you do, don't get it blocked,'" Coleman said. "So then I felt a little bit of pressure and I didn't want it to get blocked, so I took off and dove for the marker and came up about six inches short."

After his 5-yard run, the Packers took over possession. And Coleman was waiting for Grant to read him the riot act.

"He said, 'What happened?'" Coleman said. "I said, 'Well, you said you didn't want it to get blocked and I didn't get it blocked.' He said, 'If you run, next time you better make sure you make it.'"

Coleman, who had starred in football and track at Florida A&M and is the cousin of former baseball star Vince Coleman, was a very good athlete. So for the next decade he usually did make a first down when he had to take off.

Mostly, though, Coleman punted just the way Grant wanted him to do. He didn't boom the ball, but averaged 40.8 yards throughout his Minnesota career while often pinning teams deep into their own territory.

Monday Night Football broadcaster Howard Cosell called him "Coffin Corner Coleman." But that nickname never really stuck.

"We called him 'Touch' because he could put the ball anywhere he wanted on a 90-percent consistent basis," said former Vikings running back Chuck Foreman. "If Bud said, 'Put the ball on the 10-yard line,' Greg would say, 'Hey, I can do it inside the 2.'"

Coleman also was a pioneer. He was the first full-time Black punter in NFL history.

"When I was going to all-star games and working out, people would say, 'You've got to be a defensive back, you've got to be a wide receiver,'" said Coleman, originally drafted in the 14th round by Cincinnati in 1976. "I said, 'I'm a punter and a kicker,' and they would say, 'Dude, you must be crazy, there ain't no Black punters and kickers.' But I was determined that I wasn't going to play another position. All that did was fuel my conviction."

Coleman didn't end up kicking in the NFL, but he remains Minnesota's all-time leader with 29,391 punting yards. He also played a role in the clarification of an NFL rule.

For years, Coleman had success leaving his leg in the air and drawing penalties when there was contact with a defender. He sometimes would hit the ground in such a manner that wide receiver Ahmad Rashad said he was worthy of an Academy Award.

"Other coaches would get pissed off at me," Coleman said. "Mike Ditka [of Chicago], he would get furious. So they passed a rule that became known as the Greg Coleman Rule that you can't leave your leg up or lean into a defender in an attempt to draw a flag."

MITCH BERGER

Mitch Berger was known for his booming leg. In fact, if there was a spot on the Vikings all-time All-Star team for a kickoff specialist, Berger would claim it hands down.

In 1998, Berger set an NFL record that since has been tied of 40 touchbacks in a season. And teams that season kicked off from the 30-, rather than the 35-yard line.

"If we had kicked off that year from the 35, I would have had 100 of them," said Berger, whose Vikings had 112 kickoffs during a season in which they set the NFL scoring record with 556 points.

As a punter, Berger had his share of booming boots, but touchbacks, of course, aren't good in that role. It did take Berger a few years to hone a punting style that would keep him on a team.

Berger was drafted in the sixth round out of Colorado by Philadelphia in 1994 but lasted just six games with the Eagles. He bounced around, having tryouts with five teams, before he finally landed another regular-season spot with the Vikings in 1996.

"I actually called the special teams coach on all 30 teams myself or the head of pro personnel and only two coaches called me back," Berger said. "One was from Houston [the Oilers] and the other was Gary Zauner, the special teams coach at Minnesota."

Berger averaged 41.1 yards a boot as a Vikings rookie and had two punts blocked. But by 1999 he averaged 45.4 yards and became the only Minnesota punter ever to make a Pro Bowl. Playing from 1996–2001, he averaged 43.5 yards in six seasons and never had another punt blocked after his rookie season.

Berger went to play 14 seasons in the NFL before retiring after the 2009 campaign. He won a Super Bowl with Pittsburgh following the 2008 season.

Punters usually don't get much publicity, but Berger did when the Vikings in 1998 went 15–1 and advanced to the NFC Championship Game. The Vikings had plenty of games that season that were nationally televised or seen by most of the nation.

Berger made it a habit of storing a Snickers bar in an extra pair of shoes he had on the sideline. And invariably he would munch on it after a kickoff or punt.

"We were on Fox like every week and John Madden was covering all our games, and I had one kickoff where I kicked the ball out of the end zone, and Madden made a big deal of it," Berger said. "Then the cameras caught me sitting on the bench and unwrapping a Snickers bar, and Madden was breaking it down on the air. And the next thing you know I made the All-Madden Team as a kickoff specialist and it was sponsored by Snickers and I became the Snickers kicker."

As it turned out, the 1998 season did not end well for the Vikings. In the NFC Championship, they were stunned 30–27 in overtime by Atlanta. Gary Anderson, who had made all 35 of his field-goal attempts during the regular season, missed a 39-yard attempt late in regulation that could have wrapped up the game. Berger was the holder on the kick and had a clean hold.

That championship game did provide one distinction for Berger. It marked the only time in his career he put a kickoff through the goalposts, the equivalent of an 80-yard field goal.

CHRIS KLUWE

During his playing days, Chris Kluwe was known as much for his zaniness as for his punting ability.

Kluwe, Minnesota's punter from 2005–2012, wore No. 5 for his first six seasons. Then Donovan McNabb showed up to start at quarterback after starring for 11 seasons in Philadelphia and spending one year in Washington.

McNabb had worn No. 5 throughout his NFL career, and wanted to continue that. So he talked to Kluwe about changing numbers.

"Most guys sell their jersey number either for cash or a new addition to their house or something," Kluwe said. "I didn't really care what number I wore as long I was out on the field, so I'm not going to try to get an arm and a leg out of this. Plus, I mean, it's Donovan McNabb."

So Kluwe came up with an agreement for McNabb to get No. 5 and he switched to No. 4. McNabb had to donate $5,000 to muscular dystrophy; say the name of his rock band, Tripping Icarus, during five separate press conferences; and give him an ice cream cone.

"I just threw the ice cream thing in for fun because there was a cafeteria with a freezer that was packed with ice cream and all he had to do was walk up to it, and grab me an ice cream cone," Kluwe said.

The charity donation went off without a hitch. McNabb mentioned the name of Kluwe's band in a few press conferences, sometimes repeating it several times. He didn't do it at five separate sessions, but Kluwe was okay with that.

Kluwe didn't actually get the ice cream cone until 2014, three years after McNabb's career was over and two years after Kluwe's had ended. McNabb was then a Fox Sports broadcaster, and the treat was provided during a break from an interview with Kluwe. The ex-punter was giving his share of national interviews that year.

After averaging a solid 44.4 yards gross per punt in his seven Minnesota seasons, Kluwe was released in May 2013 after the Vikings had surprisingly drafted punter Jeff Locke in the fifth round. Kluwe wasn't able to land another NFL job during the 2013 season, so on January 1, 2014, he dropped a bombshell.

Kluwe wrote a first-person story for *Deadspin* in which claimed he had been released by Minnesota because of his outspoken views supporting same-sex marriage. He claimed that then Vikings special teams coordinator Mike Priefer had made homophobic remarks, including once saying in a meeting room, "We should round up all the gays, send them to an island, and then nuke it until it glows."

Kluwe threatened to sue the Vikings before a settlement was reached in August 2014. The Vikings agreed to donate more than a half million dollars to LGBT causes and Priefer was suspended for three games although it was reduced to two after he completed sensitivity training. Kluwe received no money and said he was pleased that then Vikings executive Kevin Warren apologized in the settlement for the team getting opinions during legal proceedings from "any third party out there that said he was a punter in decline."

"I wasn't super stressed because I knew I was telling the truth," Kluwe said of the legal fight. "I told my lawyer that I wanted to be perfectly clear that I wasn't trying to get money out of this. I just wanted it to be clear that, 'Hey, I got let go for non-football related reasons.'"

Kluwe knew his career would end once he wrote the *Deadspin* story, and it did. He does, though, still hold some Vikings punting records. Among them, his gross career average remains the highest for those with at least 250 punts, and his 47.6-yard gross average in 2008 remains the best for a season.

"He was a really good punter," said former Vikings kicker Ryan Longwell. "He could really boom the ball and he had five-second hang time down the field."

AND THE WINNER IS . . .

Greg Coleman's longevity with the Vikings and his ability to pin foes deep in their own territory before it was fashionable in the NFL makes him the choice.

Coleman's statistics weren't super impressive when they are compared to some punters in today's game. But consider he played in an era before anybody paid a lot of attention to net punting average.

Coleman also provided the Vikings with a running threat they've never had from any other punter. He had 10 carries in his Minnesota career, and rolled up 85 yards.

PUNTERS WHO DID NOT MAKE THE CUT

As Minnesota's first player who was exclusively a punter, Bobby Walden averaged a solid 42.9 yards per boot from 1964–1967. But he is remembered most for spending 1968–1977 with Pittsburgh. While with the Steelers, he made one Pro Bowl and was on two teams that won a Super Bowl.

Like Walden, Harry Newsome played four seasons with the Vikings, averaging 43.8 yards per punt from 1990–1993. Also like Walden, Newsome spent time with Pittsburgh. He was with the Steelers from 1985–1989, which included leading the NFL with a 45.4-yard average in 1988.

18

THE MINNESOTA VIKINGS
ALL-TIME ALL-STAR TEAM

Head coach: Bud Grant

OFFENSE
Quarterback: Fran Tarkenton
Fullback: Chuck Foreman
Halfback: Adrian Peterson
Tackles: Ron Yary, Gary Zimmerman
Guards: Randall McDaniel, Steve Hutchinson
Center: Mick Tingelhoff
Tight end: Steve Jordan
Wide receivers: Randy Moss, Cris Carter, Ahmad Rashad
Kick returner: Cordarrelle Patterson

DEFENSE
Defensive ends: Carl Eller, Chris Doleman
Defensive tackles: Alan Page, John Randle
Linebackers: Matt Blair, Scott Studwell, Anthony Barr
Cornerbacks: Bobby Bryant, Carl Lee
Safeties: Paul Krause, Harrison Smith
Punter: Greg Coleman

SOURCE NOTES

Most of the material for the book came from more than 50 interviews with current and former Minnesota Vikings executives, coaches and players.

I also relied on websites, newspapers, magazines, and some of the notable books that have been written on the Vikings over the years. Websites, newspapers, and magazines that proved helpful included Vikings.com, ProFootballReference.com, ProFootballFocus.com, NFL.com, ESPN.com, the *St. Paul Pioneer Press* (TwinCities.com), *New York Times* (NYTimes .com), *Washington Post* (WashingtonPost.com), *Sports Illustrated* (SI.com), and *Viking Update*.

BOOKS USED INCLUDED:

Bruton, Jim. *A Tradition of Purple. An Inside Look at the Minnesota Vikings.* Champaign, IL: Sports Publishing, 2007.

Bruton, Jim. *Vikings 50: All-Time Greatest Players in Franchise History.* Chicago: Triumph Books, 2012.

Craig, Mark. *100 Things Vikings Fans Should Know & Do Before They Die.* Chicago: Triumph Books, 2016.

Grant, Bud, with Jim Bruton. *I Did It My Way.* Chicago: Triumph Books, 2013.

Reusse, Patrick. *Minnesota Vikings: The Complete Illustrated History.* Chicago: MVP Books, 2010.

Silverman, Steve. *The Good, the Bad & the Ugly: Heart-Pounding, Jaw-Dropping and Gut-Wrenching Moments from Minnesota Vikings History.* Chicago: Triumph Books, 2007.

Tarkenton, Fran, with Jim Bruton. *Every Day Is Game Day.* Chicago: Triumph Books, 2009.

Williamson, Bill, with Eric Thompson. *Tales from the Minnesota Vikings Sideline*. New York: Sports Publishing, 2017.

All other sourcing has been credited in the book when needed.

ACKNOWLEDGMENTS

I've been covering the Vikings since 2013 for the *St. Paul Pioneer Press*, and this is my first book on them. It was exciting delving as deep as I ever have into Vikings history, including speaking to dozens of legendary players.

Vikings fans are among the most passionate in the NFL, and hopefully this is a book that can add to their knowledge of the team. The Vikings make a point of regularly bringing back their great players and introducing them at games, so that has allowed many young fans to gain an appreciation for players who starred before they were even born.

I wish to thank the many current and former Vikings players, coaches, and executives who were very generous with their time in interviews. And special thanks to former star wide receiver and legendary broadcaster Ahmad Rashad, who wrote the foreword.

Condolences to the families of kicker Fred Cox, who died in November 2019; defensive end Chris Doleman, who died in January 2020; and linebacker Matt Blair, who died in October 2020. All three former players had learned of their selections to the all-time All-Star Team.

I am grateful to Niels Aaboe at Lyons Press for the opportunity to write this book and for his direction. I'd like to thank *Pioneer Press* editor Mike Burbach, sports editor Tad Reeve, deputy sports editor John Shipley, and newsroom office manager Barb Regal, who was generous with her time in helping with photos for the book. I'd like to thank the *Pioneer Press* for providing numerous photos and the photographers who took such great shots over the years. A tip of the hat to the Vikings public relations staff for their help during the process.

I also would like to thank my mother, Nancy Lensen-Tomasson, and brothers, Lars and Leif Tomasson, for their support during the project.

As for those named to the all-time All-Star Team, there no doubt will be some disagreements but feel free to debate the team as much as you like. And there's no question that, with the Vikings having plenty of current rising stars, names on an all-time All-Star Team certainly could end up changing as the decade moves along.